Military Leadership Lessons
of the Charleston Campaign,
1861–1865

ALSO BY KEVIN DOUGHERTY

*Military Decision-Making Processes:
Case Studies Involving the Preparation, Commitment,
Application and Withdrawal of Force* (McFarland, 2014)

*The United States Military in Limited War:
Case Studies in Success and Failure,
1945–1999* (McFarland, 2012)

Military Leadership Lessons of the Charleston Campaign, 1861–1865

KEVIN DOUGHERTY

McFarland & Company, Inc., Publishers
Jefferson, North Carolina

LIBRARY OF CONGRESS CATALOGUING-IN-PUBLICATION DATA

Dougherty, Kevin.
    Military leadership lessons of the Charleston Campaign, 1861–1865 / Kevin Dougherty.
        p.   cm.
    Includes bibliographical references and index.

    ISBN 978-0-7864-7926-9 (softcover : acid free paper) ∞
    ISBN 978-1-4766-1453-3 (ebook)

    1. Charleston (S.C.)—History—Civil War, 1861–1865.
2. Charleston (S.C.)—History—Siege, 1863. 3. Command of troops—History—19th century. I. Title.
E470.65.D68 2014
973.7'457—dc23   2014004111

BRITISH LIBRARY CATALOGUING DATA ARE AVAILABLE

© 2014 Kevin Dougherty. All rights reserved

No part of this book may be reproduced or transmitted in any form or by any means, electronic or mechanical, including photocopying or recording, or by any information storage and retrieval system, without permission in writing from the publisher.

On the cover: the Confederate flag flying at Fort Sumter, April 15, 1861, following the surrender of Major Anderson and his Union troops; troops prepare to load cannon (Library of Congress, Alma A. Pelot, photographer); background: map of Charleston Harbor area (Library of Congress)

Manufactured in the United States of America

McFarland & Company, Inc., Publishers
  Box 611, Jefferson, North Carolina 28640
    www.mcfarlandpub.com

To the Citadel cadets
and graduates who
did their duty defending Charleston
and to the cadets of today

Table of Contents

Introduction   1

Part One: Understanding Charleston

1. Leadership During the Civil War   7
2. Charleston Campaign Overview   25
3. The Key Players   32

Part Two: Leadership Vignettes

4. James Buchanan and Ignoring Responsibility   45
5. Robert Anderson and Embracing Responsibility   52
6. Gideon Welles and Strategic Vision   65
7. Robert E. Lee and Prioritization   72
8. John Pemberton and Strategic Leadership Skills   78
9. Robert Smalls and Seizing the Moment   86
10. James Chesnut and Mentorship   90
11. Thomas Lamar and Charismatic Leadership   96
12. David Hunter and the Need for Cooperation   104
13. Gabriel Rains and Alternative Solutions   110
14. Samuel Du Pont and Synchronization with Superiors   116
15. Adolphus LaCoste and Maximizing Resources   123
16. John Dahlgren and Command Presence   129
17. Quincy Gillmore and Frame of Reference   136
18. Robert Shaw and Moral Leadership   144

19. William Carney and Personal Bravery — 152
20. Clara Barton and Servant Leadership — 158
21. Johnson Hagood and the Go-to Guy — 164
22. Edward Serrell and Charles Sellmer and Problem-Solving — 171
23. Thomas Lockwood and the Entrepreneurial Spirit — 178
24. George Dixon and the Power of Persuasion — 186

Part Three: Summary

25. The Fall of Charleston — 195

Notes — 201
Bibliography — 214
Index — 220

Introduction

The opening shots of the Civil War were fired in Charleston, South Carolina, by cadets from the Citadel to dissuade the *Star of the West* from resupplying the beleaguered Federal garrison at Fort Sumter. Although the Confederates succeeded in forcing Major Robert Anderson to surrender his command, the tables were soon turned and Charleston found itself subjected to a siege that lasted 587 days as part of the longest campaign of the war.[1] Much occurred that lengthy time span. Military and political considerations became inseparably intertwined. Personalities clashed. Commanders came and went. New technologies were experimented with. Social causes were advanced. Civilians became part of the battlefield. Ordinary individuals performed superhuman tasks. Amid this rich drama, countless examples of leadership in action emerged in both positive and negative forms. It is this aspect of the campaign that *Military Leadership Lessons of the Charleston Campaign, 1861–1865* endeavors to explore.

The outcome of several Civil War battles can be easily explained by one side's superior leadership over the other. In *Leadership Lessons: The Campaigns for Vicksburg, 1862–1863* (Casemate, 2011), the author examines thirty leadership vignettes to help explain the Federal victory at Vicksburg while demonstrating timeless leadership lessons that apply to battlefield and non-battlefield situations. The present work continues this methodology with a different campaign. Some of the participants, such as John Pemberton, appear in both campaigns. Technological issues are also common to both situations, as is the challenge of achieving unity of effort. There are civilians present on both battlefields and politicians influencing military decision-making in both campaigns. Of course there are individual heroics at Vicksburg, Charleston, and anywhere else soldiers fight and die. There are also differences between the two campaigns. Although important at Vicksburg, the role of the U.S. Navy is larger at Charleston. The strength of the defense is more pronounced at Charleston. The participation of black soldiers is better chronicled and more well-known at Charleston. The result is a reinforcement of some leadership lessons learned at Vicksburg and the presentation of some experiences unique to Charleston. Certainly this book continues to testify to the criticality of leadership in battle and the transferability of its lessons to all situations and walks of life.

Following a format similar to the Vicksburg study, the Charleston Campaign is explored through this lens of leadership. Part One of the book is called "Understanding Charleston." It contains a discussion of leadership during the Civil War, a campaign overview, and a brief introduction to the key players.

The first chapter familiarizes the reader with the challenges, characteristics, and styles associated with leadership during the Civil War in general. It specifically notes the impact of frame of reference and background, technology, strategy and doctrine, the environment, and the men at and around Charleston.

The second chapter outlines the Charleston Campaign by explaining the strategic significance and context of Charleston, the Fort Sumter crisis, the Federal blockade strategy, the opposing forces and the terrain, the failed attempts to capture Charleston by the Federal Army and Navy working together and separately, and the Confederate defenses. It notes that in the end, the fate of Charleston was decided not by a climactic clash of the long-stand-ing opponents at the scene, but by the approach of Major General William Sherman's army from Savannah, Georgia. After this, the third chapter introduces ten of the key players on both the Federal and Confederate sides to facilitate the understanding of readers new to the campaign.

Part Two, "Leadership Vignettes," presents 21 scenarios that span the actions of the most senior leaders down to those of individual soldiers. Each focuses the campaign overview to the specific situation in order to provide the appropriate context, explains the action in the terms of leadership lessons learned, and concludes with a short, bulleted list of "take-aways" to crystallize the lessons for the reader. The book ends with summary information and a set of conclusions about leadership during the Charleston Campaign.

Military Leadership Lessons of the Charleston Campaign, 1861–1865 is intended to appeal to a variety of readers. Civil War historians will appreciate its detail in recounting the campaign. Students of the military art will be drawn to its emphasis on the importance of leadership in determining a battle's outcome. Leaders will find practical examples of positive and negative leadership in action in the vignettes. Although it featured some of the day's most advanced technological applications, the Charleston Campaign was decided by more than just shot and shell, and this book offers the unique perspective of the campaign as a leadership laboratory.

Part One

Understanding Charleston

1

Leadership During the Civil War

Leadership is the process of influencing others to work towards organizational goals. It provides purpose, direction, and motivation. In war, it is the most dynamic element of combat power. Civil War leaders at Charleston and elsewhere were shaped by their frame of reference and background, technology, strategy and doctrine, the environment, and their men. The lessons they learned during the campaign are transferrable to a variety of leadership situations, both in battle and elsewhere.

Frame of Reference and Background

The officers and men who served at and around Charleston were all products of various educational, military, and life experiences that informed and inspired their conduct in their Civil War circumstances. Among the most powerful influences was military training at the United States Military Academy, the United States Naval Academy, or one of the state military colleges. An equally strong factor was prior service in the Mexican War or on an earlier Civil War battlefield. At Charleston, leaders drew on these formative experiences to provide context and a frame of reference to the new challenges they were facing.

Many Civil War generals were products of the United States Military Academy at West Point, New York. Of the Civil War's sixty major battles, West Pointers commanded both sides in fifty-five. A West Pointer commanded on one side in the other five. All told, 151 Confederate and 294 Federal generals were West Point graduates.[1] At Charleston, West Pointers included Robert

Anderson (Class of 1825) and David Hunter (Class of 1822) on the Federal side, and John Pemberton (Class of 1837) and Pierre Gustave Toutant Beauregard (Class of 1838) on the Confederate side.

Founded in 1802, West Point had a long tradition of producing engineers skilled in the construction of fortifications. David Harris (Class of 1833) served as Beauregard's chief engineer at Charleston. On the Federal side, Quincy Gillmore (Class of 1849) applied his impressive engineering background and expertise to destroying Confederate fortifications with artillery fire.

Founded in 1845, the "Naval School" became the United States Naval Academy in 1850. The relatively young naval academy did not exist in time for many of the senior naval leaders at Charleston to be educated there, but Samuel Du Pont, commander of the South Atlantic Blockading Squadron, was on the board that helped found the school. The institution being located in Annapolis, Maryland, Southern sympathies were strong at the academy, as they were throughout Maryland. Fearing attack, authorities moved the academy to Newport, Rhode Island, for the duration of the war. From its new location, the academy continued its mission, graduating officers such as John McGlensey (Class of 1861), who served aboard the *Nantucket* at Charleston.

On the other hand, 95 naval academy graduates and 59 midshipmen resigned from the U.S. Navy and joined the Confederacy. Among those was John Grimball (Class of 1858), who became one of the officers of the *Lady Davis,* South Carolina's first Civil War vessel of war. In the early period of the war, the *Lady Davis* captured several Federal vessels off Charleston.[2] Another graduate was Richard Bacot, who had entered the academy in 1859 and resigned the day South Carolina passed its ordinance of secession. Governor Francis Pickens ordered him to Fort Sumter to assist in training artillery gunnery and help police the coast.[3] However, their inability to mount any conventional naval threat against the Federal blockade of Charleston soon led officers like Grimball and Bacot to go elsewhere to serve the Confederate cause.

In addition to the Federal academies, a variety of military schools throughout the nation provided trained officers for each side. One of the biggest of these schools was the Citadel. On January 28, 1861, the South Carolina General Assembly combined the corps of cadets at the Citadel in Charleston and the Arsenal in Columbia into the Battalion of State Cadets. The two institutions were designated as the South Carolina Military Academy, and the Battalion of State Cadets was made a part of the state's military organization. By 1864, there were 296 cadets enrolled at the South Carolina Military Academy.

The Citadel's most famous involvement in the Civil War occurred on

January 9, 1861, when cadets manning an artillery battery on Morris Island fired the first hostile shots of the growing sectional crisis, repulsing the supply ship, *Star of the West*, that had been sent to reinforce the isolated Federal garrison at Fort Sumter. Officers of the Citadel helped establish artillery positions and direct fire during the bombardment of Fort Sumter, and some cadets attached themselves to various military units that participated in the action. Among those associated with the Citadel who played key roles at Charleston were Cadet George Haynesworth, who is credited with firing the first shot against the *Star of the West*, and Johnson Hagood (Class of 1847), who commanded the 1st South Carolina Volunteers.

Another of the state military schools was the Virginia Military Institute, which provided 1,781 of its 1,902 matriculates from 1839 to 1865 for service in the Confederate army. Included in that number at Charleston was John Waddy (VMI Class of 1853), who served on Pemberton's staff.

Second only to West Point in providing officers in the Union army was Norwich University in Vermont. Norwich had been founded in 1819 as the "American Literary, Scientific, and Military Academy" by Captain Alden Partridge after he served a frustrating and controversial period as superintendent of West Point from 1815 to 1817. At least 705 Norwich graduates and former cadets served in the Civil War. As geography would suggest, the vast majority fought for the Union, but at least fifty-six sided with the Confederacy. Perhaps the most famous Norwich graduate at Charleston was Truman Seymour (Class of 1844), who was among the original besieged Federals at Fort Sumter and later was severely wounded in the assault on Fort (often called Battery) Wagner. William Davis (Class of 1842) was another Norwich man who distinguished himself during the siege.[4]

Not all Civil War generals, however, were products of a professional military education and background. The rapid expansion of both the Federal and Confederate armies necessitated the formation of many volunteer regiments which were often commanded by the energetic officer that raised them. The military qualifications of such individuals were obviously a mixed bag. On the Federal side, William Birney, son of the famed abolitionist James Birney, held a dual appointment as colonel of the 22nd U.S. Colored Infantry and a brigadier general of volunteers. Unquestionably loyal to the Federal cause, Birney proved less reliable as a general and was so uninspired in his conduct at Dawhoo Creek that he was reassigned to Florida.[5] On the Confederate side, community leaders flocked to the cause and assumed positions as officers. Many proved quite competent, such as Colonel Thomas Lamar, an erstwhile planter who became the hero of the Battle of Secessionville while serving with the 1st South Carolina Artillery.

Many Civil War leaders, both from military professional and political backgrounds, were shaped by previous service in the Mexican War, a conflict which Herman Hattaway and Archer Jones consider "was in a real sense a dress rehearsal for the Civil War leadership."[6] Some 194 Federal generals and 142 Confederate generals served in the Mexican War.[7] What they carried forward from Mexican War to the Civil War varied based on their specific experiences, but in many cases the influence was profound. Samuel Du Pont's Mexican War experience with blockading was particularly relevant to his work on the Federal side at Charleston.

Given the soft support for the Mexican War, especially in the northeastern states, President James Polk decided to avoid a heavy reliance on the militia and increase the size of the army by volunteers. The response was strong in the southern states, and South Carolina raised the Palmetto Regiment. Among the regiment's eleven companies, Company F consisted of volunteers from Charleston, and sixteen years later some of these veterans served the Confederacy as members of the Charleston Battalion. John Easterby was one example.[8]

Other leaders at Charleston were shaped by prior experiences on other Civil War battlefields. Quincy Gillmore, for example, would attempt to replicate the artillery success at Charleston that he had earlier enjoyed at Fort Pulaski. Although every situation is unique, the Confederates and Federals at Charleston drew upon their backgrounds and experiences to guide their actions in their present circumstances.

Technology

The Charleston Campaign showcased a number of novel technologies, with the Federal forces possessing significant naval and artillery advantages. The Confederates responded with asymmetric weapons including mines and submarines. Leveraging technology became one of the most significant leadership challenges during the campaign.

It had long been held as a military dictum that coastal forts were superior to ships so much so that one gun on land was considered to be equal to four on water. This assumption was so powerful that the entire coastal defense of the United States had been planned according to this precept. However, at Hatteras Inlet off the North Carolina coast in August 1861, Flag Officer Silas Stringham had used superior ordnance and steam power to overwhelm the Confederate defenders in a navy-dominated victory. Samuel Du Pont repeated Stringham's tactic with even greater effect at Port Royal, South Carolina, in

1. *Leadership During the Civil War*   11

The breached walls of Fort Pulaski represent the destructive power of rifled artillery and the new threat it posed to the Confederate coastal defense system (Library of Congress, Prints & Photographs Division).

November. Steam power, by freeing ships from the restrictions of wind and current, had made possible the technique of firing while moving, and it represented an important innovation in Federal naval warfare. Russell Weigley writes, "This was a bad discovery for the Confederacy, which had inherited the traditional United States system of coastal defense."[9]

The Federals demonstrated another technological advancement at Fort

Pulaski, Georgia, where an impressive bastion with brick walls seven-and-a-half feet thick and thirty-five feet high guarded the approaches to Savannah. The Confederates had great confidence in Fort Pulaski because so far in the history of warfare there was not a single instance in which cannon and mortar had breached heavy masonry walls at ranges beyond 1,000 yards. This assumption was shattered on April 11, 1862, when, from a distance of over a mile away, Captain Quincy Gillmore, with an arsenal that included rifled artillery, reduced the mighty fort to a pile of rubble and compelled its surrender. It was, Gillmore noted, "the first example, in actual warfare, of the breaching power of rifled ordnance at long range."[10] This new development rendered many fortifications that once were considered impenetrable suddenly vulnerable. First, Hatteras Inlet and Port Royal had demonstrated that steam power had reversed the historic balance between ship and fort. Now, Fort Pulaski had shown the vulnerability of masonry to rifled artillery. As Daniel Brown concludes, "An entire defense system, which had taken nearly fifty years to perfect, was made obsolete in less than two days."[11]

Secretary of the Navy Stephen Mallory saw an opportunity for the Confederacy to offset this huge Federal advantage by building ironclads. As early as 1822, naval theorists had begun proposing wooden ships be replaced with iron ones, and the French had employed ironclads during the Crimean War. Still, the new technology attracted little attention in America, and on the eve of the Civil War, the tradition-bound United States Navy still relied on wooden ships.

While the war was still in its infancy, Mallory argued,

> I regard the possession of an iron-armored ship as a matter of the first necessity.... If we ... follow their [the United States Navy's] example and build wooden ships, we shall have to construct several at one time; for one or two ships would fall easy prey to her comparatively numerous steam frigates. But inequality of numbers may be compensated by invulnerability; and thus not only does economy but naval success dictate the wisdom and expediency of fighting with iron against wood.[12]

As he explained to his wife, "Knowing that the enemy could build one hundred ships to one of our own, my policy has been to make ships so strong and invulnerable as would compensate for the inequality of numbers."[13]

When the Federals abandoned Gosport Navy Yard on April 20, 1861, they burned and scuttled the *Merrimack,* a 350-ton, 40-gun U.S. steam frigate, in hopes of rendering it useless to the Confederates. In spite of this effort, Confederate engineers were able to raise the hulk and found it to be in good shape except for the upper works, which had been destroyed by the fire.

With Mallory's urging, naval constructor John Luke Porter and Lieutenant John Mercer Brooke converted the *Merrimack* into an ironclad that was rechristened the CSS *Virginia*. Having learned of the Confederates' efforts to build an ironclad, the Federals, led by Swedish-American inventor John Ericsson, began a similar project. Overcoming a three-month Confederate head start, Ericsson built the *Monitor* in less than 100 days, and rushed it south just in time to prevent the *Virginia* from single-handedly destroying the Federal fleet. On March 9, 1862, the two strange-looking monsters battled to a tactical draw and ushered in a new era of naval warfare. Both the Federals and the Confederates soon embarked on ambitious programs to build or buy ironclads.

After the *Virginia*'s initial success at Hampton Roads, the Confederacy began a rather haphazard effort to build additional ironclads. Throughout the war, the Confederacy initiated production of fifty-two ironclads and completed almost thirty of them. A lack of sufficient iron plate or an engine plagued many construction efforts, and other partially completed ironclads had to be destroyed to prevent Federal capture. The Confederates were able to employ two small ironclads at Charleston. These were the six-gun *Chicora* and the four-gun *Palmetto State*. While they had isolated success raiding wooden blockaders, they certainly could not go toe to toe with Federal ironclads, and Commander John Randolph Tucker kept his two rams near Fort Sumter to help defend obstructions and dissuade a Federal attack.[14]

The Federal Navy also began producing ironclads, and the superior Northern industrial might quickly outstripped the Confederate effort to field this revolutionary naval technology. Indeed, Secretary of the Navy Gideon Welles believed that Charleston's stout defenses could be matched by ironclads including the *New Ironsides*, the navy's most powerful monitor. Du Pont was skeptical, but he agreed to try if Welles could provide the necessary quantities. "The limit of my wants in the need of ironclads," Du Pont wrote Welles, "is the capacity of the [Navy] Department to supply them."[15] Ultimately, Du Pont received all but one of the navy's new ironclads, making his fleet at Charleston the first integration of the revolutionary monitor technology into the navy's larger organization.

Amid pressure from President Lincoln and Welles, Du Pont acquiesced to conduct a limited test of the ironclads against Fort McAllister on the Ogeechee River in Georgia. On January 27, 1863, he sent the ironclad *Montauk*, the gunboats *Seneca*, *Wissahickon*, and *Dawn*, and the mortar schooner *C.P. Williams* to attack Fort McAllister. Sunken obstacles that appeared to be torpedoes blocked the *Montauk*'s advance, so the ironclad blasted the fort from a distance for four hours with no noticeable effect. The Confederate fire was accurate, striking the *Montauk* fourteen times, but also doing no damage.

The next day, Du Pont learned from a runaway slave the position of the torpedoes that had blocked the previous attack. Armed with this new intelligence, the Federals tried again on February 1. The *Montauk* advanced to within 600 yards of the fort, and both sides unleashed accurate fire for four hours. The *Montauk* was hit forty-eight times but it retired without serious damage. Fort McAllister was also still sound. The results seemed to support Du Pont's earlier reluctance. Of the experiment he lamented, "If one ironclad cannot take eight guns, how are five to take 147 guns in Charleston Harbor?"[16]

Unable to penetrate the formidable position by naval attack, the Federals subjected Charleston to siege. During siege operations, a military force surrounds and blockades a city with the intent of compelling the enemy occupants to surrender by exhausting their supplies. During the Civil War, sieges were conducted in the formal European style, which had remained relatively unchanged for two centuries.[17] An approach trench was dug toward the objective, and at certain intervals, parallels were dug to the left and right. Artillery and mortar fire shelled the objective from behind the parallels. As successive parallels closed the distance to the objective, they could be used as jumping off points to launch ground attacks.

At Charleston, the Federal forces blockaded the harbor and gained footholds on the marshy islands around it, and then pounded the city with fire from both land and water. The Confederates resisted the siege from fortified and entrenched positions and used their own sizeable artillery capability to ward off the attackers. There was a variety of artillery employed during the campaign, all with different capabilities and limitations. Getting the maximum effect from these assorted assets presented a leadership challenge for both sides.

Parrott guns were invented by Robert Parrott, an 1824 graduate of the United States Military Academy who served as an artillery and ordnance officer before resigning from the army in 1836. From that time until 1867, he served as superintendent of the West Point Foundry, which became a leading producer of ordnance for both the army and the navy. As a private contractor, Parrott was unrestrained by government bureaucracy and budget, and he began experimenting early with rifled cannon.

Parrotts of all calibers are basically the same. They have a long cast iron tube with a wrought iron reinforcing band over the breech. Bands were nothing new, but Parrott's contribution to the process was the method of attaching the band. In most cases, the band of metal was heated, slipped on the tube, and then allowed to cool. During the procedure, the tube remained stationary. Parrott's innovation was to rotate the tube horizontally on rollers and keep its inside cool with a stream of water. As the hot band was slipped on, the tube rotation caused the band to clamp uniformly to the breech instead of hanging from one spot and cooling there first, as happened with a stationary tube. Parrott believed this process gave his rifles superior strength.[18]

Both the army and the navy had versions of the Parrott. Sizes included 4.2-, 6.4-, 8-, and 10-inch.[19] Perhaps the most famous Parrott at Charleston was the massive 8-inch "Swamp Angel" that bombarded the city from the Marsh Battery on Morris Island. Among the munitions fired by the Swamp Angel were shells carrying incendiary material designed to explode over a target and start a fire. Such rounds were called "Greek fire."[20]

The main piece of shipborne naval artillery was the Dahlgren gun, invented by John Dahlgren, who would succeed Du Pont as the Federal naval commander at Charleston. Dahlgrens represented "the ultimate refinement in smoothbore muzzle-loaded artillery." At the start of the war, the standard size was the 9-inch, but the navy soon added 11- and 15-inch guns to its inventory. The Dahlgrens were extremely effective against other ships, in part because their projectiles could be skipped over the surface of the water to ensure a hull hit. The spinning action of rifled pieces made this technique impossible. Dahlgrens could also be used against land defenses, especially when mounted in ironclads. The USS *Keokuk*, for example, had two 11-inch Dahlgrens.[21]

Smoothbores like the Dahlgrens dominated the prewar army and were effective at short ranges. Rifled pieces, however, offered the advantages of heavier projectiles and greater accuracy. Rifled artillery also had much better penetrating capability against masonry fortifications.[22] A great variety of rifled pieces were present in the Charleston Campaign, but the Federal industrial strength gave that side a clear advantage.

The Confederacy in part turned to overseas markets to help offset its limited production capability. Blakely rifles were cast at the Low-Moor Iron Works in England according to specifications established by Captain Alexander Blakely. Some 400 Blakely rifles were exported during the Civil War era, and many were purchased by the Confederacy.[23] One arrived in time to shell the U.S. Army at Fort Sumter, having been "presented to the State of South Carolina by a citizen resident abroad, in commemoration of the 20th December, 1860." In addition to being extremely accurate, Blakelys were efficient guns that required only a half pound of powder.[24] From its position at Cummings Point, this gun was able to create penetrations up to twenty inches into Fort Sumter's walls, and one of its shots blasted through the main gate.[25]

The Confederates also attempted to import Whitworth guns from Britain only to have a shipment captured as the *Princess Royal* attempted to run the blockade at Charleston in early 1863.[26] The Federals incorporated two of the prizes into their Naval Battery on Morris Island, but found the weapons sadly deficient. Brigadier General John Turner reported the pieces "very unsatisfactory in point of accuracy" and there being "much difficulty experienced at times in loading." It was "found necessary to abandon their use entirely, in consequence of their repeated and constant premature explosion."[27] By August 31, a disgusted Gillmore concluded "the Whitworth guns are of no use, and can be taken away."[28]

James rifles, named for Major General Charles James, were another weapon present at Charleston. These pieces represented efforts to reclaim worn-out smoothbores by improving them with rifling. In 1860, Secretary of War John Floyd reported as follows:

> Experimental firing with rifle cannon leaves no doubt that the accuracy and effectiveness of our artillery may be vastly increased at comparatively small expense without discarding from use the good and serviceable cannon of our present models; requiring only that they be rifle-grooved to adapt them to use as rifled cannon with James' elongated expanding projectiles. This easy and cheap mode will convert the smooth-bored into rifled cannon, throwing nearly double the weight of metal without increasing strain....[29]

Nonetheless, the James was not one of the Civil War's more common pieces, perhaps because the bronze rifling eroded too quickly.[30] Produced at the Ames Manufacturing Company of Chicopee, Massachusetts, some found their way into the Confederate army after capture. For example, the James at Battery Haskell had been taken at Shiloh.[31]

The Confederacy had some domestic capability to produce rifled pieces, namely the Brooke rifles that were the work of Confederate naval officer John Mercer Brooke. Banded Brooke guns were as efficient and durable as the Parrott but could not be manufactured as quickly. Thus, at many places such as Charleston, the Confederates resorted to rifling and banding less-reliable smoothbores.[32] Even then, the pieces were hard to come by. Beauregard was so desperate for ordnance that on July 23, 1863, he requested the immediate delivery of a 7-inch Brooke condemned by the army at Savannah, stating he was "willing to run the risk."[33] Indeed, the risks were very real. Three days later a 6.4-inch Brooke burst at Battery Simpkins on Shell Point, killing the cannoneer and wounding three others. Brooke blamed the accident on improper ramming.[34]

Along with Brooke rifles, the Confederates mounted heavy seacoast guns including 10-inch Columbiads on the top tier of Fort Sumter. Columbiads saw their first wartime service during the War of 1812 and are considered the first piece of purely American-designed ordnance. They were large caliber, long pieces, but their distinguishing features were elevating ratchets that ran all the way up the face of the breech. This design allowed Columbiads to elevate to thirty-nine inches as opposed to the fifteen inches permitted by guns with elevating mechanisms placed under the breech. Because Columbiads could fire heavy charges at high angles of elevation, they were ideal for seacoast defense.[35] From their perch high atop Fort Sumter, they could deliver plunging fire onto the decks of attacking ships.[36]

Columbiads were improved by the work of Thomas Rodman, who developed a method of making cannon by casting in iron around a water- or air-chilled core. This technique caused the inside of the barrel to cool first and compress because of the contraction of the outside metal. The result was a gun that could withstand more internal pressure without breaking.[37] "Confederate Rodmans" were not cast with the Rodman process of hollow casting. Instead, they were cast solid and therefore were not as strong as their northern counterparts. When the Confederates evacuated the area on February 17, 1865, a total of fifteen 10-inch Columbiads were found on Sullivan's Island, of which four were mounted inside Fort Moultrie.[38] Columbiads have qualities of the gun, howitzer, and mortar.[39] Although the terms are often used interchangeably, there is a difference between a gun and a howitzer. Guns have a relatively flat trajectory, while howitzers have a greater arc.[40]

Guns fire several different types of munitions, but one commonly used against infantry assaults in the Civil War was canister. Canister consisted of iron top and bottom plates over which were bent the ends of a cylinder made from sheet tin. Inside were four tiers of iron balls, with each layer containing seven balls. One centered ball was surrounded by the other six, and solidly packed sawdust kept the balls from moving. To accommodate the rivets for the handle, the center ball on the top tier was left out. The result was a count of twenty-seven balls per round.[41] Canister turned smoothbores into formidable weapons at short ranges. The balls scattered in the form of a cone immediately upon leaving the muzzle, resulting in a shotgun effect that was especially deadly at ranges between 100 and 200 yards. Beyond that, the dispersal diminished the impact, although canister was still effective out to 400 yards.[42]

At the beginning of the Battle of Secessionville, Colonel Thomas Lamar took personal command of an 8-inch Columbiad and delivered a devastating blast of canister into the center of the Federal assault at a range of two hundred yards. Lamar then turned the piece over to Lieutenant J.B. Humbert, ordering him to "give them canister freely, which he did."[43] When service-issued canister was not available, enterprising gunners often made field expedient versions out of glass, nails, and the like.

Howitzers are typically smoothbore cannon that were generally lighter than guns of the same caliber and, at short ranges, considerably more effective. Their higher trajectory also made them more useful in sieges.[44] Among the howitzers present at Charleston were two that were part of the Surf Battery in the second parallel of the Federal works on Morris Island.[45]

The Surf Battery also housed three Requa batteries. These batteries were constructed by the Billinghurst Company of Rochester, New York, and represented a predecessor to the machine gun. Intended to replace the short-range field guns in defensive positions, they consisted of twenty-five rifle barrels arranged horizontally and attached to a field carriage. They were effective to ranges of 1,300 yards and were operated by a three-man crew which could fire 175 shots per minute by feeding clips of twenty-five cartridges.[46]

In the first parallel of Federal works on Morris Island and elsewhere at Charleston were mortars. Mortars come in a variety of sizes. The ones at Battery Weed, for example, were 10-inch siege mortars.[47] Whereas guns fire on a fairly flat trajectory and howitzers have a slightly greater elevation, mortar rounds travel in a pronounced arc. This path makes the mortar especially useful in reaching defilade positions.

Gillmore found lighter mortars most effective at Charleston. Although he had available the large 13-inch seacoast mortars which could fire a 200 pound shell 4,200 yards at a forty-five degree elevation, he did not use them.[48] Gillmore opined that Fort Pulaski had demonstrated "at long ranges, mortars are not efficient, on account of the inaccuracy of their fire" against casemated works.[49]

The Federals used lighter mortars against Fort Wagner, and Gillmore declared the Coehorn mortar in particular "a most valuable weapon in siege operations. From its lightness and portability it is peculiarly well adapted to the attack, and should follow close on the heels of the sappers."[50] The Coehorn mortar was a bronze Model 1841 named for the 17th century Dutch artillerist Baron van Menno Coehoorn. Weighing just 296 pounds and equipped with handles to allow two men to carry it short distances, the Model 1841 was well-suited to throwing projectiles at a high arc into enemy trenches. It could fire a 24-pounder shell a maximum range of 1,200 yards.[51]

As in the case of warships, the Confederates simply could not match the Federal artillery. Major General Jeremy Gilmer lamented, "As long as the contest is one of work and shooting at long range, no people can beat the infernal Yankees."[52] Instead, the Confederates fought back by asymmetric means, defending Charleston's rivers and harbor with naval mines called "torpedoes" in the lexicon of the day. Brigadier General Gabriel Rains was instrumental in planning the torpedo defenses at Charleston, and in many cases his work was decisive. During the February 28, 1863, attack on Fort McAllister, one Federal naval officer said torpedoes were "strewn about like autumn leaves."[53] The *Montauk* was badly damaged by a torpedo, and the *Weehawken* and the *Patapsco* would eventually be sunk by torpedoes.

Other asymmetric weapons used by the Confederates at Charleston were torpedo boats and submarines. Often mistaken for a submarine, the *David* was designed to operate low in the water as a surface vessel. She carried an explosive charge on the end of a spar projecting forward from her bow and made at least three attacks against Federal vessels. More famous was the *H.L. Hunley*, a 40-foot long, 3.5-foot wide, 4-foot deep cigar-shaped submarine. On the night of February 17, 1864, the *Hunley* exploded her 130-pound spar torpedo, sinking the 1,934-ton screw sloop *Housatonic*.

Thus the Charleston Campaign was awash with technological developments that constituted a genuine revolution in military affairs. Technology, however, represents only capability. Transferring that potential into action is the work of leadership.

Strategy and Doctrine

The ability of leaders to realize the potential of the wealth of technology available in and around Charleston would be greatly affected by the strategy and doctrine by which the campaign was waged. Indeed, properly aligning technology, strategy, and doctrine is a challenge faced by all generations of military leaders, not just those in the Civil War.[54] Those involved in the Charleston Campaign labored under the disadvantage of not having the benefit of the planning and procedural systems that had since been ingrained in the United States military.

From the very beginning of the Civil War, Federal strategy recognized that success would come from the work of both the army and the navy. General-in-Chief Winfield Scott proposed the "Anaconda Plan," which involved two parts: a tight blockade of the Confederacy's ports and then a move of an army of 60,000 men, accompanied by gunboats, down the Mississippi River to seize and hold it from Cairo, Illinois, to the Gulf of Mexico. Like the big snake it was named after, the Anaconda Plan would squeeze the Confederacy into submission.

To plan the blockade envisioned by the Anaconda Plan and proclaimed by President Lincoln on April 19, 1861, Secretary of the Navy Gideon Welles convened a "Blockade Board" headed by Captain Samuel Du Pont. The board quickly and efficiently focused the Federal effort on key ports such as Charleston, and "created a roadmap for the Union Navy to conduct a major portion of its early strategic responsibilities and stood as the role model for later naval boards and commissions."[55]

While Du Pont and the board recognized the need for cooperation between the army and navy, jointness as understood in the modern sense was far from achieved. There was not a national level joint staff to develop joint

Although Scott's Anaconda Plan was rejected by President Lincoln as being too time-consuming, it was a similar strategy that eventually brought victory to the Federal forces (Library of Congress).

doctrine or advise the president, or joint task forces at the operational level to plan and command joint operations. Thus, the planning and execution of joint operations were totally dependent on ad hoc actions by the responsible commanders. As Scott Stuckey observes, "Neither command arrangements nor doctrine for joint operations existed at the time [of the Civil War]. Successful joint operations, like much else, would have to be improvised by those on the scene."[56] Achieving the unity of effort required for success under such circumstances would prove elusive for such commanders at Charleston as David Hunter and Samuel Du Pont.

Environment

What brought the Federal and Confederate military might to Charleston was both Charleston's political and practical importance. As it was the very birthplace of secession, both sides recognized Charleston as a symbol of either nationhood or rebellion. It was a place that many Confederates emotionally had to defend and many Federals emotionally had to destroy. Beyond this political importance was Charleston's military and economic value. As one of only ten Southern seaports that had rail or water connections with the interior, Charleston was a vital part of the Confederacy's logistical and transportation network.[57]

Charleston was a model Old South city in terms of its aristocracy, architecture and arts, and culture. It was also a city where slavery thrived, and it became the center of proslavery and secessionist apologists. Newspaper editor Robert Barnwell Rhett used the pages of his *Charleston Mercury* to do much to advance the agenda of the fire-eaters.

Still, it was a twist of fate that made Charleston the birthplace of secession. Infuriated by Abraham Lincoln's election, South Carolina held a secession convention in the state capital of Columbia on December 17, 1860. Then an outbreak of smallpox caused the convention to move to Charleston, and it was there on December 20 that all 169 delegates voted to withdraw from the Union. As a result, Charleston came to symbolize disunion and the Confederacy. The hatred of Charleston in some Northern circles was vitriolic. The *New York Tribune* called "wicked" Charleston a "viper's nest and breeding place of rebellion ... deserving of holocaustic infamy."[58] Assistant Secretary of the Navy Gustavus Fox seemed to agree, writing, "the fall of Charleston is the fall of Satan's Kingdom."[59]

Beyond its symbolic significance, Charleston was important for many practical reasons. It was a good-sized Southern city with a population of 40,552 in 1860. It had a vibrant economy based on rice, cotton, slave trading, and shipping. Its industrial activity included manufacturing steamship engines, locomotives, and steamship machinery. The city also contained the Citadel, an important training ground for Confederate military leaders. Although other ports were surpassing it as a shipping center, Charleston's rail link to Savannah, Georgia, made it a vital transportation hub. Along with Wilmington, North Carolina, it would become a popular Atlantic coast blockade-running port during the war. As a result, General Robert Lee believed "the loss of Charleston would cut us off almost entirely from communications with the rest of the world and close the only channel through which we can expect to get supplies from abroad, now almost our only dependence." He admonished Major General John Pemberton to defend the city "street by street and house by house as long as we have a foot of ground to stand upon."[60]

Developments throughout the larger coastal campaign also helped to militarize Charleston. Although the Federal victories at Port Royal, New Orleans, and elsewhere were devastating to the Confederates, they did allow the defenders to concentrate their efforts at the few key ports that remained open. The result was a combination of land-based artillery, torpedoes, submersible vessels, obstructions, and prepared positions that made Charleston the Confederate city best able to withstand an assault from the sea. By 1863, these formidable defenses had been expanded into a three-tiered defensive system. Thus, to the frustration of the Federals, the "only thing that awaited the attacking force once they passed Fort Sumter was additional fortifications."[61] The result was that Charleston became "the impregnable city," and, at 567 days, the campaign to take it was the longest siege of the war.[62]

Billy Yank and Johnny Reb at Charleston

While the leader is an obviously important element of the leadership equation, the nature of the subordinates is also critical. The Federal and Confederate soldiers at Charleston brought with them their own capabilities and limitations with which their leaders would have to contend. Additionally, the common soldier had strongly developed ideas of what was required of a leader. Generally speaking, Civil War soldiers had far greater expectations of independence and individuality than do their modern counterparts, and these demands would impact leaders at Charleston. One manifestation of this phenomenon was the common practice in both armies to allow soldiers to elect their officers up to the rank of colonel.[63] Such a system resulted in a disadvantage for otherwise competent officers the men considered overly strict, but it also allowed naturally charismatic individuals to lead with the added benefit of the legitimacy of popular election. Planter-turned-politician Thomas Lamar was one such officer.

Finally, leadership is not exclusively a function of positional hierarchy or exclusive to the military. Private soldiers at Charleston such as William Carney rose to challenges in specific situations, and their individual actions also comprise an important part of the leadership story at Charleston. Civilians such as Robert Smalls and Clara Barton also excelled as leaders.

Some Civil War soldiers were already in the U.S. Army or a state militia when the war broke out. When the Battle of First Manassas dispelled any notions that the war would be a short one, both the Federal and Confederate governments began enlisting large numbers of soldiers. For the most part, both nations continued the American political philosophy that the chief responsibility for raising volunteers rested with the state rather than the central government. Thus the two war departments merely levied a requirement on each state to provide a certain number of volunteer regiments. To meet the ever increasing demand for soldiers, first the Confederacy and then the Union resorted to conscription.

Few Civil War soldiers had ever been far from home, which must have made service in South Carolina somewhat of an adventure for the Federal soldiers assigned to the Department of the South. This was a secondary theater, and it was given resources according to its lower priority. When Major General David Hunter assumed command in March 1862, the combined forces of the Federal Army and Navy had occupied the strip of coastal islands from about twenty miles south of Charleston to the vicinity of Savannah, as well as some isolated coastal points in Georgia and northeast Florida. The Union had long held Key West and soon after Hunter's arrival also had taken Apalachicola and then Pensacola on the Florida panhandle. Never having more than 18,000 troops under his control, Hunter probably had the distinction of commanding the most thinly dispersed body of troops over the largest geographic area in the war. Under such circumstances, Hunter could take little offensive action.[64]

Rather than a theater of rigorous, sustained combat, the Department of South became what the *Beaufort* (SC) *Free South* declared the "Department of Experiments."[65] Indeed, the Department of the South was unique in that at the start of the Charleston Campaign it contained four black regiments: the 1st, 2nd, and 3rd South Carolina Volunteer Infantry, which had been recruited from freed slaves within the department and the 54th Massachusetts Volunteer Infantry, the fulfillment of Governor John Andrew's vision to raise a regiment of free, Northern blacks. All the black regiments were officered by whites, the most famous being Colonel Robert Gould Shaw of the 54th Massachusetts.

When the stubborn Confederate resistance compelled the Federals to send reinforcements to the Department of the South, one contingent included eight regiments of Gettysburg veterans from the Army of the Potomac, while the other half were three inexperienced brigades from Major General John Foster's command in North Carolina. Among Foster's troops was a brigade of black troops consisting of the 1st, 2nd, and 3rd North Carolina and the 55th Massachusetts. The 3rd United States Colored Troops, a regiment formed in Philadelphia, was also sent south.[66] The Federal soldiers serving at Charleston ultimately included infantry regiments from Massachusetts, Connecticut, New York, New Hampshire, Maine, Pennsylvania, Illinois, and Ohio.[67]

In addition to these volunteers, the Federal army had the advantage of being able to build on its prewar foundation, and some units at Charleston, notably those of the artillery, consisted of regular soldiers. For example, Major General Gillmore had at his disposal the 1st and 3rd United States Artillery regiments as well as a variety of volunteer artillery units, the largest contingent being from Rhode Island.[68] If nothing else, the soldiers of the Department of the South were a varied group.

On the other hand, most of the Confederate soldiers at Charleston were from South Carolina or nearby states such as Georgia, and North Carolina, with a few from Florida. Indeed, many were local Charlestonians, including those of the Charleston Battalion (formally the First South Carolina Battalion), which traced its roots to 1775 and was commanded by Lieutenant Colonel Peter Gaillard.[69] For men raised in the tradition of Southern chivalry, serving near and defending one's home was a particular honor.[70] The fact that so many of Charleston's defenders had close ties to the area is an interesting component of the campaign.

Even within a fairly homogenous group like the Charleston Battalion there was some diversity. Approximately one-third of the battalion's officers were slave holders, and at least thirty-three blacks served in the battalion, usually as musicians or cooks.[71] The significant number of immigrants in Charleston contributed to the presence of a number of foreign-born members, especially from Ireland and Germany.[72] Most Civil War soldiers were between eighteen and thirty years old, and the available data suggests the average age of the men of the Charleston Battalion exceeded that norm.[73] While most of their comrades in arms came from rural areas and had little education, in the Charleston Battalion, Brigadier General Johnson Hagood boasted that "the average intelligence and social position of the rank and file were ... greater than most."[74]

The Balance

Amid this mix of background, organization, resources, and personal and systematic strengths and weaknesses, the stage was set for the Charleston Campaign. The siege gave the Confederates the traditional advantages associated with the defense as well as the ability to consume time in a way that they hoped would tire the Northern population of war. On the other hand, the Federals benefited from the fact that history has favored the besiegers.[75] To defeat the siege, the besieged force must either break out of the encirclement or receive relief from an outside force. Indeed, the Confederates made a concerted effort to run the blockade with individual ships; but with only a nominal navy of their own, there was little hope of compelling the Federals to abandon the siege by force. Clearly this situation gave the blockaders an advantage. So the Confederate leadership challenge was to persevere, and the Federal leadership challenge was to make it impossible for them to do so. As both sides pursued these objectives, they left future generations with a host of leadership lessons.

2

Charleston Campaign Overview

Charleston, the home of Fort Sumter, was where the Civil War's opening salvos were fired. The city defied repeated Federal attacks by land and sea, and, by the summer of 1863, its defiance left it and Wilmington, North Carolina, as the only remaining major ports of entry open for Atlantic blockade runners. The Federal effort to capture Charleston was a siege that became the longest campaign of the war. Still, Charleston held on, succumbing only to the impending approach of Major General William Tecumseh Sherman toward the end of the war.

Secession and the Fort Sumter Crisis

South Carolina had long been the champion of states' rights and Southern nationalism, dating back at least to the Nullification Crisis of 1832. It was the first state to secede from the Union, a process facilitated by its constitutional provision that legislators rather than voters selected presidential electors. When these legislators convened on November 5, 1860, to choose electors, it appeared as if Abraham Lincoln was poised to win the national election for president. Thus Governor William Gist kept the legislature in session to await the results. When Lincoln's victory was certain, Gist requested a secession convention, and the legislators called for an election of delegates. The convention met on December 17 and three days later unanimously voted to secede.

South Carolina's secession created a dilemma concerning the Federal garrison at Fort Sumter, a brick fort built on an artificial island in the middle of

Charleston's main ship channel. It was garrisoned by eighty-four soldiers under the command of Major Robert Anderson, who had relocated his force there from the more vulnerable Fort Moultrie on the night on December 26. When South Carolina seceded, it claimed the fort became state property and demanded the Federal troops there leave. In spite of little in the way of support or guidance from lame duck President James Buchannan, Anderson had no intention of surrendering his position.

In the face of Anderson's defiance, the Confederates built a series of batteries that ringed Fort Sumter. A weak Federal attempt to resupply and reinforce the beleaguered garrison by the unarmed *Star of the West* was turned back on January 9, 1861. In early March, Brigadier General Pierre Gustave Toutant Beauregard arrived to assume command of the Confederate forces, and on April 10 he issued a demand that Anderson surrender or face bombardment. On April 12, Beauregard commenced his attack.

There was little Anderson could do to resist the bombardment, and on April 13 he surrendered. In the thirty-four hour attack, the Confederates had hit Fort Sumter with approximately 4,000 shells. Anderson evacuated the position by steamer to New York on April 14 and was heralded as a hero in the North. Unfortunately, in an accidental explosion while the Federals were halfway through a planned 100-gun salute preceding the evacuation, Private Daniel Hough became the first casualty of the war. With the Federal departure, the Confederates occupied Fort Sumter and used it repeatedly to help repel Federal attempts to seize Charleston throughout the war.

The South Atlantic Blockading Squadron

The events at Fort Sumter made it clear that the unfolding sectional crisis would not be resolved peacefully. Among the decisions that followed was President Lincoln's declaration of a blockade of the southern coast on April 19. In its early days, the blockade was not particularly effective, but the work of Captain Samuel Du Pont and the Blockade Board began to result in significant improvements. One of the board's recommendations was to split the Atlantic Blockading Squadron into north and south squadrons.

Du Pont was made flag officer and given command of the South Atlantic Blockading Squadron. On November 7, he succeeded in seizing the key harbor at Port Royal, South Carolina. With the army occupying this strategic location, Du Pont was able to use it as a base to extend and improve the blockade along the Georgia and Florida coasts.

Du Pont's swift victory created a panic within the Confederacy and forced

General Robert E. Lee to consolidate its coastal defenses. Unable to defend everywhere, Lee focused the meager Confederate resources on key locations such as Charleston. The result was that the Confederacy maintained fewer ports, but the ones it held were heavily fortified.

Early Failures

Given Lee's concentration of forces, Du Pont knew that Charleston could be taken only by a joint sea and land effort. After Port Royal, he had urged the army to move on Charleston, but the army had refused and future cooperation did not appear likely. Major General David Hunter had just 10,000 troops at Hilton Head, much fewer than the job would require, and reinforcements were improbable given the competing priorities of Gettysburg and Vicksburg. At first the Federals tried to shut down Charleston on the cheap by blocking the harbor with its "Stone Fleet," hulks filled with rocks and scuttled to obstruct the main channel. However, powerful tides and storms soon washed these half-hearted attempts away.[1]

A more promising attempt was made possible on May 16, 1862, when Robert Smalls, a twenty-three-year-old slave employed by the Confederates as the pilot of the *Planter*, escaped with his vessel and brought news that the Confederates had abandoned their positions guarding the seaward approaches to James Island. This development left Charleston vulnerable to an attack from the rear across the island. Du Pont immediately saw the opportunity for a coup de main joint operation to seize Charleston, and on June 2 he landed two of Hunter's divisions, backed by considerable naval support, on James Island. However, instead of pushing forward against the meager Confederate resistance, Hunter convinced himself he was grossly outnumbered. He left Brigadier General Henry Benham in command and directed him not to attack until ordered to do so. For two weeks the Federals idled away their advantage while the Confederates reinforced the island. When Benham finally disobeyed his orders and attacked on June 16, he was badly defeated near the town of Secessionville. Among the host of brave Confederate defenders, Colonel Thomas Lamar particularly distinguished himself. Fearing a Confederate counterattack, Hunter evacuated James Island.

Du Pont was disgusted by this missed opportunity, complaining to Assistant Secretary of the Navy Gustavus Fox: "Oh those Soldiers I put them nearly on *top* of the house in Charleston, but I did not push them into the windows and they came back."[2] Secessionville was one example of the Federal difficulty in achieving unity of effort during the campaign. Indeed, the debacle reinforced Du Pont's opinion that the cooperation of a competently led army force was critical to any operation against Charleston.

Others saw promise in Admiral David Farragut's daring run past the forts at New Orleans. Secretary of the Navy Gideon Welles and others reasoned that if Du Pont similarly ran past Fort Sumter the Confederates would be forced to withdraw. Du Pont, however, felt otherwise, believing that Welles had woefully underestimated the strength of Charleston's defenses. Indeed, Fort Sumter was only a small part of a formidable defense in depth that by 1863 protected Charleston.

The outer layer of defenses consisted of fortifications which covered the mouth of the harbor and the channel from the barrier islands and Fort Sumter. These included Morris Island to the left of the harbor entrance with its Fort Wagner and Battery Gregg. Fort Sumter was immediately ahead, guarding the main harbor entrance, while Sullivan's Island and its Fort Moultrie and Batteries Bee and Beauregard stood on the left of the main entrance. Battery Gregg, Fort Sumter, and Fort Moultrie combined to deliver three-sided fire on any vessel that reached the harbor mouth.

Behind this tier was a second layer of artillery batteries in the inner harbor, sited to engage any Federal ships that might break through. These included Fort Johnson and Battery Glover on James Island, Fort Ripley and Castle Pinckney in the harbor itself, and the White Point Battery (Battery Ramsay) in Charleston. Finally, a series of land forts protected the flanks, thus barring a repeat of the strategy the British had used to seize Charleston during the American Revolution.[3]

Even nature seemed to conspire against the attackers. Fast currents and a shallow bar with irregular breaks were made even more difficult after the Confederates had removed the buoys marking the channels. As it was, the wide and deep Main Ship Channel was the only safe approach.[4] The result was that Charleston Harbor was a "bag" or "cul de sac" according to Du Pont's apt description. Once a naval force entered it, there was no clear channel that could be used to run past the fortifications, as there had been at New Orleans.[5]

Fort McAllister and the End of Du Pont

Secretary Welles believed the answer lay in ironclads, and he allotted resources to Du Pont's fleet accordingly. In spite of this influx of technology, Du Pont remained convinced that what was required was a joint operation with a robust army component. Welles favored an all-navy solution and joined Lincoln and Fox in pressing Du Pont into action.[6] Du Pont finally acquiesced

Confederate guns like this one repulsed Du Pont's trial attack at Fort McAllister and helped reinforce his assessment that the solution to Charleston would require more than just ironclads (Library of Congress, Prints & Photographs Division).

and sent the ironclad *Montauk*, the gunboats *Seneca*, *Wissahickon*, and *Dawn*, and the mortar schooner *C.P. Williams* to attack Fort McAllister on the Ogeechee River, Georgia. The Confederate forces resisted two separate attacks on January 27 and 28, 1863, leading Du Pont to lament, "If one ironclad cannot take eight guns, how are five to take 147 guns in Charleston Harbor?"[7]

Du Pont launched attacks on Fort McAllister again on February 28 and March 3 with more disappointing results, including the *Montauk* being badly damaged by a torpedo in the February 28 attack. Du Pont made an all-out attack on Charleston on April 7 without success. He wrote his wife: "We have failed as I felt sure we would."[8] Amid growing opinion in Washington that Du Pont had become defeatist, Welles replaced him as commander of the South Blockading Squadron with Rear Admiral Andrew Foote. However, when Foote died before reporting to his new post, Welles turned to Rear Admiral John Dahlgren, who assumed command on July 6.[9]

Fort Wagner

From July to September, Dahlgren kept up a bombardment of the Charleston defenses, but this time the navy would not be alone. On June 12, Major General Quincy Adams Gillmore had assumed command of the Department of the South and brought with him the excellent reputation he had earned by using long-range rifled artillery to pound Fort Pulaski into capitulation. Now he aimed to replicate this success against Forts Wagner and Sumter. On July 10, Gillmore crossed nearly 3,000 troops to the south end of Morris Island and advanced to within a half mile of Fort Wagner. In the meantime, Dahlgren's ironclads dueled with Fort Wagner for nearly twelve hours. Gillmore's men dug trenches to shelter Parrott guns that could range both forts, but there things stalemated. Over the next two months the Federals launched at least twenty-five separate attacks to try to capture the rest of Morris Island but without success.[10]

The Federals also kept Fort Sumter under fire. On August 17, Gillmore and Dahlgren began a week-long bombardment. On August 23 and again on September 1, Dahlgren attacked Fort Sumter with his ironclads. Throughout it all, the fort held.[11]

Next Gillmore turned his attention to Charleston itself. On August 21 he sent the Confederate commander General P.G.T. Beauregard a demand for the evacuation of Fort Sumter and Morris Island within four hours. If Beauregard failed to comply, Gillmore promised to open fire on Charleston. On August 22, the Federals initiated fire from the "Swamp Angel," a massive 8-inch Parrott, which caused fires and panic in the waterfront district but little more.[12]

Other attacks continued. On September 7, Dahlgren mounted a major ironclad assault on Fort Sumter. Thinking Fort Sumter had been partially evacuated, the next two days he sent 400 sailors and marines on more than thirty boats to attack Morris Island. Gillmore had planned an army operation as well, but by this time interservice rivalries had again surfaced and any cooperation between Gillmore and Dahlgren floundered. The Confederates were ready for the purely navy show and took more than 100 Federal prisoners.[13]

By now all the ironclads were in need of extensive repairs at Port Royal, and active operations ceased for several weeks. When they resumed, both Federal ships and troops continued to harass the forts. The Confederates responded by shifting heavy guns from Fort Sumter to the more powerful Forts Moultrie and Johnson and continued to plague the Federals with torpedoes and submersibles. The most famous of these was the *H.L. Hunley*, which on the night of February 17, 1864, sunk the 1,934-ton screw sloop *Housatonic*.

In the end, the Federal Navy Department decided Charleston was not worth risking the loss of its lone ironclad squadron. The capture of Charleston would have to wait for Major General William Sherman and his Carolinas Campaign sequel to his March to the Sea. On February 17–18, 1865, the Confederates evacuated, and Charleston succumbed to Federal occupation. By that time, Fort Sumter, where the war and the campaign had begun, was largely just a pile of rubble. To bring the matter full circle, when the original U.S. flag was once again raised over it on April 14, Major Robert Anderson, who had so bravely led its original defense, did the honors.

3

The Key Players

Federals

ROBERT ANDERSON (1805–1871)

Born in Kentucky and graduating from West Point in 1825, Anderson provided gallant service in the Black Hawk War and in Florida and Mexico. Anderson's reputation as an effective artillerist and his supposed Southern sympathies led secretary of war John Floyd to assign him to Charleston in the midst of the secession crisis. Floyd was disappointed if he expected Anderson to accommodate secession. Instead, with limited support and scant guidance from Washington, Anderson provided resolute service under trying conditions. Although forced ultimately to surrender Fort Sumter, Anderson returned north a hero for his resolute stand. Failing health soon forced him to resign from active service, but with the Union victory, Anderson returned to Fort Sumter exactly four years after the surrender to triumphantly raise the U.S. flag.[1]

HENRY BENHAM (1813–1884)

Graduating from West Point in 1837, Benham served in the Mexican War. After commanding a brigade in West Virginia, he reported to the Department of the South and was present for the capture of Fort Pulaski. He was relieved for disobedience of orders in initiating the Battle of Secessionville and became the scapegoat for the debacle. As a result, his appointment to brigadier general was revoked on August 7, 1862. The revocation was cancelled on February 6, 1863, and Benham was "returned to his proper sphere" as an engineer rather than a field commander.[2]

John Dahlgren (1809–1870)

Dahlgren was appointed a midshipman in 1826 and served sixteen years as an ordnance officer. During that time he invented the Dahlgren gun—a rifled cannon—and boat howitzers with iron carriages. Dahlgren's boat howitzers were the finest guns of their time in the world and were used by both Federals and Confederates throughout the Civil War. They remained in active service in the U.S. Navy until the 1880s and were copied throughout the world.

Dahlgren took command of the Washington Naval Yard on April 22, 1861. He was promoted to captain on July 16, 1862, and appointed chief of the Ordnance Bureau on July 18. Many felt Dahlgren was nothing but a shore officer and shared Admiral Samuel Du Pont's assessment that Dahlgren "chose one line in the walks of the profession [scientific ordnance work] while [Admiral Andrew] Foote and I chose another [sea duty]; he was licking cream while we were eating dirt and living on the pay of our rank."[3]

Hapless Henry Benham's tepid attack at Secessionville was too little for Admiral Samuel Du Pont and too much for Major General David Hunter (Library of Congress, Prints & Photographs Division).

Dahlgren ruthlessly exploited his ordnance achievements and his close relationship with President Lincoln, and on February 7, 1863, he was promoted to rear admiral. When Du Pont was relieved as commander of the South Atlantic Blockading Squadron, Dahlgren, in spite of his lack of experience with sea command, became his replacement on July 6. In that capacity, Dahlgren launched several attacks and siege operations against Charleston, South Carolina, but was unable to capture it.[4]

Samuel Du Pont (1803–1865)

Du Pont became a midshipman in 1815 and served in European waters, the West Indies, along the South American coast, in the Mediterranean, and in the Mexican War.[5] In the latter conflict, he gained valuable experience in blockade duty that would serve him well when he was appointed to be president of the Blockade Board in June 1861.[6] In this capacity, Du Pont was instrumental in planning the strategy for the blockade and coastal war.

Du Pont was promoted to flag officer in September 1861, and in October he commanded the fleet which captured Port Royal Sound. From there, Du Pont continued to ravage the Confederacy's Atlantic coast. Ultimately, growing tension between Du Pont and his army counterparts, as well as stiff Confederate defenses at Charleston, caused the campaign to culminate. At Charleston, Du Pont suffered a series of repulses by the Confederate defenders, and he became increasingly cautious and increasingly at odds with President Lincoln and Secretary of the Navy Gideon Welles. Du Pont was relieved of his command and served out the war on various boards and commissions.

Du Pont was a true military professional but also a man who was thin-skinned and jealous of his reputation. He was a firm believer in joint operations, understanding the concept more clearly than any other Federal commander except perhaps Lieutenant General Ulysses Grant or Admiral David Porter.[7]

A member of the talented Delaware manufacturing family, Du Pont is described by Bruce Catton as "a sailor whose social and financial standing was quite impeccable."[8] His fall from grace after Charleston led his biographer Kevin Weddle to term him "Lincoln's tragic admiral" and called his story "one of the most heartbreaking of the Civil War."[9]

Gustavus Fox (1821–1883)

Appointed a midshipman in 1838, Fox served in the Mexican War. He tired of peacetime service and resigned in 1856. At the outbreak of the Civil War, officers who had resigned in peacetime were ineligible to be restored to their former places in the navy, so Fox and others like him were recommissioned as acting lieutenants. Fox became skipper of the tug *Yankee* at Hampton Roads and soon made a name for himself as a vocal critic of the Federal failure at Fort Sumter. To both quiet Fox and mollify certain of his patrons, President Lincoln asked Secretary of the Navy Welles to give Fox some responsible job in the Navy Department. On May 8, 1861, Fox received orders appointing him as chief clerk of the Navy Department. His duties there were the equivalent of what is now performed by the entire Office of the Chief of Naval Operations. Fox became the Assistant Secretary of the Navy when the post was established later that summer.

Fox approached his duties with zeal and seemingly boundless energy, possessing what Commander Charles Davis called "a gigantic capacity for work." Fox was a godsend to Welles and the Navy Department. With a broad network of friends, Fox made things happen using a deft combination of aggressiveness and tact. Welles gave him a wide latitude and counted on his counsel for critical command appointments, strategic planning, and executing the department's technical business. President Lincoln shared Welles's high opinion of Fox, and Admiral Dahlgren once said, "Captain Fox, *he* is the Navy Department."[10]

Fox, however, would become a champion of the naval parochialism, which conflicted with Du Pont's quest for joint action at Charleston. As the two debated the proper course, Fox told Du Pont "the crowning act of this war ought to be by the navy. I feel that my duties are two fold; first, to beat our southern friends; second, to beat the Army."[11] Although Fox and Du Pont were friends, such a view clashed poignantly with Du Pont's feeling: "I have never had but one opinion—that the capture of Charleston should be effected by a joint operation of the army and navy.... We should be willing to share the laurels."[12]

QUINCY ADAMS GILLMORE (1825–1888)

Gillmore graduated first in the West Point class of 1849. He supervised harbor construction, and taught engineering and served as quartermaster at West Point before the Civil War. On August 6, 1861, he was promoted to captain and went on to serve as Chief Engineer on the Port Royal Expedition. In that capacity, he directed the bombardment of Fort Pulaski, Georgia which was the first time in history that long-distance rifled artillery defeated a masonry fort. He was appointed major general on July 10, 1863 and commanded the X Corps and the Department of the South at Charleston where he tried unsuccessfully to replicate his Fort Pulaski success. In the process, Gillmore and Admiral John Dahlgren, his navy counterpart, developed increasing problems with unity of effort.

Gillmore left the Department of the South in May 1864 to serve as a corps commander in Virginia and North Carolina and was injured while pursuing Lieutenant General Jubal Early in the Shenandoah Valley. After recovering, Gillmore returned to the Department of the South from February 9 to June 28, 1865.[13]

DAVID HUNTER (1802–1886)

Graduating from West Point in 1822, Hunter served in the army on the frontier but then resigned his commission to speculate in real estate, only to rejoin the army and serve as a paymaster during the Mexican War. While serving at Fort Leavenworth, Kansas, in 1860, Hunter established correspondence with Abraham Lincoln regarding secession rumors and was invited to make the inaugural journey with Lincoln to Washington. His relationship with Lincoln helped him receive an appointment as the fourth ranking volunteer general on May 17, 1861.[14]

In March 1862, Hunter replaced Brigadier General Thomas Sherman as commander of the newly created Department of the South. The next month, Fort Pulaski fell to troops under his command. He distanced himself from the defeat at Secessionville on June 16 by blaming Brigadier General Henry Benham for attacking in disobedience of orders and then suspended further operations directed at taking Charleston.

Hunter's career would be characterized by controversy. He had a reputation for being "independent in thought and action," and his relations with his naval counterpart Samuel Du Pont would steadily deteriorate.[15] In May 1862, Hunter would issue an order freeing slaves in his jurisdiction, which President Lincoln would have to quickly rescind. After being replaced by Major General Quincy Gillmore as commander of the Department of the South in July 1863, Hunter fought in the Shenandoah Valley.

ROBERT SHAW (1837–1863)

The son of prominent Bostonian abolitionists, Shaw attended Harvard between 1856 and 1859 but did not graduate. With the arrival of the Civil War, he enlisted in the 7th New York Infantry and later joined the 2nd Massachusetts and advanced to the rank of captain. In 1863, Massachusetts Governor John Andrew convinced Shaw to command the 54th Massachusetts Infantry, one of the first regiments of black soldiers. Shaw led these men in the attack on Fort Wagner on July 18, 1863. He was portrayed by Matthew Broderick in the 1989 film *Glory*.

ROBERT SMALLS (1839–1915)

Although born a slave in Beaufort, South Carolina, Smalls became quite accomplished in a variety of skills, including as a boat pilot. As a result of his expertise and navigational skills, he was made pilot of the Confederate gunboat *Planter* in March 1861. In an exceptionally bold move on May 13, 1862, Smalls escaped with the *Planter* and delivered her to the Federal blockading fleet. He brought with him intelligence that helped precipitate the Battle of Secessionville. Throughout the war, Smalls continued to serve the Union cause with both his seamanship and as a spokesman on behalf of black causes. After the war he became a long-time fixture in South Carolina politics.

GIDEON WELLES (1802–1878)

Spending most of his pre–Civil War life as a newspaper editor, a Democrat, and a postmaster, Welles held a minor post as head of the Naval Bureau of Provisions and Clothing during the Mexican War, but otherwise was largely untrained in naval matters. In 1854, he became a Republican and campaigned for Lincoln's election. Lincoln looked past Welles's lack of naval expertise and, seeing his administrative abilities and capability in evaluating and molding public opinion, made him his secretary of the navy. Among Welles's most important early contributions was the formation of the Blockade Board.

Welles was a firm believer in the new ironclad technology and felt it represented the solution to Charleston's stubborn defenses. He was unimpressed by Admiral Samuel Du Pont's arguments to the contrary and considered Du Pont to be overly cautious and pessimistic. Finally, on June 3, 1863, Welles relieved Du Pont. His handling of this situation did not show Welles at his best. He had become obsessed with taking Charleston and did not properly consider Du Pont's reservations as the commander on the scene. Welles also misled Congress in the subsequent inquiry by not releasing many documents that outlined Du Pont's concerns about the attack and the concerns he and his ironclad commanders shared about their ships.[16]

Confederates

PIERRE GUSTAVE TOUTANT BEAUREGARD (1818–1893)

Graduating second in the West Point class of 1838, Beauregard served as an engineer in Mexico and was the superintendent of West Point for just six days, being reassigned on January 28, 1861, on account of his Southern sympathies. He resigned from the U.S. Army on February 20 and was dashed in his hopes of receiving command of the army of his home state of Louisiana. Instead he was summoned to the Confederate capital in Montgomery, Alabama, where on February 26 President Jefferson Davis asked him to go to Charleston and take command of the Confederate and South Carolina forces there. Beauregard arrived on March 3, having been appointed the Confederacy's first brigadier general. The successful conclusion of the Fort Sumter crisis won him extravagant praise and when Virginia seceded, Beauregard was called there on May 28. His subsequent role in the Battle of First Manassas added to his fame.[17]

On August 3 Beauregard was promoted to full general, and in early 1862 he was transferred west where he served as General Albert Sidney Johnston's second in command at Shiloh. When Johnston was killed, Beauregard assumed command and delivered an uninspired performance that suggested his earlier reputation as a military genius had been exaggerated. He went on sick leave in June, turning his command over to Braxton Bragg. President Davis then accused Beauregard of leaving his post without authority and relieved him of command. Upon his recovery, Beauregard hoped to be restored to his field command in the west, but he had since fallen out of favor with Davis. Instead, he was deemed a politically expedient replacement for Lieutenant General John Pemberton at Charleston, where he arrived on September 15 to assume responsibility for the defenses of the Carolina and Georgia coasts. Feeling his talents wasted in what he described as the "Department of Refuge," Beauregard was delighted to be called to more active service in Virginia on April 20, 1864.[18]

STATES RIGHTS GIST (1831–1864)

Gist had such a unique name that diarist Mary Chesnut had to explain he "is a real personage—and not an odd name merely."[19] Benefiting from the support of Chesnut's powerful and well-connected husband, James, Gist held a variety of staff and command positions. As adjutant and inspector general of the State of South Carolina, Gist performed such tasks as helping implement the state's military draft and coordinating with General Robert E. Lee for the defense of the coast. On March 20, 1862, he was appointed brigadier general in the Provisional Confederate Army, and on April 8, he was ordered to duty at Charleston. He was placed in command of the Confederate forces on James Island and did much to prepare the defenses at Secessionville. Before the actual battle, however, Gist was superseded by a recently arrived, more senior, general. Gist was subsequently reassigned and fought at Vicksburg, Chickamauga, and Atlanta before being killed at the Battle of Franklin on November 30, 1864.

JOHNSON HAGOOD (1829–1898)

Having graduated from the Citadel in 1847, Hagood studied law, was active in the state militia, and was principally a planter. He was elected colonel of the 1st South Carolina Volunteers in 1861 and participated in the reduction of Fort Sumter. He then fought at First Manassas, and, after returning to South Carolina with his regiment, was promoted to brigadier general on July 21, 1861. He was so active on James Island and elsewhere around Charleston that Stephen Wise calls him "the department's designated troubleshooter." Towards the end of the war, Hagood also saw service in Virginia and North Carolina.[20]

Thomas Lamar (1826–1862)

A planter-turned-politician in the Edgefield District of South Carolina before the war, Lamar served on Governor Francis Pickens's staff and commanded an artillery battery on Morris Island during the Fort Sumter crisis. He then returned to Edgefield and raised a company he brought to Charleston. Lamar advanced in rank to colonel, and his unit grew to the size of a regiment. He emerged as the hero of the Battle of Secessionville and was awarded the Thanks of Congress. Lamar died of malaria on October 18, 1862.

Robert E. Lee (1807–1870)

Lee would, of course, eventually become the commander of the Army of Northern Virginia and one of the most distinguished generals in American history, but at the early stages of the Civil War, his reputation was much less luminous. He had led an unsuccessful campaign in western Virginia, which climaxed in defeat at Cheat Mountain in September 1861. In October, Lee returned to Richmond, but he did not stay long. With indications of Federal plans to attack Port Royal Sound, President Jefferson Davis ordered Lee to assume command of a newly formed department comprising the coasts of South Carolina, Georgia, and north Florida. Lee arrived at his new post on November 7, the same day Port Royal was captured by the Federals. He remained in this position until March 1862, when Davis summoned him back to Richmond to serve as his military advisor. When General Joe Johnston was wounded at Seven Pines, Lee assumed command and repulsed George McClellan's Peninsula Campaign.

Lee appreciated the problems of defending the vast Confederate coast and worked hard to consolidate and strengthen the effort. The difficulty of this undertaking was compounded with the loss of Fort Pulaski, in whose thick masonry walls Lee had placed great confidence. Even as commander of the Army of Northern Virginia, Lee could not escape the coastal war. In the summer of 1864, he sent word to Colonel William Lamb that Fort Fisher must be held. Without Wilmington open to blockade runners, Lee could not sustain his army.[21] Lee experienced the coastal war both directly in South Carolina and indirectly in Virginia.

John Pemberton (1814–1881)

Born in Pennsylvania and graduating from West Point in 1837, after serving in Mexico Pemberton married Martha Thompson of Norfolk, Virginia, in 1848. This marital connection to the South no doubt influenced Pemberton's decision to side with the Confederacy. He enjoyed a seemingly inexplicably rapid advance in rank and was sent to Charleston as commander of the Department of South Carolina, Georgia, and Florida in November 1861. He was promoted to major general on January 14, 1862.

Pemberton had great difficulty in implementing the strategy initiated by General Robert E. Lee to prioritize and consolidate the coastal defenses. Furthermore, in part due to suspicion aroused by his Northern birth, Pemberton suffered from a tempestuous relationship with Governor Francis Pickens and much of Charleston's citizenry. As a result of these difficulties, Pemberton was replaced in command by General Pierre Gustave Toutant Beauregard on September 24. In spite of his lackluster performance at Charleston, Pemberton was promoted to lieutenant general on October 13. He was reassigned to command the Department of Mississippi and Eastern Louisiana, where he experienced many of the same difficulties in defending Vicksburg as he had experienced at Charleston.[22]

After a lackluster performance commanding in the field, Gabriel Rains found his niche experimenting with torpedoes and helping develop the Confederacy's river and coastal defenses (Library of Congress, Prints & Photographs Division).

Francis Pickens (1805–1869)

Pickens was an Edgefield planter who served as minister to Russia under President James Buchanan. Upon returning to South Carolina, he quickly immersed himself in the passions of the sectional crisis. He became governor of South Carolina in December 1860 and noted in his inaugural address, "It is our sincere desire to separate from the States of the North in peace, and leave them to develop their own civilization to their own sense of duty and of interest. But if, under the guide of ambition and fanaticism, they decide otherwise, then be it so." Pickens played an active role in the Fort Sumter crisis. He demanded President Abraham Lincoln order Major Robert Anderson back to Fort Moultrie from Fort Sumter. He gave the orders to erect and man the batteries on Morris Island that would repulse the *Star of the West*. He offered his military advice to Brigadier General P.G.T. Beauregard. After Fort Sumter surrendered, Pickens debated with General Robert E. Lee about his prioritized defensive plan. Pickens was even more interventionist with Major General John Pemberton, and Pemberton's dissatisfaction and complaining helped ensure his reassignment. Much of his term was consumed by military problems, and a dissatisfied Mary Chesnut labeled him "Pickens the 1st."[23] The South Carolina General Assembly elected Milledge Bonham to replace Pickens as governor on December 17, 1862.

Gabriel Rains (1803–1881)

Rains graduated thirteenth in the West Point class of 1827 and fought in the Second Seminole War and the Mexican War. On July 31, 1861, he resigned as the lieutenant colonel of the 5th U.S. Infantry. Subsequently, he was appointed a brigadier general and commanded a brigade during the Peninsula Campaign. Clifford Dowdey describes Rains as "an old-time army man unsuited for combat,"[24] and Douglas Southall Freeman explains he "was at heart a scientist, and was more interested in explosives than in field command."[25]

In fact, Rains had made rudimentary experiments with land mines during the Seminole War and then again during the Peninsula Campaign. Such uses challenged the contemporary mores of civilized warfare, and Rains's energies were redirected to the more acceptable employment of "torpedoes" as part of water defenses. His techniques helped offset the Confederacy's conventional naval disadvantage at Charleston.

St. Julien Ravenel (1819–1882)

Ravenel was a gifted physician and scientist; one of his noteworthy accomplishments before the war was to go to Norfolk, Virginia, in 1855 to help combat the yellow fever outbreak there. During the war, he served as a surgeon in the 25th South Carolina Volunteers and as the surgeon in charge of the Confederate hospital in Columbia. Also in Columbia he supervised a laboratory which produced much of the medicine and nitrate of silver made for the army.[26]

Ravenel's greatest contribution to the defense of Charleston was in designing the *David*, a cigar-shaped boat that operated low in the water as a surface vessel. She carried an explosive charge on the end of a spar projecting forward from her bow. Although built as a private venture at Stoney Landing on the Cooper River, the *David* was put under the control of the Confederate States Navy and made at least three attacks against Federal vessels. After the war, Ravenel was critical in developing the phosphate fertilizer industry in South Carolina.

Roswell Ripley (1823–1887)

Born in Ohio and graduating from West Point in 1843, Ripley served in Mexico. Afterward, he married into the Middleton family of Charleston, South Carolina, in 1852. A year later he resigned from the army to pursue business opportunities in Charleston.

With the coming of the Civil War, Ripley joined the South Carolina state forces and, as a lieutenant colonel, occupied Fort Moultrie after the Federals vacated it in 1860. He later occupied Fort Sumter after it was surrendered. He was promoted to brigadier general on August 15, 1861, and assigned to command the Department of South Carolina and the coastal defenses of that state. He remained in that position until the arrival of Major General John Pemberton.[27]

Ripley's difficult personality caused tension with both his seniors and subordinates. His disagreements with Pemberton finally came to a head in May 1862, and Ripley was reassigned to duty in Virginia. There was no denying, however, Ripley's technical expertise as an artilleryman, and the Federal attack at Secessionville demonstrated the need for such skills. Shortly after he assumed command of the Department of South Carolina and Georgia, General Pierre Gustave Toutant Beauregard notified the Confederate authorities in Richmond he "would be pleased to have General Ripley assigned to my command for the defense of Charleston."[28] Upon returning to Charleston, Ripley did much to improve the defenses at Fort Wagner.

Part Two

Leadership Vignettes

4

James Buchanan and Ignoring Responsibility

James Buchanan was elected as the fifteenth president of the United States in 1856. He had the difficult task of leading the nation in a time when the divide between the northern and southern states was widening, and soon after his election he was faced with such sectional crises as the Dred Scott case and the controversial Lecompton constitution in Kansas. Moreover, he had to contend with the economic panic of 1857. Buchanan no doubt faced challenges that would try the best of presidents, but he failed to rise to the occasion. Arthur Schlesinger notes that "crisis widens opportunity for bold and imaginative action." He concludes, however, that Buchanan failed to show the "creative leadership" the situation demanded, and instead left it to his successor, Abraham Lincoln, "to show the difference individuals make to history."[1]

When Abraham Lincoln was elected president in 1860, South Carolina voted to secede from the United States on December 20. By February 1, 1861, Mississippi, Florida, Alabama, Georgia, Louisiana, and Texas had joined South Carolina in leaving the Union. Declaring themselves the Confederate States of America, these seven states swore in Jefferson Davis as their president on February 18. Because Lincoln would not be inaugurated until March 4, it was left to the lame duck president, James Buchanan, to deal with the crisis. The flash point was Fort Sumter off the coast of Charleston, South Carolina. There Major Robert Anderson and an intrepid garrison of eighty-four soldiers maintained a beleaguered Federal outpost that South Carolina now claimed belonged to her.

Many historians credit Buchanan with deciding upon a wise and statesmanlike course of action given the circumstances. His strategy appears to have been to rely on peace, conciliation, and delay in hopes of preserving the Union without bloodshed. While the policy may have been sound, Buchanan proceeded to execute it with "all his characteristic feebleness, hesitation, and timidity."[2]

Buchanan was no stranger to politics, having served in a variety of posts that spanned four decades. Throughout it all, he had escaped much of the rough and tumble that now plagued him. Known as the "Old Public Functionary," Buchanan "liked to conduct government on a gentlemanly basis."[3] He seemed unable to deal with the tumult in which he now was immersed. Among Buchanan's most serious problems was that several of his key cabinet members had pronounced loyalties to the fledgling Confederate cause. His secretary of the treasury was Thomas Howell Cobb of Georgia. His secretary of the interior was Jacob Thompson of North Carolina and later Mississippi. His secretary of war was John Floyd of Virginia.

Floyd, whom Ulysses Grant called "as earnest—to use a mild term—in the cause of Southern secession as Mr. Davis or any Southern statesman," was perhaps the worst in this area.[4] Known for his carelessness and disorganization, already Floyd's "neglect had left the War Department in anarchy."[5] Now in the time of sectional crisis, Floyd's mismanagement was compounded by his sectional loyalties. On the eve of the Civil War, he transferred muskets and other ordnance to southern states that would likely secede, leaving Grant to complain that Floyd "scattered the army so that much of it could be captured when hostilities should commence, and distributed the cannon and small arms from Northern arsenals throughout the South so as to be on hand when treason wanted them." Despite his obvious disdain for Floyd, Grant held Buchanan responsible for allowing such behavior. According to Grant, "The President did not prevent his cabinet preparing for war upon their government, either by destroying its resources or storing them in the South until a de facto government was established with Jefferson Davis as its President."[6]

Fort Sumter historian W.A. Swanberg agrees that Floyd was "the worst possible man to head the War Department at this critical time, and he should have been removed long before on the ground of incompetence alone." Swanberg claims Buchanan failed to do so because he "liked him personally and could not bring himself to dismiss him."[7] Mrs. Floyd also was a frequent visitor to the White House and was a friend of the president's.[8] Eventually, Floyd, Thompson, and Cobb followed their states into secession, but by then, Grant complained, "the harm had already been done. The stable door was locked after the horse had been stolen." All the while, Grant claimed, "the Administration of President Buchanan looked helplessly on and proclaimed the general government had no power to interfere; that the Nation had no power to save its own life."[9] Whether due to a lack of will and courage, misguided personal feelings, or perhaps some other reason, Buchanan failed to remove Floyd from his post when duty and good judgment demanded it.

Floyd did further disservice to Buchanan by advising him in early November 1860 that reports the forts at Charleston might come under attack were exaggerated. Floyd writes that he "assured [Buchanan] that the rumor was altogether without foundation, and gave it as my opinion that there was no danger of such an attempt being made.[10] Abner Doubleday, then a captain at Fort Moultrie, had a different opinion. "The muttering of the storm was heard all around us," Doubleday recalled, "and yet not one word of counsel or encouragement came from Washington."[11] Aging general-in-chief Winfield Scott had submitted a rather fanciful recommendation in late October that nine key forts in the South, including Moultrie and Sumter, be reinforced; but when pressed as to what manpower would be available for such an enterprise, Scott could come up with only 400 men. Fort Sumter alone required a wartime garrison of 650 men, so Scott's recommendation was unrealistic. Although this option was insufficient, Buchanan still had the problem of what to do.[12] He cautioned Floyd: "If those forts should be taken by South Carolina in consequence of our negligence to put them in defensible condition, it were better for you and me both to be thrown into the Potomac with millstones tied about our necks."[13] Nonetheless, Buchanan ultimately "determined not to touch the *status quo* at Charleston as long as our troops should continue to be hospitably treated by the inhabitants and remain in unmolested possession of the forts."[14]

Instead of reinforcing Charleston, Floyd tried to calm the situation by dispatching native Charlestonian Colonel Benjamin Huger as a sort of goodwill ambassador to oversee the fifteen men stationed at the city's arsenal. In an action even more significant, Floyd replaced Colonel John Gardner as commander of Fort Moultrie with Major Robert Anderson. The day after Lincoln's election, Gardner had attempted to transfer quietly some ammunition from the arsenal to Fort Moultrie. A hostile crowd blocked the move, and, rather than supporting Gardner, Floyd blamed him for stirring up trouble. Floyd clearly felt that Anderson, a Kentuckian by birth and husband of a Georgian, would present a more conciliatory presence in Charleston.[15] Moreover, until 1860, Anderson had owned a few slaves in Georgia, and Doubleday reported his new commander was still "a strong pro-slavery man."[16] It was with no small amount of self-satisfaction that the intriguing Floyd boasted of Anderson, "I selected him myself."[17]

As events unfolded, Floyd would soon come to realize that Anderson had no intention of placating the belligerent South Carolinians. Anderson quickly set out to improve discipline, inspect and repair defenses, and request reinforcements. He soon ascertained that Fort Moultrie was a poor location.

On his own initiative and without orders, he located to Fort Sumter on December 26. Floyd was beside himself, complaining to Buchanan that "the solemn pledges of this government had been violated" and insisting "one remedy only is left, and that is to withdraw the garrison from the harbor of Charleston altogether."[18]

Buchanan found himself caught between pro–Southern officials such as Floyd, who demanded he order Anderson back to his original position, and Northern advisors who insisted with equal vigor he do no such thing. Allan Nevins colorfully describes Buchanan as a "weary, vacillating, alarmed potentate, the center of a paralyzing storm … unable to make up his mind."[19] In the midst of this crisis, charges surfaced that Floyd was connected to the embezzlement of government bonds by Goddard Bailey, a distant relative. Again Nevins is unsparing in his critique of Buchanan: "Any other President would have summoned the Secretary to a private interview, given him a bad half hour, and directed him to write his resignation."[20] Instead, Buchanan assigned the task to Vice President John Breckenridge, who found Floyd unwilling to resign. Buchanan's indecision soon drew criticism on many fronts. Newspaper editor

In the lower left of this Kimmel and Forster allegory "The Outbreak of the Rebellion in the United States, 1861" President Buchanan is asleep and Secretary Floyd rakes coins into a bag (Library of Congress, Prints & Photographs Division).

Horace Greeley, for example, complained to Illinois congressman Elihu Washburne in a December 30 letter: "Why in the devil don't you present articles of impeachment against Buchanan and Floyd? People are becoming frantic—absolutely frantic with rage at treason. If Old Buck would show his countenance in these parts he would be hung so quick that Satan would not know where to look for his traitorous soul."[21] Floyd finally resigned as secretary of war on December 31, ridding Buchanan of one of his most unhelpful advisors and "giving Union men full control of the Union's cabinet."[22]

With the departure of Floyd, Buchanan began to receive more resolute advice, notably from Secretary of State Jeremiah Black and Attorney General Edwin Stanton. Both advocated forceful action in Charleston and their determination soon manifested itself in Buchanan. In response to demands to remove Anderson from Charleston, Buchanan declared, "This I cannot do; this I will not do." Instead, Fort Sumter would be defended "against hostile attacks from whatever quarter they may come."[23] On December 31, the reinvigorated president issued orders to the War and Navy departments to send the sloop of war *Brooklyn* to Charleston with troops and supplies.

Gradually, however, even this bold move suffered from compromise and indecisiveness. The *Brooklyn* was a powerful screw steamer of 2,070 tons. In January 1861, her armament consisted of twenty-two 9 inch Dahlgren guns, one heavy 12 pounder, and one light 12 pounder.[24] She would have presented a formidable challenge to the Confederates at Charleston and sent a clear message that the United States meant business. Instead, Winfield Scott began to worry about the deep-draft vessel's ability to get over the bar at Charleston Harbor. Moreover, use of the *Brooklyn* would smack of coercion. Scott recommended—and Buchanan "yielded reluctantly"—replacing the *Brooklyn* with the *Star of the West*, a merchant steamer with "no guns, no protection, and no business venturing where shots might be fired at her."[25] This decision "changed the open, forthright reinforcement of one of the nation's forts into a clandestine enterprise as sneaky as a smuggler's voyage."[26] It also delayed the operation for two more days and would further sap Anderson's strength and increase that of the Confederates. When the *Star of the West* finally embarked from New York late on January 5, the 200 "well-drilled recruits" she carried were ordered to hide below the decks when she reached Charleston.[27] The operation was "a perfect example of too little and too late" and seemed to indicate "the United States Government ... did not have the courage to do its duty honestly and openly."[28]

Perhaps it was a foregone conclusion that such a diluted effort would fail. By the time the *Star of the West* was approaching Fort Sumter, the Confederates had received numerous warnings of her arrival, including from

Secretary of the Interior Thompson, who finally resigned in protest. On January 9, Captain John McGowan, a civilian merchant skipper, headed the *Star of the West* into the main channel, paralleling Morris Island. When she was about two miles off Fort Sumter, the ship was greeted by fire from a battery on Morris Island manned by Citadel cadets. Although Major Anderson had received no official word of the resupply effort, he now ordered his men to their stations, but there was little they could do. Without instructions from Washington and fearful of igniting a civil war, Anderson held his fire.

The *Star of the West* cleared the guns on Morris Island after suffering two insignificant hits, but now found herself under fire from Fort Moultrie. McGowan decided he had had enough and turned his ship and headed out the channel and back to New York. Although the firing on the *Star of the West* clearly established a casus belli, Buchanan did nothing.[29] To many critics, the entire affair "was so bungled in conception and execution as to make the American eagle appear a sorry bird indeed."[30]

Leadership Lessons

W.A. Swanberg describes the *Star of the West* fiasco as "a story of what might have been had ordinary initiative and enterprise been shown." He chronicles a long list of "ifs" that may have resulted in a different outcome: If the *Brooklyn* had been sent instead of the *Star of the West*.... If the operation had not been delayed.... If a naval captain had been in charge.... If Anderson had been advised of what was going on....[31] All of these measures were entirely within President Buchanan's ability to influence in the immediate matter of Fort Sumter.

Allan Nevins is equally critical of Buchanan writ large, declaring the president to have failed in four critical points. According to Nevins, Buchanan neglected to rally the country with a spirited appeal to national sentiment. He failed to reorganize his cabinet by removing its pro–Southern members and replacing them with those who would promote unity and decision. He did not reinforce Anderson and therefore send a clear message to all that, whatever else, disunion would result in a fight. Finally, and most important, Nevins thinks, Buchanan did not press "with instant vigor his plan for a national convention to formulate a scheme of adjustment" that would have neutralized the radical secessionists and the radical Republicans then in Congress who "were committed to oppose any practicable scheme of accommodation."[32]

Of course Swanberg and Nevins, as all historians do, have the benefit of hindsight, and Buchanan is not without his defenders. Even his harshest critics admit he was in a most difficult spot.³³ Yet, instead of taking action of the sort Swanberg and Nevins recommend or even some other option, Buchanan did nothing. Rather than thinking about what he could do to affect positively the situation, he surrendered the initiative to his adversaries. In the process, Buchanan "so exaggerated what the South might do that he was often immobilized."³⁴

According to Attorney General and Secretary of State Jeremiah Black, Buchanan "was convinced that if no movement were made looking to the increase of our force at that point, the revolutionary states would await the advent of the new administration."³⁵ In adopting this course, Buchanan was what Peter Northouse describes as the "laissez-faire leader [who] takes a 'hands-off—let-things-ride' approach." According to Northouse, "This leader abdicates responsibility, delays decisions, gives no feedback, and makes little effort to help followers satisfy their needs." Laissez-faire leadership "represents the absence of leadership" and is the complete opposite of transactional-transformational leadership.³⁶

Jean Baker astutely identifies the problem with Buchannan's laissez-faire leadership, writing, "To be sure, to do nothing was to do much, because Buchanan was granting the future Confederate States of America precious time to organize and prepare for war." Because Buchanan failed to act decisively, "a confrontation that might have dwindled away against one state became more certain."³⁷ Seeing Buchanan's inaction, other southern states, especially those on the border, were emboldened to follow South Carolina's lead. As Edward Pollard describes it, Buchanan "drew the wind for southern sails by his complacent attitude."³⁸ Thus the new president, Lincoln, was forced to deal with a "Confederacy that was much more powerful than it might have been."³⁹ Buchanan seems to have little remorse concerning the mess he had left for his successor. On his last day of office, he told Lincoln, "If you are as happy in entering the White House as I shall feel on returning to Wheatland [Buchanan's Pennsylvania home], you are a happy man."⁴⁰

Take-aways

- Problems usually don't just go away on their own. Leaders must take action.
- Leaders are only as good as those around them.
- Individual leaders make a difference.
- Good leaders prepare a transition plan for their successor.

5

Robert Anderson and Embracing Responsibility

With the sectional crisis growing daily, Major Robert Anderson was ordered to Charleston Harbor to assume command of Castle Pinckney, Fort Moultrie, and Fort Sumter. With only the vaguest of instructions from Washington, Anderson did his duty as he understood it. He surrendered only after enduring a thirty-four hour bombardment that showed further resistance was futile.

Major Anderson was on furlough in New York City on November 15, 1860, when he was ordered to "forthwith proceed to Fort Moultrie, and immediately relieve Bvt. Col. John L. Gardner."[1] Gardner was a veteran of the War of 1812 and the Mexican War, but Abner Doubleday, a captain in his command, believed that "now, owing to his advanced age, [he] was ill fitted to weather the storm that was about to burst upon us."[2] Although Gardner was a native of Massachusetts, Doubleday considered him to be politically "quite southern, frequently asserting that the South had been treated outrageously in the question of the Territories, and defrauded of her just rights in other respects."[3] Nonetheless, the garrison commander found himself at odds with the local population after his seemingly reasonable step on November 8 of attempting to move ammunition from the U.S. Arsenal to Fort Moultrie turned into a debacle. Although Gardner later exacted an apology from Mayor Charles Macbeth for the interference, the uproar put Gardner on the wrong side of Secretary of War John Floyd, who dispatched Major Fitz John Porter on an inspection tour of the defenses. Porter was unimpressed, reporting on November 11 that "the unguarded state of the fort invites attack, if such design exists, and much discretion and prudence are required on the part of the commander to restore the proper security without exciting a community prompt to misconstrue actions of authority. I think this can be effected by a proper commander...."[4] By this point, Floyd had probably already decided that Gardner was not "a proper commander."

Robert Anderson, on the other hand, had both political and military reasons to commend him for this difficult posting. As a Kentucky-born, pro-slavery husband of a Georgian, Anderson, Floyd hoped, had the background and capacity to appease the hostile South Carolinians. If push came to shove, however, Anderson was also a respected officer, who more resolute heads than Floyd considered up to the challenge. Captain Doubleday wrote, "We had long known Anderson as a gentleman; courteous, honest, intelligent, and thoroughly versed in his profession."[5] He had graduated from West Point in 1825 and been promoted to major in 1857 after service in the Black Hawk War, Florida, and Mexico. An expert artilleryman, he had been a member of various artillery boards and an artillery instructor at West Point. Moreover, in spite of his connections to the South, Anderson was unquestionably loyal to the Union.[6]

Robert Anderson was the stalwart commander of the Federal garrison at Fort Sumter (Library of Congress, Prints & Photographs Division).

He would need all his abilities and more in his new assignment. Duty in Charleston had long been regarded as "a veritable country club," especially when contrasted with a remote and rugged post on the frontier.[7] The garrison enjoyed friendly relations with the city, and the leisurely pace allowed the soldiers to enjoy all of Charleston's charm, society, and entertainment.[8] In such a comfortable environment, Porter found the noncommissioned officers and privates "do not move with an alacrity and spirit indicating the existence of a strict discipline."[9] Furthermore, Gardner resided with his family outside of Fort Moultrie, which gave him a sense of personal detachment from any threat to its safety. On one occasion, when a hostile secessionist crowd gathered near the fort, Gardner "sent word to [Doubleday] to assume command at once in his place," rather than personally handling the crisis.¹⁰ By all accounts, Gardner had been a gallant soldier in his younger days, but, "after almost a half century in the army," W.A. Swanberg declares, Gardner's "martial spirit was pretty well played out."¹¹ Putting it perhaps a little more gently, the newly arrived garrison surgeon Dr. Samuel Crawford reported, "the old and worthy soldier ... was slow to awaken to the reality" of the new situation.¹² The end result was that Anderson inherited an unsatisfactory position.

Anderson wasted no time inspecting his new command. By November 23 he had seen enough to send a report to Washington. Of the general situation, Anderson said, "There is not so much of feverish excitement as there was last week, but that there is a settled determination to leave the Union, and to obtain possession of [Fort Moultrie], is apparent to all." "The clouds are threatening," he warned, "and the storm may break upon us at any moment." Although he desired "so far as honor will permit—to avoid collision with the citizens of South Carolina," he felt the best way of preventing such a clash was to so strengthen his defenses so as to create "an attitude that it would be madness and folly to attack us." For his part, he acknowledged the deficiencies already reported by Porter and set out to immediately correct these and other weaknesses. More, however, would be required, and he told the War Department, "I do, then, most earnestly entreat that a re-enforcement be immediately sent to [Fort Moultrie], and that at least two companies be sent at the same time to Fort Sumter and Castle Pinckney—half a company, under a judicious commander, sufficing, I think, for the latter work."¹³

Having informed his superiors of the situation as he understood it, Anderson then asked for guidance. He saw two possible courses that might unfold. The first was the positive one. "With these three works garrisoned as requested, and with a supply of ordnance stores, for which I shall send requisitions in a few days," Anderson wrote, "I shall feel that, by the blessing of God, there may be a hope that no blood will be shed, and that South Carolina will not attempt to take these forts by force, but will resort to diplomacy to secure them." On the other hand, there was a negative possibility as well. "If we neglect, however, to strengthen ourselves," Anderson warned, "she will, unless these works are surrendered on their first demand, most assuredly immediately attack us." Either way, Anderson knew what was at stake and all its implications. "I will thank the Department to give me special instructions," he calmly but clearly asked, "as my position here is rather a politico-military than a military one."¹⁴

Anderson's report is exemplary in its clarity, objectivity, and completeness. He is reporting facts that he has verified by personal observation. He identifies problems and recommends solutions. He maintains an objective and respectful tone rather than allowing himself to resort to emotion. He clearly understands the limits of his authority and requests guidance on how to act on behalf of the secretary of war or the president. In the language of modern day military communications, Anderson is seeking to understand his "commander's intent." The commander's intent is "a clear, concise statement of what the force must do and the conditions the force must meet to succeed with respect to the enemy, terrain, and the desired end state."[15] A clearly stated commander's intent allows subordinates to exercise initiative in a decentralized and fluid environment.[16]

Anderson sent another report on November 28, again requesting reinforcements and asking for specific guidance if South Carolina attempted to enroll in state military service some of the men who had been working on Fort Moultrie. Anderson was also having serious doubts if Fort Moultrie was worth further effort. As if thinking out loud, he wrote, "I am inclined to think that if I had been here before the commencement of expenditures on this work, and supposed that, this garrison would not be increased, I should have advised its withdrawal, with the exception of a small guard, and its removal to Fort Sumter, which so perfectly commands the harbor and this fort."[17]

Although Anderson's report of November 23 has been lauded as "one of the most important reports ever penned by an American officer, the fruit of careful deliberation by an able commander at the scene, stated with the highest degree of emphasis and warning," it failed to inspire Secretary Floyd to provide the clear guidance and support he owed Anderson.[18] Instead, on December 1, Anderson received word that Colonel Benjamin Huger would be sent to help assuage the emotions some of his fellow Charlestonians had displayed after Gardner's aborted attempt to move supplies from the arsenal. Anderson may have drawn some comfort from the presence of Huger, who had been a classmate of his at West Point, but beyond that, Floyd provided little substantive help. The secretary "believed, from information thought to be reliable, that an attack will not be made on your command." But, if such "convictions unhappily prove untrue," whatever actions Anderson took "must be such as to be free from the charge of initiating a collision." Floyd provided no guidance as to what these actions might be, other than to say, "If attacked, you are, of course, expected to defend the trust committed to you to the best of your ability."[19]

Anderson had already clearly stated in his report of November 23 that, given his present understrength complement of what he estimated to be about sixty men, "if beleaguered, as every man of the command must be either engaged or held on the alert, they will be exhausted and worn down in a few days and nights of such service as they would then have to undergo."[20] That would be the extent of Anderson's defense "to the best of your ability" unless he received his requested reinforcements. These Floyd denied, opining that reinforcements would "but add to [the] excitement, and might lead to serious results."[21]

The longer Anderson was in Charleston, the more he was convinced that the situation would soon reach a climax. The same day he received the disappointing message from Floyd, Anderson wrote the War Department: "The question for the Government to decide—and the sooner it is done the better—is, whether, when South Carolina secedes, these forts are to be surrendered or not. If the former, I must be informed of it, and instructed what course I am to pursue. If the latter be the determination, no time is to be lost in either sending troops, as already suggested, or vessels of war to this harbor. Either of these courses may cause some of the doubting States to join South Carolina."[22] In the meantime, Anderson promised to "go steadily on, preparing for the worst, trusting hopefully in the God of Battles to guard and guide me in my course."[23]

By December 6, Anderson was clearly feeling the weight of the crisis. "Our time is short enough for what we have to do," he wrote. He also was more concerned with details and continued pressing the War Department for clarity. "I have not yet commenced leveling off the sand hills which, within one hundred and sixty yards to the east, command [Fort Moultrie]," he reported. "Would my doing this be construed into initiating a collision? I would thank you also to inform me under what circumstances I would be justified in setting fire to or destroying the houses which afford dangerous shelter to an enemy, and whether I would be justified in firing upon an armed body which may be seen approaching our works."[24] He also was becoming increasingly convinced that Fort Sumter was more important than Fort Moultrie. On December 9 he told Floyd, "I hear that the attention of the South Carolinians appears to be turned more toward Fort Sumter than it was, and it is deemed probable that their first act will be to take possession of that work."[25]

Belatedly Floyd gave Anderson some sort of guidance. As a security safeguard, Floyd directed Major Don Carlos Buell, a member of the adjutant general staff, to commit the instructions to memory and verbally and in person communicate them to Anderson. On December 9, Buell reached Charleston and told Anderson:

> You are aware of the great anxiety of the Secretary of War that a collision of the troops with the people of this State shall be avoided, and of his studied determination to pursue, a course with reference to the military force and forts in this harbor which shall guard against such a collision. He has therefore carefully abstained from increasing the force at this point, or taking any measures which might add to the present excited state of the public mind, or which would throw

any doubt on the confidence he feels that South Carolina will not attempt, by violence, to obtain possession of the public works or interfere with their occupancy. But as the counsel and acts of rash and impulsive persons may possibly disappoint those expectations of the Government, he deems it proper that you should be prepared with instructions to meet so unhappy a contingency. He has therefore directed me verbally to give you such instructions.

You are carefully to avoid every act which would needlessly tend to provoke aggression; and for that reason you are not, without evident and imminent necessity, to take up any position which could be construed into the assumption of a hostile attitude. But you are to hold possession of the forts in this harbor, and if attacked you are to defend yourself to the last extremity. The smallness of your force will not permit you, perhaps, to occupy more than one of the three forts, but an attack on or attempt to take possession of any one of them will be regarded as an act of hostility, and you may then put your command into either of them which you may deem most proper to increase its power of resistance. You are, also authorized to take similar steps whenever you have tangible evidence of a design to proceed to a hostile act.[26]

Anderson received more guidance on December 14, in response to his November 28 query about potential attempts by South Carolina to enroll his workers, and his December 6 query about clearing his fields of fire: If the request for enrollment was bona fide, Anderson was to allow it; leveling the sand dunes at this point would be unwise; instead, it would be better for Anderson, in the event of an attack, to destroy the houses with his guns since the other party had established itself at that point as being guilty of "initiating a collision."[27]

This belated flurry of guidance "showed Floyd in a better light," and at least gave Anderson "one escape from the trap."[28] Floyd had given Anderson permission to consolidate his small force where he thought his chances of defense were greatest. Anderson had already been pursuing this line of thought, and even Buell offered, "My personal advice is that you do not let this opportunity to escape you."[29] By this point Anderson likened his position at Fort Moultrie to "a sheep watching the butcher sharpening a knife to cut his throat."[30] Unlike a sheep, he was ready to move.

President Buchanan was not aware of the guidance Floyd had sent to Anderson via Buell, and when the cautious president learned of it, he took issue with the instruction "to defend yourself to the last extremity." The last thing Buchanan wanted was Anderson's men decimated. Floyd was forced to clarify this part of the guidance, telling Anderson in a message that reached him on December 23:

In the verbal instructions communicated to you by Major Buell, you are directed to hold possession of the forts in the harbor of Charleston, and, if attacked, to defend yourself to the last extremity. Under these instructions, you might infer that you are required to make a vain and useless sacrifice of your own life and the lives of the men under your command, upon a mere point of honor. This is far from the President's intentions. You are to exercise a sound military discretion on this subject.

It is neither expected nor desired that you should expose your own life or that of your men in a hopeless conflict in defense of these forts. If they are invested or attacked by a force so superior that resistance would, in your judgment, be a useless waste of life, it will be your duty to yield to necessity, and make the best terms in your power.

This will be the conduct of an honorable, brave, and humane officer, and you will be fully justified in such action. These orders are strictly confidential, and not to be communicated even to the officers under your command, without close necessity.[31]

Anderson had already made it clear that to mount any sort of a credible defense he would need reinforcements, and these requests had been repeatedly denied. Rather than give Anderson the men he said he needed, Washington had only sent vague and contradictory orders that seemed to say "defend the forts ... but in heaven's name do not offend anyone." As Swanberg states, these "were the instructions of a superior who did not choose to take a clear stand but preferred to throw responsibility on his subordinate."[32]

The situation was exasperating for poor Anderson. He wrote Washington on December 22: "I must confess that I think where an officer is placed in as delicate a position as the one I occupy that he should have the entire control over all persons connected in any way with the work intrusted to him. Responsibility and power to control ought to go together." He clearly thought Fort Sumter was his most defensible position and would move there "were I to receive instructions so to do."[33] To his great credit, Anderson had the moral courage to make this important decision himself when his superiors failed him. On December 26, he told Doubleday: "I have determined to evacuate this post immediately, for the purpose of occupying Fort Sumter; I can only allow you twenty minutes to form your company and be in readiness to start."[34] After an expeditious and pleasantly uneventful movement, Anderson wrote Washington from Fort Sumter: "I have the honor to report that I have just completed, by the blessing of God, the removal to this fort of all of my garrison, except the surgeon, four non-commissioned officers, and seven men.... The step which I have taken was, in my opinion, necessary to prevent the effusion of blood."[35]

Although Anderson and his officers shared a small flask of brandy and toasted "to the success of the garrison," Anderson's move drew alarm and criticism from many other quarters. Robert Barnwell, James Adams, and James Orr, who were in Washington as a commission to represent the interests of South Carolina, protested to Buchanan:

Since our arrival an officer of the United States acting, as we are assured, not only without but against your orders, has dismantled one fort and occupied another, thus altering to a most important extent the condition of affairs under which we came.

Until those circumstances are explained in a manner which relieves us of all doubt as to the spirit in which these negotiations shall be conducted, we are forced to suspend all discussion as to any arrangements by which our mutual interests might be amicably adjusted.

And, in conclusion, we would urge upon you the immediate withdrawal of the troops from the harbor of Charleston. Under present circumstances they are a standing menace which renders negotiation impossible, and, as our recent experience shows, threatens speedily to bring to a bloody issue questions which ought to be settled with temperance and judgment.[36]

Floyd, as expected, joined his fellow Southerners in protesting what he claimed, in spite of his earlier guidance, was Anderson's unauthorized action. More disappointing was President Buchanan's exclamation: "My God! Are calamities never to come singly! I call God to witness, you gentlemen, better than anybody, know that this is not only without but against my orders. It is against my policy."[37]

Given the fait accompli, however, President Buchanan somehow found enough moral courage to tell the South Carolina commissioners, "In the harbor of Charleston we now find three forts confronting each other, over all of which the Federal flag floated only four days ago; but now over two of them this flag has been supplanted, and the palmetto flag has been substituted in its stead. It is under all these circumstances that I am urged immediately to withdraw the troops from the harbor of Charleston, and am informed that without this, negotiation is impossible. This I cannot do; this I will not do."[38] By January 1 the South Carolinians informed the president, "By your course you have probably rendered civil war inevitable."[39] And so it was.

When Anderson made his move to Fort Sumter, he reported having about four months' worth of supplies on hand.[40] The failure of the *Star of the West* mission on January 9, 1862, had added nothing to Anderson's daily-decreasing stockpile. On April 1, Anderson notified Washington that he had told Assistant Secretary of the Navy Gustavus Fox "that if I placed the command on short allowance I could make the provisions last until after the 10th of this month; but as I have received no instructions from the Department that it was desirable I should do so, it has not been done." On April 3, Anderson added more urgently that his situation required him to "most respectfully and urgently ask for instructions what I am to do as soon as my provisions are exhausted. Our bread will last four or five days."[41] On April 4, Anderson received his first communication from the new secretary of war, Simeon Cameron. It reflected Washington's continuing detachment from the reality of Anderson's situation:

> Your letter of the 1st instant occasions some anxiety to the President. On the information of Captain Fox he had supposed you could hold out till the 15th instant without any great inconvenience; and had prepared an expedition to relieve you before that period.
>
> Hoping still that you will be able to sustain yourself till the 11th or 12th instant, the expedition will go forward; and, finding your flag flying, will attempt to provision you, and, in case the effort is resisted, will endeavor also to re-enforce you.
>
> You will therefore hold out, if possible, till the arrival of the expedition. It is not, however, the intention of the President to subject your command to any danger or hardship beyond what, in your judgment, would be, usual in military life; and he has entire confidence that you will act as becomes a patriot and soldier, under all circumstances.
>
> Whenever, if at all, in your judgment, to save yourself and command, a capitulation becomes a necessity, you are authorized to make it.[42]

The Lincoln Administration had been in office for a month, and this initial communication from Cameron certainly could not have given Anderson any more confidence in support from Washington than the little he had mustered under Buchanan and Floyd.

To make matters worse, the Confederates were becoming increasingly hostile and increasingly restrictive about Anderson's contact with the outside world. By April 9, Secretary of War Leroy Walker decided that Fort Sumter "must be completely isolated" and ordered Brigadier General P.G.T. Beauregard to do so.[43] On April 11, Beauregard sent three of his aides to inform Anderson:

> The Government of the Confederate States has hitherto forborne from any hostile demonstration against Fort Sumter, in the hope that the Government of the United States, with a view to the amicable adjustment of all questions between the two Governments, and to avert the calamities of war, would voluntarily evacuate it.
>
> There was reason at one time to believe that such would be the course pursued by the Government of the United States, and under that impression my Government has refrained from making any demand for the surrender of the fort. But the Confederate States can no longer delay assuming actual possession of a fortification commanding the entrance of one of their harbors, and necessary to its defense and security.
>
> I am ordered by the Government of the Confederate States to demand the evacuation of Fort Sumter. My aides, Colonel [James] Chesnut and Captain [Stephen] Lee, are authorized to make such demand of you. All proper facilities will be afforded for the removal of yourself and command, together with company arms and property, and all private property, to any post in the United States which you may select. The flag which you have upheld so long and with so much fortitude, under the most trying circumstances, may be saluted by you on taking it down.[44]

Although Surgeon Crawford wondered, "Was ever such terms granted to a band of starving men?" all of Anderson's officers recommended refusing the demand.[45] Anderson agreed and informed Beauregard his was "a demand with which I regret that my sense of honor, and of my obligations to my Government, prevent my compliance."[46] Anderson confided in Colonel Chesnut: "I shall await the first shot, and if you do not batter us to pieces, we shall be starved out in a few days."[47]

Chesnut and his party returned to Charleston and reported what Anderson had said about being "starved out." This condition presented one last possibility of a peaceful resolution in the eyes of the Confederates. Shortly before 1:00 a.m. on April 12, Chesnut and three other Confederate representatives returned to Fort Sumter and delivered to Anderson a note from Beauregard stating, "If you will state the time with which you will evacuate Fort Sumter, and agree in the meantime that you will not use your guns against us unless ours shall be employed against Fort Sumter, we will abstain from opening fire upon you." Anderson consulted with his officers and was advised by Surgeon Crawford that the men could last about five days—the last three without food. After much thought, Anderson replied that he would evacuate Fort Sumter by noon on April 15, "should I not receive prior to that time controlling instructions from my Government or additional supplies."[48]

Chesnut and his fellow messengers considered Anderson's reply and decided that it was inconsistent with the instructions they had been given. Instead, Chesnut wrote and at 3:20 a.m. handed Anderson the following: "Sir: By authority of Brigadier General Beauregard, commanding the Provisional Forces of the Confederate States, we have the honor to notify you that he will open fire of his batteries on Fort Sumter in one hour from this time."[49] Anderson then accompanied the Confederates back to their boat and bid them farewell, saying, "If we never meet in this world again, God grant that we may meet in the next."[50]

The bombardment commenced at 4:30 a.m. with a signal shot fired from the Confederate mortar battery on James Island. After that "the fire soon became general from all hostile batteries."[51] In the meantime, the ad hoc Federal relief expedition was arriving off the bar. Anderson's men could see the *Baltic*, *Harriett Lane*, and *Pawnee*, but the vessels remained anchored. Anderson and his men weathered the storm alone until it became obvious that the cause was hopeless. Shortly after 1:00 p.m. on April 13, Brigadier General James Simons dispatched Colonel Louis Wigfall and Gourdin Young to Fort Sumter, where Wigfall told Anderson, "You have defended your flag nobly, sir. General Beauregard wishes to stop this, and to ask upon what terms you will evacuate this work." His options exhausted, Anderson acquiesced to surrender and evacuate

Generals Robert Anderson and Quincy Gillmore, near the center of this photograph, prepare to raise the flag over Fort Sumter on April 14, 1865 (Library of Congress, Prints & Photographs Division).

the fort. His command would be allowed to leave with their arms and all company property. Anderson was also accorded the final courtesy of departing with a salute to the flag. Shortly after Wigfall and Young departed, another Confederate contingent consisting of Richard Pryor, William Miles, and Captain Stephen Lee arrived under orders by Beauregard. There was some confusion when it became apparent Wigfall had lacked authority from Beauregard to arrange terms, but the matter was quickly settled. Anderson would surrender under the previously arranged conditions.

In the thirty-four hour attack, the Confederates hit Fort Sumter with approximately 4,000 shells. Anderson evacuated the position by a steamer to New York on April 14. In an accidental explosion while the Federals were halfway through a planned 100-gun salute, Private Daniel Hough became the first casualty of the war.

Anderson was hailed as a hero upon his arrival in New York. He was appointed brigadier general on May 15 and commanded for a short time in Kentucky, where he helped solidify his native state's allegiance to the Union. In an even broader sense, Ezra Warner contends Anderson's resolute stand at Fort Sumter "served to unify the North" at a critical hour. Unfortunately, the experience was also detrimental to Anderson's health, and he was relieved in October 1861 and retired in 1863. He was able, however, to return to Fort Sumter on April 14, 1865, to raise the United States flag he had hauled down exactly four years before.[52]

Leadership Lessons

Immediately upon arriving at his new command, Anderson assessed the situation. He found many security, discipline, readiness, and materiel deficiencies, and he established a program to make corrections. While Anderson could rely on his own expertise to assess much of the artillery situation, elsewhere he made excellent use of Surgeon Crawford to assess the health and medical situation.

Anderson's assessment did more than merely improve the status quo. As he gained situational awareness, he became increasingly convinced that Fort Sumter offered a better alternative to his inherited position at Fort Moultrie, and he made this significant change. Anderson assessed not just what his situation was, but also what it could be. He identified a problem and developed a solution.

Anderson did an excellent job of keeping his superiors informed. He clearly communicated his observations, made recommendations, and requested guidance. He did so with the greatest of self-control as he contended with the slow transit of communications compounded by insufficient answers. Throughout the entire ordeal, he remained astutely aware of the political sensitivity of the situation and the potential second and third order effects of even his smallest actions.

In an uncertain and ambiguous environment, Anderson did his duty as he understood it. In the process, he had to resolve myriad conflicts that pulled him every which way. He was a United States Army officer, but one with certain

Southern sympathies. He was subordinate to the authorities in Washington, but superiors like Floyd had failed in their reciprocal obligations to him. He had a duty to defend his fort, but at the same time he was responsible for the lives of his men. Perhaps weighing most heavily in Anderson's calculus was the conundrum presented by his duty to resist rebellion while simultaneously giving the nation every last opportunity to peacefully resolve the mounting sectional crisis. Rushworth Kidder notes that while "right-versus-wrong" choices certainly present moral temptations, they really leave no doubt about the proper resolution. Instead, he argues, "The really tough choices ... don't center on right versus wrong. They involve right versus right. They are genuine dilemmas precisely because each side is firmly rooted in our basic, core values."[53] Such was the situation Anderson faced, and it is hard to imagine anyone handling it better under the circumstances.

Take-aways

- Leaders carefully assess the situation based on their own expertise and the advice of their staff and then develop a plan of action.
- Leaders look beyond the status quo in considering a solution.
- Leaders keep superiors informed in a way that allows the superiors to make decisions.
- Leaders understand the bigger picture and know the limits of their authority.
- The most challenging duty involves resolving "right-versus-right" dilemmas.

6

Gideon Welles and Strategic Vision

On April 19, 1861, six days after the loss of Fort Sumter, President Abraham Lincoln issued a proclamation declaring the blockade of the Southern states from South Carolina to Texas. On April 27, the blockade was extended to Virginia and North Carolina. The purpose of the blockade was to isolate the Confederacy from European trade. Responsibility for its execution fell to Secretary of the Navy Gideon Welles.

President Lincoln's proclamation boldly stated that "a competent force will be posted so as to prevent entrance and exit of vessels from the ports" under blockade. Declaring a blockade and making it effective, however, were two different things, especially since Secretary of the Navy Welles had at the time but twelve ships available for blockade duty. All the rest were either in ordinary (maintenance or overhaul) or in overseas squadrons. To make matters worse, many of the navy's ships were large, slow, deep-draft steam frigates that were ill suited as blockaders. With 189 harbor and river openings along the 3,549 miles of Confederate shoreline between the Potomac and the Rio Grande, the existing navy lacked the resources and organizational structure the task required. To bring some strategic focus to the problem, Welles turned to the Blockade Board.[1]

The Blockade Board (also called the Navy Board, the Strategy Board, and the Committee on Conference) was first envisioned by Alexander Bache, superintendent of the U.S. Coast Survey. Assistant Secretary of the Navy Gustavus Fox was also a proponent of the idea, but in spite of the contributions of Bache and Fox, Kevin Weddle, perhaps today's leading authority on the Blockade Board, concludes, "Welles must receive the lion's share of the credit for having the vision to sanction the board officially and for acting on its recommendations."[2]

Welles must also be credited with appointing four excellent members to the board. Captain Samuel Du Pont, a professional naval officer, was its head. Du Pont was one of the few officers with blockading experience, having learned many of its logistical difficulties during the Mexican War.[3] Indeed, two days before Du Pont arrived in Washington to assume his duties on the board, he recalled his previous blockading experience in a letter to a friend: "During the Mexican War I had two hard years' work at it, with endless correspondence with naval and diplomatic functionaries, for I established the first blockade on the western coast."[4] Professor Bache, who had the initial idea of the board, was the second member, and he brought to it his specialized knowledge of the Confederate coast. Without Coast Survey maps, an effective blockade of the Southern ports would have clearly been impossible.[5] The third member was Major John Barnard, an army engineer in charge of the defenses of Washington and an expert on coastal topography and the construction of coastal defenses and harbor improvements. Rounding out the board was Commander Charles Henry Davis, a scientific expert who had been the head of the Naval Almanac, an agency that produced navigational and astronomical tables that would be valuable to blockade planning.[6] Weddle declares that "Welles could not have appointed a more competent group."[7]

Secretary Welles's initial guidance to the board was expansive. He instructed Du Pont:

> The Navy Department is desirous to condense all the information in the archives of the Government which may be considered useful to the Blockading Squadrons; and the Board are therefore requested to prepare such matters as in their judgment may seem necessary: first, extending from the Chesapeake to Key West; second, from Key West to the extreme southern point of Texas. It is imperative that two or more points should be taken possession of on the Atlantic Coast, and Fernandina and Port Royal are spoken of. Perhaps others will occur to the board. All facts bearing on such a contemplated movement are desired at an early moment. Subsequently, similar points in the Gulf of Mexico will be considered. It is also very desirable that the practicability of closing all the Southern ports by mechanical means should be fully discussed and reported upon.[8]

Welles was clear that he expected the board to tackle two of the blockade's key challenges: a lack of local information and a lack of logistical bases. He focused the effort by ordering the board to plan for the seizure of additional bases, first in the Atlantic and then in the Gulf. It was a far-reaching task, but Welles's guidance was clear and helpful.[9]

There was much to be done to bring order to the presently porous blockade. Du Pont was shocked that squadron commanders seemed content to merely cruise aimlessly up and down the coast with a few vessels. Part of the problem was that initially the Federals had only Hampton Roads, Virginia, and Key West, Florida, available to them. These widely separated bases made it almost impossible to maintain an effective blockade. Indeed in the early days of the war, "some ships spent nearly as much time going to and from these bases for supply and repair as they did on blockade duty."[10] This situation would be exacerbated in foul weather when blockading ships would need ports of refuge along the stormy Atlantic. Clearly, the navy would need additional bases for the blockading squadron to both shut down Confederate blockade running and to resupply the Federal ships.

Shelby Foote writes that "out of this double necessity the blockade gained a new dimension, one in which the army would have a share. Not only could harbor entrances be patrolled; the harbors themselves might be seized, thus reducing the number of points to be guarded and at the same time freeing ships for duty elsewhere."[11] Thus was born a strategy that would result in a series of army-navy operations directed against critical locations along the Southern coast. It was the Blockade Board that provided this direction.

The board held its first meeting on June 27, 1861, and presented its first two reports to Welles on July 5 and 13. The first report confirmed the need for additional bases, stating, "It seems to be indispensable that there should exist a convenient coal depot on the southern extremity of the line of Atlantic blockades ... [and it] might be used not only as a coal depot for coal, but as a depot for provisions and common stores, as a harbor of refuge, and as a general rendezvous, or headquarters, for that part of the coast."[12] Fernandina, Florida, was the board's recommendation to meet this requirement.

The second report focused on the need for a second base farther north. First, the board recommended closing the inlets between the Cape Hatteras barrier islands. Then it examined three potential bases along the South Carolina coast: Port Royal Sound, Bull's Bay, and Saint Helena Sound. Seizing a base deep in the South would be risky and would require a formidable ground and naval force, but the strategic payoff would be great. Although the board recognized the superiority of the harbor at Port Royal Sound, it also assumed the Confederates would mount a difficult defense there. Thus, the board recommended seizing Bull's Bay.[13]

The board issued two more reports on July 19 and 29. Perhaps the most important of the many recommendations in these reports was that responsibility for the Atlantic blockade be divided between two squadrons. This arrangement would streamline command and control and reduce the burdens placed on the commanders. Later, the board would recommend the Gulf Blockading Squadron also be divided into two separate commands.[14]

On August 6, the board issued its first report on the Gulf. The geographic complexities of the Mississippi River Delta made this region particularly difficult to blockade, and the board was quick to point out "the blockade of the river ... does not close the port [of New Orleans]." Because the capture of New Orleans would require such a large naval and military force, the board recommended action against New Orleans be delayed until "we are prepared to ascend the river with vessels of war sufficiently protected to contend with the forts." In the meantime, the board recommended seizing Ship Island, a barrier island midway between New Orleans and Mobile. Ship Island would serve as the headquarters and logistical base for the Gulf Blockading Squadron and would be useful as a jumping off point for any future attack against either New Orleans or Mobile.[15]

Du Pont's stellar work on the board catapulted him ahead of several more senior officers when it came time to select a commander for the important Port Royal Expedition. It also caused him to divide his attention between the board and his sea command, and it was not until September 3 that the board completed its second Gulf report. This report summarized the geography and topography of the rest of the Gulf, including the Florida Keys and the entire coast of Texas. Finally on September 19, the board made its last report which supplemented the first Gulf report by carefully outlining the defenses of Ship Island. Du Pont was now fully engaged in his Port Royal Expedition duties, but he asked the Department of the Navy to allow the board to make one more report—a manual for the conduct of blockading. In a rare oversight, Secretary Welles failed to act on Du Pont's request, and this report was never finished.[16]

The Blockade Board was a resounding success, producing what Weddle described as "a military (naval) strategy that was fully coordinated with the national strategy and government policies."[17] Indeed, the Department of the Navy accepted most of the board's recommendations. Welles split the Atlantic Blockading Squadron into the North and South Atlantic Blockading squadrons, commanded respectively by Flag Officers Louis Goldsborough and Du Pont. Likewise, the Gulf Blockading Squadron was divided into the East and West Gulf Blockading squadrons under Flag Officers William McKean and David Farragut respectively. The Lincoln administration and the War and Navy departments also took swift action on the board's recommendations for joint operations, seizing Hatteras Inlet in August 1861, Port Royal and Ship Island in November, and Fernandina in March 1862. Welles also used the model of the Blockade Board to establish other boards and commissions such as the Board of Ironclad Vessels and the Board of Naval Examiners. Finally, the board succeeded in its mission of condensing the wealth of information on the Confederate coast into a useable form that was readily available to the squadron commanders. In praising the work of the Blockade Board, Weddle argues "the

Civil War saw no comparable organization, staff, or agency that systematically formulated naval or military strategy."[18]

Indeed, the Blockade Board was certainly a result of the "outstanding leadership" Welles provided the Navy Department, something James McPherson sharply contrasts with the War Department.[19] Likewise, Weddle calls it "one of the most interesting historical ironies of the war that the Union army, with a well-developed bureaucracy, a body of strategic writing and theory, and a general-in-chief, was unable to formulate a coherent military strategy until the war was almost three years old. On the other hand, the U.S. Navy, with none of the army's advantages, developed a superb strategic concept in less than three months that lasted, with few changes, until the end of the war."[20] Clearly, Welles used the Blockade Board to provide much needed direction and focus to the navy's war effort.

The beached remains of the British-built blockade runner *Ruby* are shown here after she ran aground on Folly Island upon passing the Federal squadron, June 10–11, 1863 (Library of Congress, Prints & Photographs Division).

Leadership Lessons

Strategic leaders provide their organization with a "vision" which helps focus effort and map progress toward a desired future. The vision is both an image of a future state and a process the organization will use to guide future development. It provides direction, purpose, and identity. To this end, Weddle praises Welles for providing "guidance that was clear, concise, and coordinated with Lincoln's strategic concept."[21] Welles effectively fulfilled a vision's purpose of providing "a 'strategic umbrella' under which specific tactics can be worked out as opportunities arise or barriers appear."[22] A vision also requires an implementing strategy or plan to ensure its attainment.[23] Through the Blockade Board, Welles was able to provide "the basis for a broad strategic plan to maintain the blockade."[24]

Strategic leaders must recognize that they operate in a complex web of overlapping and sometimes competing constituencies.[25] Although Professor Bache deserves much credit for coming up with the initial idea of the Blockade Board, "Welles's vision and administrative abilities allowed him to see the value of Bache's idea and act upon it, despite the myriad competing demands for his attention and the shortage of experienced officers necessary to man such a commission."[26] Through the Blockade Board's reports, Welles was able to present a "firm, logical line" where once had been a confusion of chaos and problems.[27]

Unfortunately, with Du Pont's departure for the Port Royal Expedition, the Blockade Board ceased to function. In the absence of the initial detailed and deliberate planning effort, the Federal coastal campaign progressed in a much more haphazard fashion. In September 1862, Du Pont pleaded with Assistant Secretary Fox to not "go it half cocked about Charleston—it is a bigger job than Port Royal.... You & I planned the first.... Let us consult together again."[28] Instead of what he had seen in the careful planning of the Blockade Board, Du Pont lamented that now the "desire of the President and others '*to strike a blow*' somewhere" was not accompanied by having "someone [who] would sit down and study how the blow was to be given." The result, according to Du Pont, was that Charleston was a "chaotic conception" rather than the result of a military plan.[29] In Du Pont's mind, the outcome was predictable.

Du Pont's criticism of the decline in the quality of the Federal planning effort shows the criticality of sustained effort. Strategic leadership is a process, not a destination. There is no end point. Unfortunately, the Blockade Board discontinued as a planning body long before its work was complete, "leaving its early promise ... never fully realized."[30] Donald Stoker correctly asserts, "Its continuance would have been a good thing for the navy."[31]

Take-aways

- Strategic leaders must develop a strategic vision that provides direction, purpose, and identity.
- The vision is followed by a strategy or plan for implementation.
- Strategic leaders build teams of capable subordinates to fulfill the vision.
- Strategic leadership is a process, not a destination.

7

Robert E. Lee and Prioritization

Just two days before the Federal attack on Port Royal, President Jefferson Davis appointed General Robert E. Lee to command the Department of South Carolina, Georgia, and East Florida. Lee left immediately for Charleston, but he arrived too late to do anything about Port Royal. Instead, he accepted the lessons of the Confederate defeat and made adjustments as he could.

The victory at Port Royal gave the Federals an excellent harbor that became the home base for the South Atlantic Blockading Squadron for the remainder of the war. Moreover, it struck a blow in both the sentimental heartland of secession and in an important cotton-producing region. Within three days, the Federals moved up the rivers and inlets and occupied the towns of Beaufort and Port Royal, putting them in a position to threaten either Charleston or Savannah. The local population was thrown into a panic, and Confederate confidence was shattered. By December, planters along the Georgia-South Carolina coast were burning cotton to prevent its capture.[1]

Lee inherited an immense challenge in his new command. The Federal victory at Port Royal necessitated a radical change in the entire Confederate strategy for the defense of its coasts, and Lee had few factors in his favor. As Emory Thomas notes,

> Nature seemed to conspire against Confederate capacity to defend this coastal region. Barrier islands lay miles from the mainland separated from the major landmass by salt marshes, sounds, and meandering tidal streams, and separated from each other by wide channels. The Federal Navy enjoyed dominance in these waterways as in the near-shore waters and ocean beyond. To defend this coast, the Confederates would have to mount batteries of guns everywhere and the new nation (or any nation for that matter) did not have enough guns with enough range to cover every channel, sound, and creek.[2]

7. Robert E. Lee and Prioritization

The scant Confederate defenses, including Battery Beauregard, proved no match for Du Pont's attack on Port Royal (Library of Congress, Prints & Photographs Division).

Lee concluded that his enemy "can be thrown with great celerity against any point, and far outnumbers any force we can bring against it in the field."[3] This fact confirmed for Lee that the Confederacy could not use a merely defensive strategy. It simply was not strong enough to defend everywhere.[4] Lee decided to concentrate his defensive efforts at Georgetown, Charleston, Savannah, and along the Charleston and Savannah Railroad.[5]

Such logic would later influence Lee, as commander of the Army of Northern Virginia, to adopt his strategy of the offensive-defensive. In the current emergency, it led him to initiate three measures. These were to strengthen the defenses at Fort Pulaski, Georgia and Charleston in order to withstand a more serious bombardment than they had been built to sustain, to obstruct the waterways that might be used by Federal ships, and to assemble the scattered Confederate forces at the most probable points of Federal attack.[6] Later Lee would put into effect a longer-range plan by ordering the withdrawal inland of garrisons and guns on outlying positions. This move was part of Lee's plan to hold only key locations such as Charleston. Finally, at Savannah and along the southern part of the Charleston and Savannah Railroad, Lee built a strong defensive line upon which he could concentrate his forces. Rendering his 1861 annual report as head of the Charleston and Savannah Railroad, Thomas Drayton had prophesized that if South Carolina's secession resulted in war, "this much neglected railway will be the cheapest and most formidable earthwork that could have been devised to give confidence and security at home and repel invasion from abroad."[7] Lee would put Drayton's theory to the test, resisting a Federal advance first with his scattered, primarily cavalry, forces and then rushing forward reinforcements via the railroad to the threatened point. This would force the Federal army to fight without the assistance of its powerful navy.[8]

Lee established his headquarters at the small village of Coosawatchie at the head of navigation on the Coosawatchie River. He took advantage of the fact that the Federals did not follow up their Port Royal success with a full-scale invasion and made numerous trips to inspect and supervise the defensive preparations. He also began collecting forces until he had a strength of some 25,000 troops. Although he now outnumbered the Federals, the training of

The Charleston and Savannah Railroad was a critical component of Lee's plan to defend the South Carolina and Georgia coasts (Library of Congress, Prints & Photographs Division).

his men and the preparation of his defenses progressed painfully slowly. Given his situation, Lee was relieved when the Federals sank their Stone Fleet in the Charleston Harbor on December 20. Interpreting this as a sign the Federals were for the moment content to restrict traffic in and out of Charleston Harbor rather than to use it as an attack route, Lee turned his attention to other vulnerable locations.[9]

Lee based his plan on the coastal defense theories of the venerable Colonel Joseph Totten, who was now the chief engineer of the U.S. Army. Decades earlier, Totten had championed a system of harbor forts that would delay an attacker's advance until the local militia could rally to the defense. Forts Sumter and Pulaski were part of Totten's system. Lee's plan was to add the element of railroad transportation to Totten's original idea. He would garrison Charleston and Savannah with a force strong enough to resist an initial assault and then rush reinforcements to the scene by rail. The result was that, "from this point on, Charleston's harbor works and the railroad were linked together."[10]

Lee had divided the coast of South Carolina into five military districts, and he placed Brigadier General Roswell Ripley in command of the Second Military District. Ripley was headquartered in Charleston and his responsibilities included the area from the South Santee River to the Stono River and up Rantowles Creek.[11] After the alarm created by Port Royal, Ripley was ordered by Lee to "prosecute vigorously the completion of the water and land defenses of Charleston."[12] Ripley had done much before Lee's arrival, including strengthening Fort Moultrie by putting sand against its sea face and erecting earthworks around it. To protect James Island, Ripley built up Fort Johnson. He had constructed several batteries on Cole's Island at the mouth of the Stono River to protect the entrance of the Stono and block the approaches to Folly and Morris Islands.[13]

Ripley's plan was an attempt to provide a defense in depth and to cover as many waterways as he could. He felt the defense of Charleston depended largely on preventing enemy ships from gaining footholds on the outer barrier islands such as John's Island, Battery Island, Church Flats, and Edisto Island. Lee's vision of concentrating the meager Confederate resources required Ripley to contract his lines. Lee explained: "Your plan of occupying the country between the Edisto and Combahee and occupying Edisto Island would be advantageous, if you had sufficient troops and guns to retain such an extent of country; but unless you can make the line sufficiently strong, or at least have the means of withdrawing the troops, it will, I fear, expose them to be taken in detail. If all the force was concentrated at advantageous points, I think the defense of the approaches would be more effective."[14] Ripley explained to Lee in reply that "if more troops can be got, to hold in advance and reoccupy

Edisto, it seems to me as far forward as we can go with safety from Charleston the better we are for its defense."[15]

Ripley was not alone in such logic. Governor Francis Pickens and many citizens who did not want to see their land unprotected favored the forward defense. But even Ripley had to admit the logistical reality. Although he had reported to Lee in December "that the line of intrenchments for the defense of [Charleston] may be considered as completed except those between the Cooper and Ashley Rivers," he also was forced to confess he was "entirely without troops to defend them, those not required at the forts and batteries being advanced on James Island and beyond the Stono to check the approach and marauding parties of the enemy."[16] The tyranny of finite resources made a forward defense untenable, and the Confederate leaders in Richmond saw Lee's pragmatic approach as the correct one. The Confederate defeat at Forts Henry and Donelson exacerbated the problem. On February 18, the secretary of war, Judah Benjamin, ordered Lee to "withdraw all forces from the islands in your department to the main-land, taking proper measures to save the artillery and munitions of war."[17] The next day, Lee advised Ripley:

> From the progress of the war, it seems plain that the enemy, when ready to move against Charleston, should he select it as a point of attack, will advance in great force. We should therefore be prepared to concentrate rapidly in his front, on the lines that can be best defended, so as to be able to contend to the utmost of our strength. Beyond these lines every preparation should be made to withdraw guns and munitions of war when it becomes necessary or when the route of defense, our lines could be contracted, and exposed or distant points abandoned.
>
> The batteries at Cole's Island, for instance, would not be available, provided the enemy should advance by the Edisto, and, unless arrangements are made to withdraw them, would be lost. If they can be reached in great force by the enemy's gunboats they might be suppressed, and the Stono seized as an avenue of approach. If it is necessary to maintain these batteries, they should be made as strong as possible and their communications rendered practicable in case of a reverse. So at other exposed points.
>
> I am in favor of abandoning all exposed points as far as possible within reach of the enemy's fleet of gunboats and of taking interior positions, where we can meet on more equal terms. All our resources should be applied to those positions. I wish you therefore to review the whole subject, and see what changes or improvements can be made, both as to the importance and strength of the positions retained.[18]

More adjustments followed. On February 24, Secretary Benjamin advised Lee:

> The recent disaster to our arms in Tennessee forces the Government to the stern necessity of withdrawing its lines within more defensible limits, so as to enable us to meet with some equality the overpowering numbers of the enemy. The railroad line from Memphis to Richmond must be defended at all hazards. We can

only do this by withdrawing troops from the seaboard. You are therefore requested to withdraw all such forces as are now employed in the defense of the seaboard of Florida, taking proper steps to secure the guns and munitions of war, and to send forward the troops to Tennessee, to report to General A.S. Johnston, by the most expeditious route.[19]

Lee executed these orders, and on March 1 reported "troops not necessary to prevent the enemy from penetrating into the interior will be forwarded to General Johnston."[20] Having made the hard decisions necessary to consolidate his department and put it in the most efficient defensive posture possible, Lee was called to Richmond for duty as President Davis's military advisor. On March 4, Major General John Pemberton assumed command of the Department of South Carolina, Georgia, and East Florida.[21]

Leadership Lessons

According to Stephen Covey, leaders must be able to not just establish priorities. They then must be able to organize and execute around those priorities.[22] In many cases, it is the ability to follow through that presents the real challenge. Lee was able to fulfill all three of Covey's requirements.

Lee assessed the situation presented by the Federal ability to attack most anywhere and the Confederate inability to defend such a wide front. He decided to prioritize the finite Confederate resources at Georgetown, Charleston, Savannah, and along the Charleston and Savannah Railroad. He then organized around those priorities by using a version of Totten's coastal defense plan, updated to incorporate railroad transportation. Under pressure from Governor Pickens, Ripley, and others who unrealistically clung to the idea of a much broader defense, Lee stuck to his guns and enforced the priorities he had set. He demonstrated not only the conceptual agility to prioritize but the discipline to follow through.

Take-aways

- Resources are finite and force leaders to make decisions about how to employ them.
- When leaders make these hard choices, they must expand their conceptual framework to compare the relative abilities of competing options to contribute to accomplishment of the higher goal.
- Leaders must set priorities and then organize and execute around them. The latter two requirements may be the most challenging.

8

John Pemberton and Strategic Leadership Skills

With Lee's departure for Richmond, responsibility for the defense of Charleston passed to John Pemberton. It was a difficult job under any circumstances, but it was one made more so by Pemberton's lack of the interpersonal and conceptual skills required of a leader at the strategic level.

John Pemberton was a captain in the U.S. Army before he tendered his letter of resignation on April 24, 1861. A Pennsylvanian, Pemberton's decision to join the Confederacy is usually attributed to the fact that his wife was a Virginian. In support of this theory is the fact that Pemberton waited until after Virginia had seceded to make his decision.

Upon reporting to Richmond, Pemberton was nominated by Virginia Governor John Letcher to be a lieutenant colonel of volunteer state troops. Pemberton was assigned to the command of General Joseph Johnston, who tasked Pemberton to supervise an instructional camp near Norfolk. Johnston's advocacy is often considered to be a significant reason for Pemberton's rapid rise in rank.[1]

On May 8, Pemberton became a lieutenant colonel of artillery in the Provisional Army of Virginia. On June 15, he was designated a major in the Confederate States Army. Just two days later, he bypassed the intermediate ranks of lieutenant colonel and colonel and was promoted to brigadier general. Pemberton's biographer, Michael Ballard, concludes, "There is no clear answer to why Pemberton moved up in rank so quickly."[2]

Pemberton remained in the Norfolk area until November, when President Jefferson Davis reorganized the coasts of South Carolina, Georgia, and north Florida into a single department and named General Robert E. Lee as its commander. Responding to South Carolina Governor Francis Pickens's complaint that Lee lacked brigadier generals, President Davis dispatched Pemberton to Charleston on November 29. Pemberton was promoted to major general on January 14, 1862.

Lee gave Pemberton command of District Four, which consisted of the coastal region south of Charleston from the Ashepoo River to the Port Royal Sound area. Pemberton established his headquarters at Coosawatchie, where Lee also had his headquarters. As a result, Pemberton had ample opportunity "to observe, implement, and learn about Lee's strategic concepts in defending the coast against Yankee gunboats." Between Lee's example and Pemberton's own experience with Federal tactics, Pemberton became convinced of the futility of trying to use outlying forts and batteries to stop the enemy's powerful vessels and infantry.[3] He also learned from Lee that the situation required an enemy-based rather than a terrain-based defense. For example, on February 20, Lee reminded Pemberton that "the disposition of the troops, therefore, should look rather to their concentration to resist the enemy than to hold the country."[4]

John Pemberton's command in Charleston was marred by a tense relationship with Governor Francis Pickens and others (Library of Congress, Prints & Photographs Division).

As a subordinate, Pemberton showed an ability to execute Lee's concept for the defense. However, when Pemberton replaced Lee as department commander in March, he struggled to implement the strategy as his own. His difficulty stemmed from his discomfort with the uncertainty of the situation in which he found himself and in his inability to forge positive relationships with those around him. Pemberton, "who was much better at dealing with the known than with the suspected," had a difficult time in uncertain environments.[5] Pickens considered him now to be "confused and uncertain about everything."[6] There was such doubt among the civil authorities that Mayor Charles MacBeth pointedly asked Pemberton if he intended to defend Charleston or withdraw his force in the event of a Federal attack. On May 2, Pemberton replied:

> I cannot at this time express my intentions as to the course to be pursued in the event of the enemy's gunboats passing our forts and presenting themselves in front

of the city. This calamity may not occur at all; it may be very remote; it is possibly near at hand. The circumstances of to-day may be materially changed before the enemy is prepared to make his attack. The force at my disposal may be somewhat increased or much diminished. You will readily perceive how important a bearing these and other conditions which I occur to you must have upon my decision when the time arrives to declare it. I do not, however, hesitate to say that in my opinion it is advisable that women and children should leave the city at once.[7]

Such a response was hardly the reassurance MacBeth had hoped for.

The loss of Fort Pulaski on April 10 and the capture of the *Planter* on May 13 further damaged Pemberton's reputation. He tried to restore some confidence in a May 22 letter to Confederate congressman William Porcher Miles and Judge A.G. Magrath, saying, "The disposition evinced by so many distinguished citizens of the State to defend Charleston to the last extreme meets with my entire sympathy and concurrence. It is possible that 'a single regard to military duty' may require the withdrawal of Confederate troops, but this I confidently hope will not be the case."[8] In light of the fact that men like Magrath and Miles would feel the need to seek such reassurance, Pemberton's tempered explanation was unsatisfying.

Pemberton's increasing concerns about his ability to defend Charleston were becoming painfully obvious to a variety of observers. Governor Pickens tried to steel Pemberton's resolve, telling him on May 23, "I hope and pray that it is well known that the defense is to be desperate, and if [the Federals] can be repulsed even with the city in ruins we should unanimously prefer it. It is due to our cause and our country that we should make a desperate fight in Charleston. We can afford to lose our city, but not our honor. I will stand by you in anything you desire."[9] From his new position in Richmond, Lee seconded Pickens's urgency, advising Pemberton on May 29:

> The importance of defending both Charleston and Savannah to the last extremity, particularly Charleston, is earnestly brought to your attention. The loss of Charleston would cut us off almost entirely from communication with the rest of the world, and close the only channel through which we can expect to get supplies from abroad, now almost our only dependence. You will therefore make use of every means at your command to put these cities in the most perfect state of defense. Your attention is particularly called to the river and harbor obstructions. These should be rendered as strong as it is possible for them to be made. Spare no labor or expense upon them. It is also of the greatest importance that the discipline of the garrisons of the different works should be brought to the highest state of perfection. Let it be distinctly understood by everybody that Charleston and Savannah are to be defended to the last extremity. If the harbors are taken the cities are to be fought street by street and house by house as long as we have a foot of ground to stand upon. The State authorities of both South Carolina and Georgia will doubtless lend you every means at their command to aid you in your operations.[10]

In fact, Pemberton was following the same strategic concept initiated by Lee, but he lacked Lee's leadership skill of blending strategy and public diplomacy. His biographer concludes Pemberton's problem was that "he approached his job from a purely military point of view." Unlike Lee, he never "understood that public support and morale were necessary to favorable military results."[11]

Without a doubt, Pickens could be irritating, stubborn, overbearing, and difficult to get along with. He was the type of man that Ballard assesses "a Southerner like Robert E. Lee did not necessarily like but certainly understood." Pemberton, perhaps at a disadvantage because of by his Northern birth, simply never understood Pickens, and their relationship suffered because of it.[12] For example, Lee suggested to Pemberton, "in order to preserve harmony between the State and Confederate authorities," it would be advisable for Pemberton to notify Governor Pickens "whenever you determine to abandon any position of your defenses, in order that he may give due notice to the inhabitants to look out for their security."[13] Such considerations seemed to be largely lost on Pemberton.[14] The result was that Pickens became increasingly adversarial toward Pemberton. Pemberton also found himself at odds with Brigadier General Roswell Ripley. Ripley "was the sort who seldom got along with superior officers," and he had earlier had disagreements with Lee. Like Pemberton, Ripley was a native Northerner, but even that bond did little to facilitate their relationship.[15]

Ripley and Pickens soon found common cause in objecting to Pemberton's March 27 decision to abandon the batteries on Cole's Island as part of the overall strategy of relying on an inner defensive line. In light of the protests, Pemberton conceded to delay the order until additional progress was made on the inner defenses, but the seeds of discord were already sown. On April 27, Pemberton moved his headquarters from Pocotaligo to Charleston. There he found a host of problems ranging from lax discipline to slow progress on the city's defenses, which he blamed on Ripley.[16]

The independent-minded Ripley chafed under Pemberton and requested reassignment. On April 28, Pemberton acknowledged the request, but informed Lee, "I do not think General Ripley can be spared at this time. His knowledge of everything connected with Charleston and its defenses is of great value. I know of no one now within the department who can replace him."[17] In spite of this concession, the tension between the two men continued. On May 8, Pemberton sent Ripley a tersely worded note about the disposition of Cole's Island, explaining, "I have been thus particular in my instructions because you have suggested that they be given."[18]

Pickens and other supporters of Ripley elevated the matter to Lee, who obviously had more pressing concerns. One suggestion advanced by Miles and

MacGrath was to give Ripley "the direct control and responsibility for the defense of Charleston District, independent of General Pemberton." On May 15, a visibly vexed Lee told Pickens, "This it is impossible to do while General Pemberton is in command of the department. One or the other must be removed."[19] The die thus cast, on May 29 Lee notified Pickens: "General Ripley has been relieved from duty in Charleston and ordered elsewhere and another competent officer will be sent to replace him."[20]

Ripley's departure did not end Pemberton's problems. On June 11, Pickens sent President Davis a confidential message stating, "I fear Charleston is to be sacrificed by a total incompetency in the officer commanding and a total want of knowledge of the country."[21] In a more thoughtful vein, Congressman Miles wrote Lee:

> It is with extreme reluctance that I address you this letter, but I think it my duty to say what I am about to communicate. General Pemberton does not possess the confidence of his officers, his troops, or the people of Charleston. Whether justly or unjustly, rely upon it the fact is so. I speak with positive certainty. It is useless to inquire into all the reasons for this unfortunate condition of sentiment in both soldiers and people. Such is the deplorable fact.[22]

Not even the successful repulse of the Federal attack at Secessionville on June 16 could reverse the turn in sentiment against Pemberton.

Pemberton was under attack from seemingly all quarters. Mary Chesnut wrote: "Crimination and recrimination. Everybody's hand against everybody else. Pemberton said to have no heart in this business, so the city cannot be defended."[23] Chesnut's fellow diarist Emma Holmes, wrote: "Everybody has lost confidence in Pemberton and many even suspect treachery, though it cannot be proved of course."[24] Pemberton's personality also failed to endear him to his men. With his managerial approach to command, he seldom visited the lines and failed to establish a rapport with the soldiers. Instead, he left them with the impression he was detached and uncaring. Lieutenant Colonel John Pressley, for example, wrote passionately of a particular incident in which he felt Pemberton "was utterly regardless of the entreaties of the men."[25]

Indeed, Pemberton's poor interpersonal relations skills may stem from the fact that "he was a bureaucrat at heart." Upon assuming command of the department, he inexplicably reorganized it into a more complex structure. Unable to uncover a reason for the change, Ballard muses Pemberton may have done it "for no other reason than the challenge of doing" so,[26] but it certainly was indicative of Pemberton's tendency to immerse himself in minute details that should have been routinely delegated to staff officers. Instead, Pemberton busied himself with minor matters at the expense of strategic concepts and building relationships with those around him.

President Davis had long been regarded as a champion of Pemberton, but he could no longer tolerate such deteriorating conditions. He dispatched General Samuel Cooper to investigate the situation. The adjutant general of the Confederate Army concluded the following:

> I have great confidence in the zeal and untiring efforts of General Pemberton to do all that lies in his power and the energy of his will to effect the object we so anxious hope for. I know that he feels—honestly feels—the weight of the responsibility which rests upon him, yet bears that responsibility with calmness and a determination to discharge his duty honestly and faithfully; but with such an opposition as constantly surrounds him it would be difficult for any commander situated as he is to affect much.[27]

Amid such an environment, Pemberton must have felt some relief when, on August 28, he was informed that he was being replaced as commander, by General Pierre Goustave Toutant Beauregard. Beauregard assumed command on September 24, and Pemberton departed for a brief stay in Virginia. On October 13, Pemberton was promoted to lieutenant general and ultimately superintended the surrender of the Confederate forces at Vicksburg, Mississippi.

Leadership Lessons

The "skills approach" to leadership argues that effective leadership depends on technical, human, and conceptual skills. Technical skills involve having knowledge about and being proficient in a specific type of work or activity. Pemberton's technical skills involved military administration and bureaucracy as well as artillery and defense of a static location. Human skill is having knowledge about and being able to work with people. Pemberton was deficient in this category as illustrated by his difficult relationship with Governor Pickens, General Ripley, and others. Conceptual skills are abilities to work with ideas, abstractions, and concepts. Pemberton had little of this characteristic. He was comfortable with a fixed set of factors, including mission, intelligence, and geography. The much more demanding and ambiguous concepts associated with commanding a large force in the field were foreign to him.

Different levels of leadership require different combinations of skills. Low leadership levels require high competencies in the areas of technical and human skills, but there is less of a need for conceptual skills. Middle levels retain the high requirement for human skills while technical demands are lowered to, and conceptual demands are raised to, middle levels. Top leadership positions place a premium on human and conceptual skills but a low priority on technical skills.[28]

Level of Leadership	Relative Percentage of Skills Required		
	Technical	*Human or Personal*	*Conceptual*
Top/Strategic	Low	High	High
Middle/Organizational	Medium	High	Medium
Low/Direct	High	High	Low

Strategic leaders must be able to operate in an environment characterized by volatility, uncertainty, confusion, and ambiguity (VUCA).[29] The leader must be able to sift through the "noise" and "become the master of information and influence."[30] Pemberton lacked such ability. He was a deliberate, inflexible leader who had to understand fully the situation in order to make informed decisions. Without this understanding, Pemberton naturally feared the worst and tended toward paralysis. None of his previous experiences had prepared him for his current scope of responsibilities and pressures. Ballard concludes that the burden of command eventually overwhelmed Pemberton, and the lack of confidence others had in him seemed to drain his own self-confidence.[31]

Dr. William Cohen is a professor of marketing and leadership at California State University, Los Angeles, and a retired major general in the U.S. Air Force Reserve. In his book *The Stuff of Heroes*, Cohen lists eight universal laws of leadership, one of which is to "expect positive results."[32] Pemberton's pessimism violated this law and detracted from his interpersonal skills.

Cohen is quick to point out that merely expecting positive results will not necessarily ensure their achievement. There may be circumstances beyond the leader's control that prevent a positive outcome in spite of the leader's expectations. However, Cohen is adamant that a leader who does not expect positive results will not get them. "So while expecting positive results may not always lead to success," Cohen explains, "failing to expect positive results will almost always lead to failure."[33] General Colin Powell agrees, calling optimism "a force multiplier." He considers a leader's positive enthusiasm and confidence to be a factor that multiplies the effectiveness of other capabilities in the organization. When leaders view the situation with hopeful expectation, those around them catch the same positive attitude.[34] On the other hand, Powell considers cynicism, doubt, and negativity to be "force shrinkers." Leaders who view the world negatively are likely to demoralize and reduce the effectiveness of their organization.[35] Pemberton is an example of the latter phenomenon.

Pemberton's skill set was not conducive for high level leadership. His strength lay in technical skills, the characteristic needed at lower rather than higher levels. His weaknesses were in the human and conceptual dimensions, which were what the situation at Charleston most required. In the absence of those necessary skills, Pemberton focused on his technical skills, which were inappropriate for the fluid situation he then faced. According to Ballard, Pemberton "viewed his job as that of an administrator, not a combat general."[36] He was a poor fit for the role in which he was placed, and, as John Maxwell notes, "when people aren't where they do things well, things don't turn out well."[37] That is exactly what happened to Pemberton, first at Charleston and later at Vicksburg.

Maxwell also highlights the responsibility of the leader to put people in situations where they can maximize their effectiveness. Because higher levels of leadership require different skills, leaders should not select subordinates for promotion based primarily on *performance* at lower levels. Instead, promotion should be more heavily based on the *potential* to serve in positions of greater responsibility. This focus on potential requires leaders to be very aware of subordinates' human and conceptual skills rather than the often more obvious technical skills. Pemberton certainly had shown little potential for department command before assuming his position at Charleston. His performance there showed even less potential to adequately master the responsibilities that awaited him at Vicksburg.[38]

Take-aways

- Top leadership positions place a premium on human and conceptual skills and a lower priority on technical skills.
- You can manage things, but you must lead people.
- Leaders must actively nurture relationships in the organization.
- Leaders must equip and select subordinates for positions of increased responsibility.
- Promotion should be based primarily on potential rather than performance.

9

Robert Smalls and Seizing the Moment

On May 13, 1862, Robert Smalls, a twenty-three-year-old slave impressed into duties as pilot of the Confederate *Planter*, escaped with the ship and its black crewmembers into the Federal blockade lines. Smalls brought with him news that the Confederates had abandoned their positions guarding the seaward approaches to James Island, leaving Charleston vulnerable to an attack from the rear across the island. While the resulting Federal attempted coup de main to seize Charleston was a dismal failure, Smalls was elevated to the status of a national hero.

Robert Smalls was born into slavery in Beaufort, South Carolina, in 1839. As much as possible under the system of slavery, Smalls benefited from a positive relationship with his master, John McKee. Indeed, biographer Andrew Billingsley credits the "entrepreneurial base" Smalls would later develop to his formative experiences as one of McKee's "favored house servants."[1] Billingsley describes the kind McKee as "a substitute father figure" who taught Smalls "some rudimentary skills in management" as part of his household duties.[2] Thus, even given the disadvantages of slavery, Smalls was by all accounts "a man of exceptional ability."[3]

Smalls continued his development when he moved with McKee to Charleston in 1851. He worked as a waiter at the Planter Hotel and a lamplighter before obtaining his goal of working on Charleston's waterfront. First as a stevedore, then as a supervisor and rigger, Smalls "developed a remarkable set of skills on the waterfront." Ultimately he became a wheelman, or boat pilot.[4] By the time the Civil War broke out, Smalls "had completely mastered the harbors and waterways of the South Carolina and Georgia seacoasts" and found himself as a crewmember on the *Planter*.[5]

Drawing less than four feet of water, the *Planter* was ideally suited for the shallow coastal waters of South Carolina. She could carry fourteen thousand bales of cotton or one thousand men and was fast and maneuverable. John Ferguson was the pilot. His crew included three of his own slaves and five more, including Smalls, that he had contracted for from other owners. When the war broke out, Ferguson leased the *Planter* to the Confederate Navy for $100 per day.[6]

On May 12, the *Planter* was ordered to Cole's Island to pick up four guns there and transport them to the Middle Ground Battery, also known as Fort Ripley. It was late by the time the guns were taken on board, so the *Planter* proceeded to Charleston where she tied up at her usual berth at Southern Wharf. In spite of standing orders requiring officers to remain on board, the captain, mate, and engineer left Smalls in charge of the *Planter* and the rest of the black crew, and went to spend the night at their homes. Smalls saw his opportunity. He was joined by fellow black crewmen John Smalls (no relation), J. Samuel Chisholm, Abraham Allston, Gabriel Turno, Abraham Jackson, and Alfred Gradine. In what must have been a painful decision, David Jones opted not to join the escape for fear of his family's future. Smalls accepted Jones's decision, and released him based on his pledge of secrecy. Jones kept his word.[7]

At about 3:00 a.m. the next morning, Smalls and his colleagues began to build up steam, and as soon as there was ample pressure in the boiler, they backed the *Planter* away from her berth. Blowing the ship's whistle as was the usual routine, Smalls advanced a short distance upstream before turning and heading for the lower harbor. A sentinel posted about fifty yards away observed the *Planter*'s departure, but the sentinel noting nothing out of the ordinary, he sounded no alarm. Smalls proceeded slowly passed Fort Ripley and steamed on toward Fort Sumter.

Before making his dash to safety, Smalls made one very daring stop. Easing along the shore to the north Atlantic wharf, he dispatched two of his men in a rowboat to where the Confederate ship *Etowah* was moored. Smalls had enlisted two of the ship's black stewards in his plan and, with their help, had hidden several family members and friends onboard the *Etowah* the night before. All told, Smalls's "family of liberation" consisted of sixteen souls. With this precious cargo safely on the *Planter*, Smalls eased passed Castle Pinckney and was again allowed to proceed without delay.

As the *Planter* came into sight of Fort Sumter, Smalls donned the captain's straw hat and gold-trimmed jacket, and stood on the bridge. He struck the white captain's familiar pose with his arms folded across his chest but was careful to keep his back to the fort. Smalls again sounded the ship's whistle, convincing the fort's guard that the *Planter* was one of the guard ships going to the bar to take up her usual position. Instead, Smalls steamed straight out to sea through the Swash Channel toward the Federal blockade fleet. By the time the Confederates realized something was happening, the *Planter* was safely out of the range of Fort Sumter's guns.

Smalls's next problem was to avoid being mistaken by the Federals as a blockade runner. Indeed, as the *Planter* approached, the USS *Onward* moved into position to intercept her. When Smalls signaled his intentions by lowering his South Carolina and Confederate battle flags and running up a white sheet his wife, Hannah, had brought for this purpose, the *Onward*'s captain held his fire and boarded the *Planter*. A crew was put onboard, the American flag was raised, and the *Planter* was taken to Port Royal, where she arrived at about 10:00 p.m. after her fifteen-hour odyssey. Smalls was brought to see Flag Officer Samuel Du Pont, who told him he "would take care of him and his people, that he was a hero."[8]

Smalls informed Du Pont that Cole's Island had been evacuated, and Du Pont sent the *Unadilla*, *Pembina*, and *Ottawa* into Stono Inlet to verify the report. When the gunboats were not fired upon, the Federals recognized the importance of this change in the Confederate defenses. Indeed, Brigadier General Henry Benham had already been contemplating offensive action. He noted this new information "seems to assure us of the evacuation and destruction of the batteries at Stono Inlet." Based on this information, Benham made some modifications to the plan and submitted it to Department of the South commander, Major General David Hunter, on May 17.[9]

Smalls's leadership and daring in delivering the *Planter* to the Federals brought him national attention. Du Pont ensured Smalls received $1,500 in prize money, and the *Planter*, along with Smalls, then entered into federal service.[10] After participating in a minor expedition to test Confederate defenses up the North Edisto River in June, Smalls was transferred to DuPont's flagship, *Wabash*, to serve as pilot. Smalls was often called away from military service, however, to serve as a spokesman on behalf of the advancement of blacks.[11] For example, he and Mansfield French travelled to Washington and met with Secretary of War Edwin Stanton on August 20, 1862, to discuss options for enlisting blacks in the army.[12] Throughout the duration of the war, Smalls continued to mix military service and advocacy work on behalf of the freedmen. The experience left him well-postured to "transform wartime fame into political power," and after the war he began a decades-long career as a member of the South Carolina house of representatives and senate and as a U.S. congressman.[13]

Leadership Lessons

Initiative is "the ability to be a self-starter—to act when there are no clear instructions, to act when the situation changes or when plans fall apart." As critical to leadership and organizational growth as initiative is, however, it must be combined with good judgment to be productive. The goal then is not mere impulsive or ill-advised action, but initiative balanced with sound judgment to produce "disciplined initiative."[14] Disciplined initiative requires opportunity, ability, action, and risk management.

Smalls showed this disciplined initiative in escaping with the *Planter*. He was presented an opportunity by the negligence of the ship's white officers in leaving the *Planter* unattended. (Indeed, as a result of a court-martial two of the officers were sentenced to imprisonment and fines, and Major General John Pemberton railed against their "inexcusable and gross neglect of duty."[15]) Life presents many such opportunities, but not everyone is equipped to take advantage of them. Smalls's carefully honed skills as a pilot and his awareness of harbor procedures gave him the ability to make something of the opportunity that was before him. Still, ability and action are two distinct entities, and many a perfectly capable individual has remained inert as opportunity passed by. Smalls, even within the confines of slavery, had developed the leadership traits necessary to act on the opportunity and ability he now had. This required not only confidence in himself, but also the ability to convince others to follow him in his plan. Of course, while the potential payoff of a successful escape was priceless, the risk of failure was equally great. A slave attempting to escape, especially under the traitorous conditions Smalls was proposing, was taking his life in his own hands. Smalls mitigated these risks by such measures as careful planning, secrecy, camouflage, teamwork, and avoiding undue attention. Such prudent risk management is what separates disciplined initiative from a foolhardy gamble.

By all accounts, Robert Smalls was a religious man, so he may very well have been familiar with Mordecai's admonition to his niece Queen Esther that "who knows but that you have come to your royal position for such a time as this?"[16] Like Esther, Smalls found himself in an unexpected and risky situation, but one for which he was prepared. He seized a fleeting opportunity and led himself and others to freedom through disciplined initiative.

Take-aways

- Leaders must be ready to seize unexpected opportunity.
- Disciplined initiative is action balanced by judgment.
- A moment of action may be the result of a lifetime of preparation.

10

James Chesnut and Mentorship

The information Smalls brought to the Federal command helped lead to the Battle of Secessionville on James Island, where Brigadier General States Rights Gist had commanded the Confederate forces. The influential South Carolina politician James Chesnut was instrumental in effecting Gists's rise to this position of authority. Indeed, Chesnut's involvement in the career development of a promising subordinate is a positive example of mentorship.

The interestingly named States Rights Gist was born in Union District, South Carolina, in 1831, the son of future South Carolina Governor William Gist. After graduating from South Carolina College in 1852, the younger Gist studied law at Harvard. He returned to South Carolina to practice law and served in the South Carolina militia. He became a brigadier general in 1859, and on January 29, 1861, he officially became adjutant and inspector general of the State of South Carolina, after informally holding that position for the proceeding few weeks. In the midst of the Fort Sumter crisis, he busied himself with myriad conferences and details about such matters as the progress of work on fortifications, the procurement of munitions, and the fledgling chain of command. Once Major Robert Anderson surrendered, Gist turned his attention to processing, equipping, and mobilizing the rush of volunteers.[1]

When South Carolina sent troops to Virginia, Gist went with them, helping to set up two camps of instruction for the new recruits. While in Richmond, Gist met with Secretary of War Leroy Walker and President Jefferson Davis. As a result of that meeting, Davis informed General Joseph Johnston "General Gist, the adjutant-general of South Carolina, goes to your headquarters to make himself useful to you in any way he can serve you, and it gives me pleasure to commend him to your polite attention."[2] On the strength of this recommendation, Gist found himself as a volunteer aide to Brigadier General Barnard Bee. At the Battle of First Manassas, Gist assumed command of the 4th Alabama Regiment when all its field grade officers became casualties. He was wounded in the fighting, but not before he attracted the notice of General P.G.T. Beauregard, who recognized him as "a young man whom I had known as adjutant general of South Carolina, and whom I greatly esteemed."[3]

After the battle, Gist went to Richmond to recover from his wound and then back to South Carolina to his position as adjutant general. His biographer Walter Cisco notes that it was a new Gist now: "The antebellum functionary decked-out in blue-uniformed elegance had been replaced by the hard-driven agent of a revolutionary government."[4] Gist was certainly busy. He met with Governor Francis Pickens's executive council. He helped organize training centers. He prepared reports and correspondence. He planned South Carolina's military draft.[5] He coordinated with General Robert E. Lee, assuring the newly assigned department commander "of the most hearty and sincere co-operation of the State authorities in all possible matters; of their earnest desire to carry out your designs and wished when made known to them, and their readiness to respond to an call you may make upon them to the utmost extent of their ability. Permit me to add that they do this the more cheerfully, as you possess their entire confidence."[6] If General Dwight Eisenhower is correct that one develops as a decision-maker by "[being] around people making decisions," then Gist certainly had such an opportunity.[7]

Gist's hard and efficient work did not go unrewarded. On March 20, 1862, he was appointed brigadier general in the Provisional Confederate Army. On April 8, he was ordered to duty at Charleston.[8] Many saw Gist's promotion as a fortuitous opportunity to balance the northern-born Major General John Pemberton with a native son when Pemberton replaced Lee as commander of the Department of South Carolina, Georgia, and East Florida on March 4. Such political explanations notwithstanding, Gist had performed well as adjutant and inspector general. The *Charleston Mercury*, for example, concluded he had "discharged the extremely laborious and the difficult duties of his office with both ability and fidelity."[9] Yet, that Gist had such opportunities thus far and the ones that lay ahead of him was in part due to the mentorship of the influential James Chesnut.

Perhaps less well-known than his diarist wife, Mary, it was Chesnut's position that gave Mary much of the access, perspective, and insights that make her writings so valuable. James Chesnut practiced law in Camden before being elected to the state house of representatives, serving from 1842 to 1854. He was involved early in the mounting sectional tension as a delegate to the Nashville Convention in 1850. He served in the state senate from 1854 to

1858, when he was elected to the United States Senate to fill the vacancy caused by the death of Josiah J. Evans. Chesnut left the Senate on November 10, 1860, the first Southern senator to resign. He returned to South Carolina and became a delegate to the Secession Convention, where he served on the committee that drafted the ordinance.

Chesnut was elected as a delegate to the Confederate Provisional Congress in January 1861 and served on the committee writing the Confederate constitution. As a colonel, he served as an aide to General Beauregard at Fort Sumter. In this capacity he was involved in frequent negotiations with Major Robert Anderson, the Federal commander, including being part of the delegation that demanded the fort's surrender on April 12, 1861. Chesnut again served on Beauregard's staff at the Battle of First Manassas in July.

Although perhaps less famous today than his diarist wife, James Chesnut was an important player in South Carolina military and political affairs (Library of Congress, Prints & Photographs Division).

In November, Chesnut failed to win election to the permanent Confederate Congress. Some credit his surprising defeat to "his reluctance to promote himself for the seat." Nonetheless, his return to South Carolina was fortuitous, as he became one of the five members of a new executive council that would wield remarkable powers in wartime South Carolina. On January 9, 1862, Chesnut became chief of the executive council's Military Department, a position that effectively supplanted the governor as the state's commander in chief. Although President Davis commissioned Chesnut as an aide-de-camp with the rank of colonel on April 19 and asked him to come to Richmond, Chesnut remained in South Carolina to continue his important work with the executive council.

When the council dissolved on December 18, Chesnut went to Richmond and joined Davis's staff. He advised the president on military matters, visited the various departments, and reported on military conditions. Of much significance was his role as liaison between the Confederacy and the South Carolina government. On April 23, 1864, he was appointed brigadier general and assigned to command the reserve troops in South Carolina, a position he held through the remainder of the war.[10]

Chesnut became a champion of Gist and did much to facilitate his young charge's development.[11] It was likely that it was Chesnut who arranged for Gist to meet with President Davis when Gist was in Richmond in the summer of 1861, an introduction that led to Davis's referral of Gist to General Johnston and his service at First Manassas. As adjutant general, Gist worked closely with Chesnut when Chesnut occupied his critical role on the executive council. It was under Chesnut's direction that Gist prepared the plan for South Carolina's military draft.[12] Chesnut was impressed by Gist. Cisco notes "Chesnut saw in Gist genuine ability and commitment and felt justified in staking his reputation on the young man." Chesnut may very well have written directly to President Davis recommending Gist's appointment to a brigadier generalship, implying intentionally or not that he spoke for the entire executive committee.[13] It is known that on March 14 Chesnut wrote his friend William Porcher Miles, a South Carolina congressman and chairman of the powerful Military Affairs Committee of the Confederate house of representatives: "It is more than probable that my friend genl. S.R. Gist [,] Adj. Genl. of the state [,] will be urged by his friends for the appointment of Brigadier Genl. in the Provisional Army: I could speak of him & his qualifications in the highest & sincerest terms; but to you who know him it is unnecessary. I invoke your aid to enlist our Delegation in his behalf, and to present him to the President. No better appointment from this state could, in my opinion, be possibly made."[14] Such a strongly worded recommendation seemed to have carried its intended weight when Gist was appointed brigadier general on March 20. It is unlikely that without Chesnut's support, Gist would have found himself in May 1862 headquartered at Secessionville in command of the Confederate forces on James Island.

In this new posting, Gist inherited a defensive line that roughly split James Island in half. One line ran from a point on the Stono River near Wapoo Cut south to the banks of Newtown Cut. Further to the east, another line faced south and west and arched around to Lighthouse Inlet. This line was anchored by two fortifications of its flanks. To the north was Fort Pemberton and to the south was what would become the Tower Battery. Located at the neck of the Secessionville peninsula, well south and forward from the main line's left flank on Lighthouse Inlet, Tower Battery occupied a critical location. It not only covered the southern portion of the Confederate line with enfilading fire, it also provided access to a water route to the Confederate rear. The Tower Battery was an isolated but extremely important part of the Confederate defense.[15]

Gist attacked his duties with vigor. On May 14, he pulled most of the 24th South Carolina Regiment off Cole's Island and repositioned them near Secessionville. He replaced them with two rifle companies under Lieutenant Colonel Ellison Capers but instructed them to withdraw in the face of a significant attack.[16] This reduction in force on Cole's Island helped Gist reinforce positions on James Island. He also reported to Pemberton that he had "detached four companies from [Colonel Thomas] Lamar's battalion to take charge of and man the lines east of James Island Creek."[17] This force would be of critical importance to the upcoming Battle of Secessionville.

Leadership Lessons

Gist's biographer concludes Chesnut's "political influence gave States Rights Gist the boost he needed."[18] In so doing, Chesnut assumed a mentorship role in Gists's life. A mentor is "a leader with greater experience than the one receiving the mentoring [who] provides guidance and advice."[19] Both in political and military life, Chesnut had greater experience that he shared with Gist in informal settings as well as in their formal relationship through Chesnut's position on the executive council. Moreover, mentoring is "a future-oriented developmental activity focused on growing in the profession."[20] Chesnut fulfilled this aspect of mentorship in his efforts to help place Gist in increasing positions of responsibility.

Some observers carefully distinguish between the specific function of mentoring and the senior leader's general responsibility of providing for the organization's future by "growing future senior leaders...[:] the process whereby senior leaders identify promising juniors for key developmental and career enhancing positions."[21] Indeed, as General Bill Creech expresses it, "the first duty of a leader is to create more leaders."[22] Mentorship, however, should not be a way for subordinates "to connive their way into the good graces of powerful and influential superiors and hence receive special treatment and favors."[23] Such politically motivated "sponsorship" is not to be confused with merit-based mentorship.[24] Unfortunately, there were many incidents of cronyism masquerading as mentoring in both the Federal and Confederate armies, and there appear to have been some critics who felt Chesnut's support of Gist was a product of undue political influence. Chesnut's wife, however, counters such claims, wondering "what have these comfortable stay-at-home patriots to say of General Gist now" after Gist had served the cause well and died at the forefront of his brigade at the Battle of Franklin in 1864.[25]

Former Chief of Staff of the Army General Edward Meyer considers "door opening," or "providing opportunity for an individual," to be a key facet of mentorship. However, Edgar Puryear, Meyer's interviewer, explains that by this Meyer's means "providing the opportunities for assignments that might assist in professional growth" and these are usually "the toughest and most demanding jobs and working longer hours than most of a person's counterparts."[26] Gist certainly earned his stripes as adjutant and inspector general before securing his appointment to brigadier general and his command at James Island. Indeed, Gist appears to have been a worthy candidate for Chesnut's mentorship and a good example of how such attention can develop both the individual and foster organizational growth.

Take-aways

- Mentors assist less experienced leaders to grow personally and professionally.
- Mentorship is one way senior leaders ensure the future health of the organization.
- Mentorship is not intended to be a means of gaining or giving unwarranted favor.

11

Thomas Lamar and Charismatic Leadership

Although Gist and other generals had worked feverishly before the battle, the actual fighting at Secessionville was led at the field grade level. The Federal attack was defeated in no small part thanks to the determined stand of Colonel Thomas Lamar at the Tower Battery. Lamar is an exemplary example of countless natural leaders on both sides who rose to the demands of wartime command.

Major General David Hunter had assumed command of the Department of the South at Hilton Head in March 1862. When he learned of the Confederate evacuation of Cole's Island he saw an opportunity to turn Charleston's defenses and on June 2 he transported nearly 75,000 troops to the southwestern end of James Island, from whence they would advance along the Stono River. Brigadier General Henry Benham was the operational commander of this force, with Brigadier General Horatio Wright commanding three brigades on the left and Brigadier General Isaac Stevens commanding the two-brigade main assault force.

The Federal march was slowed by heavy rains and Confederate artillery, but by June 9 Wright had advanced as far as Grimball's Plantation, where he established his headquarters and built a line of entrenchments. Confederate pickets near the Presbyterian church observed these developments. Major General John Pemberton had been slow to react to Hunter's move, but when he did realize the Federals were concentrating in the vicinity of the Stono River, he began gathering forces. He ordered Brigadier General William Duncan Smith, the latest in a string of Confederate commanders on James Island, to move a force southeast of the Presbyterian church to contest any further Federal advances. Smith placed the reinforced 1st South Carolina and Colonel

Johnson Hagood at the Presbyterian church, and Colonel Gilbert Williams's 47th Georgia to Hagood's south. On June 10, the Confederates attacked along the road leading to Grimball's. In a battle of some two hours, the Federal line held and the Confederates withdrew.[1]

In spite of this victory, the Federal command seemed to lose its enthusiasm for further offensive action.[2] Wright reported his troops were "now quite exhausted, having been actually engaged with the enemy or under his fire for several hours this afternoon," and implied his men were not in condition to continue forward as Benham had planned.[3] Hunter's aggressive spirit seems also to have run its course. He now did not think his presence was any longer required and as he departed on June 10 he advised Benham:

> In leaving the Stono River to return to Hilton Head I desire, in any arrangements that you may make for the disposition of your forces now in this vicinity, you will make no attempt to advance on Charleston or to attack Fort Johnson until largely re-enforced or until you received specific instructions from these headquarters to that effect. You will however provide for a secure entrenched encampment, where your front can be covered by the fire of our gunboats from the Stono on the left and the creek from Folly River on the right. After making all proper arrangements for the security of the camp, and the necessary provision for quartermaster's, commissary, and medical stores, if in your judgment you can safely leave the position you will return to your usual headquarters at Hilton Head, reporting to me verbally the state of affairs here; or, if delayed, reporting in writing by each boat that may leave here previously. You will be especially careful to have the free communication established and kept up by the repairs of the causeway between the old battery and Cole's Island.[4]

The action at Grimball's convinced Pemberton that the main Federal attack would occur on James Island. To meet this developing threat, he ordered Brigadier General Nathan Evans and two of his regiments to move from Adams Run to Charleston. As both Federals and Confederates built up their forces, the area around Colonel Lamar's Tower Battery became the scene of increased activity.

Work on this fort was begun in January 1862 when the 23rd South Carolina was practically the only Confederate force on James Island. Under the direction of Colonel Lewis Hatch, the regiment constructed a small earthwork, built a causeway to connect the peninsula with the main body of the island, and erected an observation. It was this seventy-five foot tall reconnaissance platform that eventually gave the fort its name. The fort itself was laid out in a rough shape of an "M," running northwest to southeast and bordered on each side by marsh. The fort's design and the terrain served to canalize any attack into a plunging, enfilading fire. About 800 yards from the Tower Battery was the small hamlet of Seccessionville, so named not in honor of the current

Major General Hunter perhaps unwisely returned to his headquarters at Hilton Head before the Battle of Secessionville (Library Congress, Prints & Photographs Division).

sectional crisis but as a result of an earlier act of younger family members "seceding" from their elders and moving away from the Fort Johnson area to the peninsula.[5]

The work Hatch started was reinvigorated when, on May 13, Brigadier General States Rights Gist reported dispatching "four companies from Lamar's battalion to take charge of and man the lines east of James Island Creek." Gist also noted placing an 18-pounder in position there.[6] By the time Lamar had made his improvements, several more pieces were added. There was an 8-inch

Columbiad on the right side of the front wall, and a rifled 24-pounder on the left. Several 18-pounders had been added to the original one, and they and another 24-pounder rounded out the front line armament. A mortar battery was positioned to the rear of the magazine almost directly behind the left front wall.[7]

While Lamar and his men had been improving their position, Federal work parties were also laboring some 2,000 yards away on the eastern tip of James Island. Lamar observed this and other activity, and on the afternoon of June 15 he notified Evans that "he was convinced that Secessionville would doubtless be attacked either on that night or on the morning of the 16th." Evans "directed him, to hold his position; that he would be re-enforced if necessary." Lamar's assessment of the situation proved to be correct, and at 2:00 a.m. on June 16, he notified Evans that the enemy was advancing.[8]

This Federal movement seemed to have contradicted Hunter's parting orders to Benham that he was to "make no attempt to advance on Charleston or to attack Fort Johnson until largely re-enforced or until you received specific instructions from these headquarters to that effect," but Benham felt the move was allowed by the same orders' requirement that he "provide for a secure entrenched encampment."[9] He believed the Confederates now "covered with their fire the whole of the position and camps of General Stevens on our right, and as these were the only or the lower positions that secured a footing upon the main portion of James Island and a direct route on firm land to Fort Johnson, which, when required, gave us the command of the city and harbor of Charleston." With the Tower Battery "being apparently made much stronger every day," he "deemed it important that a reconnaissance should be made in force at the earliest practicable period, with the object, if it were successful and the fort not too strong, of capturing and holding the same."[10]

Anticipating Benham's advance, the Confederates had reinforced Lamar's 750-man force. Of his own accord, Colonel Johnson Hagood had placed three regiments of his First South Carolina Volunteers on alert and sent a detachment of Colonel Spartan Goodlette's 22nd South Carolina regiment to the support of Lamar. Evans further ordered the Fourth Louisiana Battalion of Lieutenant Colonel John McEnery and the rest of Goodlette's regiment to "repair at double-quick and report to Colonel Lamar at Secessionville."[11]

Lamar had pickets stationed to cover the Rivers Causeway, which linked the Battery Island Road to Sol Legare Island. At about 4:00 a.m., these were driven in and reported to Lamar that the enemy was about three-fourths of a mile away and advancing. Lamar sent couriers to order Lieutenant Colonel Peter Gaillard's Charleston Battalion and Lieutenant Colonel Alexander Smith's Pee Dee Battalion forward, and to inform Evans of the situation. Lamar then moved to his batteries, where he had a detachment on duty at each gun. By now the enemy was but seven hundred yards away, advancing at the double-quick. Lamar ordered his 8-inch Columbiad loaded with grape and aimed the gun himself so as to "fire at the center of the line and thereby break it, in order to cause confusion and delay, so that I might get my infantry into position previous to their reaching my lines." Lamar reported "the shot had the desired effect" and caused the enemy to "immediately [flank] to the right and left." He then ordered the Columbiad to be loaded with canister. After again aiming it himself, Lamar left the battery, directing Lieutenant J.B. Humbert "to give them canister freely, which he did." While Lamar had been firing the Columbiad, Sergeant James Baggott of Company B was firing the 24-pounder to its left.

As Lamar headed to his infantry, he ordered Captain T.Y. Simons to go to Gaillard and Smith and tell them to hurry up their battalions. Lamar first encountered Smith and ordered him to take position on the left. The enemy had already reached the Confederate flank, but Smith's counterattack drove them from their positions. Lamar then ordered Gaillard to take a position on the right and center. Three successive Federal assaults were repulsed, with Lamar being seriously wounded in the head by a minié ball on the second attack. The Federals then attempted a flank attack on the Confederate left. Galliard's men met this threat and were soon reinforced by McEnery's Louisianans. This Federal attack was also halted. Only with the matter thus in hand did Lamar, "so much exhausted from loss of blood" from his wound, turn the command over to Gaillard and then, after Gaillard was wounded, to Lieutenant Colonel Thomas Wagner. Still, Lamar "never ceased to give orders to my batteries."[12]

The Confederate victory at Secessionville was a critical one, both in the Charleston Campaign and the broader war effort. Had the Federals carried the day, they would have flanked the Confederate defenses at James Island and been able to capture Fort Johnson and continue to Charleston. If Charleston fell, the Federals would not only have gained a significant moral victory, they would have also denied the Confederacy a critical rail and port center. The Federals could have then used these facilities to launch their own offensive, possibly requiring the Confederacy to divert resources from Virginia to South Carolina. This weakening of the Richmond defenses may well have considerably shortened the war.[13] Instead, the Federal offensive spirit was sorely checked.

Hunter was livid in his assessment that Benham had violated his orders in attacking. He cashiered Benham and placed Horatio Wright in "command of all the troops on James Island and at Legareville" on June 19. Hunter was adamant there would be no repeat of Benham's initiative, advising Wright,

"You will not attempt to advance toward Charleston or Fort Johnson till largely re-enforced and until you receive express orders from these headquarters."[14]

Leadership Lessons

In the aftermath of the Confederate victory, Pemberton called Lamar "gallant and indefatigable," and Evans heralded him as "dauntless."[15] Such praise was not misplaced, as indeed it had been Lamar and his men who had carried the day. Walter Cisco notes, "Victory was won on the parapet of Lamar's fort without the benefit of general officers."[16]

On February 8, 1864, Lamar received the Thanks of Congress for his role in the battle, and when the fort encompassing the Tower Battery was finally completed in the spring of that year, it was christened Fort Lamar. Unfortunately, both these honors occurred after Lamar had succumbed to malaria on October 18, 1862.

Lamar was properly singled out for his decisive role in the Confederate victory at Secessionville, but his battlefield performance is somewhat surprising given his "less than military background."[17] Before the war, Lamar had been a planter-turned-politician in the Edgefield district. He was elected to the state general assembly in 1860, and as the crisis unfolded at Fort Sumter, he was appointed to Governor Francis Pickens's staff. Seeking a more active role, he went on his own to Morris Island, where he secured command of an artillery battery.

After the surrender of Fort Sumter, Lamar returned to Edgefield and raised an artillery company. He was elected captain and brought his unit to Charleston, where it served at Fort Johnson. As "a tribute to Lamar's popularity and ability," this company grew into first a battalion and then a regiment. According to Patrick Brennan, author of a history of the Battle of Secessionville, the men of the 1st South Carolina Artillery were led "by the energy of their colonel."[18]

One attribute that no doubt caused the men of the 1st South Carolina Artillery to warm to their leader was Lamar's magnanimity. Although he was proclaimed as "the hero of Secessionville," the selfless Lamar refused to monopolize the credit. He closed his report of the battle with the following: "In conclusion, I would state that the great victory achieved on June 16 over such a superior force of the enemy is owing entirely to the patriotism, love of freedom, and indomitable courage of the officers and men under my command. Every man did his duty."[19]

On the strength of his background and battlefield performance, there developed a campaign in Edgefield to make Lamar a candidate for a legislative seat. Upon hearing of the movement, Lamar declined, explaining, "I can much better serve my country in the field, as long as the war lasts, and I keep my health, I prefer to continue in the military service." Ironically, it was just a week later that Lamar contracted malaria. When he died, men of both the 46th Georgia and the Charleston Battalion escorted his body in a solemn procession through the streets of Charleston.[20]

Although Lamar may have lacked the military background of some of his contemporaries, he possessed the attributes of a charismatic leader that allowed him to be an excellent battlefield commander. Charismatic leaders not only have special personality characteristics that facilitate their leadership, their charisma is also validated by their followers. Peter Northouse identifies five specific types of behaviors that charismatic leaders demonstrate.[21] Lamar exhibited all these behaviors.

First, Northouse states that charismatic leaders "are strong role models for the beliefs and values they want their followers to adopt."[22] Jay Conger adds that such leaders "build exceptional trust by demonstrating a total dedication to the cause they share with followers."[23] Lamar exhibited this behavior in declining to pursue a legislative seat in Edgefield in favor of continuing to "serve my country in the field, as long as the war lasts." In so doing, Lamar set an example of selfless service and courage for his men. Second, charismatic leaders "appear competent to followers."[24] Lamar's personally aiming the early shots in the battle demonstrated his own technical competence to his gunners. He instilled confidence in his men by his own abilities.[25] Third, charismatic leaders "articulate ideological goals that have moral overtones."[26] Lamar evoked such language in crediting the victory "entirely to the patriotism, love of freedom, and indomitable courage of the officers and men under my command. Every man did his duty." By recognizing the effect of such values at Secessionville, Lamar inspired his men to continue to operate according to such ideals. Fourth, "charismatic leaders communicate high expectations for followers, and they exhibit confidence in their followers' abilities to meet these expectations."[27] Lamar exhibited this behavior when, after aiming the Columbiad a second time, he left the battery, directing Lieutenant J.B. Humbert "to give them canister freely, which he did." Charismatic leaders like Lamar make "extensive use of personal example and role modeling ... [and] empowerment practices to demonstrate how their vision can be achieved."[28] Such empowerment influences followers to eventually perceive as feasible tasks once judged as being too difficult and this becomes a significant force multiplier.[29] In trusting Humbert to perform the task, Lamar was freed to influence the battle elsewhere. Fifth, charismatic leaders "arouse task-relevant motives in followers that may include affiliation, power, and esteem."[30] They "create among subordinates a compelling desire to be led in the direction of the vision despite its often significant hurdles."[31] This behavior was manifest in the Civil War tradition of electing officers and raising volunteers. That Lamar's rise from captain to lieutenant colonel and the growth of his unit from a company to a regiment was declared "a tribute to Lamar's popularity and ability" shows the bond Lamar had with his men and the loyalty they had to him and their unit.

The rapid need for officers resulted in both the Confederate and Federal armies including many examples of "natural leaders without military training" who sometimes "showed more valor than discretion."[32] Clearly a person can be charismatic without rising to the bar of mastering the charismatic leader behavior required by Northouse's description. Lamar is an example of a man who achieved this standard.

Take-aways

- Charismatic leadership behaviors involve a process between the leader and his followers.
- The charismatic leader uses his own energy to build energy in his followers.
- Effective communication—by word and deed—is a critical component of charismatic leadership.
- Charisma is a means, not an end, and charismatic leadership must be purposeful and directed toward accomplishing organizational goals.

12

David Hunter and the Need for Cooperation

The charismatic leadership of Lamar and the heroics of his men notwithstanding, a major factor contributing to the failed Federal attack at Secessionville was the difficulty in obtaining meaningful cooperation between Hunter's land force and Du Pont's naval force. Du Pont in particular was insistent on the need for such unity of effort, but personality, resources, and the lack of a doctrinal or organizational basis for joint operations seemed to conspire against progress in this area.

The presence of Major John Barnard on the Blockade Board had potentially represented some very limited liaison between the army and navy as they waged the coastal campaign, but in reality Barnard's main contribution was to provide specialized engineering expertise and topographical information rather than unity.[1] In fact, the general-in-chief, Winfield Scott, did not even have a counterpart commander of the navy with whom he could coordinate.[2] This situation was exacerbated by the fact that Secretary of the Navy Gideon Welles and Secretary of War Edwin Stanton did not get along. Moreover, Welles continually complained that the army did not keep him informed of its plans.[3] At Charleston, unity of effort between the army and navy would be critical, and such cooperation would rely on the individual personalities and actions of those involved rather than the joint doctrine and command relationships that guide operations today.

Indeed, at the time of the Civil War there were no formal command arrangements or doctrine to facilitate joint operations in the modern sense. Instead, successful joint operations were largely the result of improvisation and personal actions of the commanders involved. At Charleston, that meant the Department of the South commander, Major General David Hunter, and

South Atlantic Blockading Squadron commander Admiral Samuel Du Pont. In the general context of the Civil War, Scott Stuckey concludes that "in the absence of unified command or meaningful joint doctrine, the conception and execution of joint operations totally depended on ad hoc actions by the responsible commanders, and therefore upon their personal chemistry and communications."[4] In this particular situation, Hunter's biographer Edward Miller notes that "Hunter's position in the Department of the South required that he keep on good terms with Commodore Du Pont."[5]

Under the loose nature of Civil War joint operations, the key to the difference between success and failure was the ability of the commanders to achieve the principle of war unity of effort.[6] Unity of effort focuses on cooperation rather than command. Accordingly, it is distinct from the traditional principle of war unity of *command*, which requires "that all forces operate under a single commander with the requisite authority to direct all forces employed in pursuit of a common purpose." Unity of *effort*, on the other hand, "requires coordination and cooperation among all forces toward a commonly recognized objective, although they are not necessarily part of the same command structure."[7] Unity of effort was what joint operations during the Civil War required. The emphasis on cooperation rather than command is typified in Hunter's initial orders from the War Department upon assuming command of the Department of the South to "co-operate with Commodore Du Pont in the taking of Fort Pulaski and Savannah."[8] No command relationship was established subordinating one commander to the other.

This loose arrangement continued at Secessionville, which Francis DuCoin notes "constituted a genuine combined operation, but there was still no one officer in command. Instead, it depended, as all such operations did, on mutual cooperation between army and navy leaders. So long as that cooperation lasted, the operation could proceed. But any bump in the planning meant that the officers had to meet again to discuss alternatives."[9] Effective communication, personal relationship skills, consensus building, and shared purpose would all be required to gain the needed cooperation in such an environment. In the campaign for Charleston, several teams of commanders would find it difficult to achieve this effect. The first two to fail in this regard would be Du Pont and Hunter.

Du Pont had liked Hunter's predecessor, Brigadier General Thomas Sherman, and believed Sherman had been unjustly relieved.[10] Perhaps based on this feeling, Du Pont was guarded in his initial assessment of Hunter. On March 31, 1862, he wrote his wife: "*mon impression n'est pas tres haute*" [my impression is not very high].[11] On April 4, he provided a mixed assessment which indicated his loyalty to Sherman. Du Pont wrote, "All I see of [Hunter]

I like, yet I do not know him and I think all that has been done since he came here with [Brigadier General Henry] Benham, if viewed through any medium but one of strong predisposition, would show apathy and blundering for Pulaski, I consider, was taken in one sense before they came."[12] Nonetheless, Du Pont recognized the political need to publicly recognize the capture of Fort Pulaski and wrote Assistant Secretary of the Navy Gustavus Fox on April 14 to request that he publish Du Pont's complimentary report on Fort Pulaski "in order to gratify as I think it will, Genl Hunter and the army people."[13] While Du Pont's request no doubt represents a certain amount of awareness, it also smacks of condescension and insincerity.

By early summer, however, Du Pont had reconsidered his poor first impression, which he expressed in writing to his wife: "General Hunter is a man of the finest bearing, tone, and address; silent, but not like most silent men, he is uncommonly generous and benign in his intercourse. He is easy in his private means, and very independent in thought and action, has no fear of responsibility, yet very devoid of pretension."[14] Even within this revised assessment, however, are indications that Hunter and Du Pont lacked the chemistry necessary to effect unity of effort. Du Pont's declaration of Hunter as "silent" did not bode well for effective future communication between the two, and his assessment of Hunter as being "very independent in thought and action" did not suggest a penchant for cooperation.

Indeed, Du Pont and his fellow naval officers remained suspicious of their army counterparts and critical of their inaction. On May 25, Du Pont wrote Fox: "The landward defences are nothing—but these Soldiers are queer people to us."[15] Indeed, the process of arranging for the transportation of Benham's men was a tortuous affair that involved missed meetings, sharply worded letters, and general bad attitudes until the issue was finally resolved in a meeting on May 30 at Hunter's headquarters with Hunter, Benham, and Du Pont present. More than half the soldiers would travel overland and the rest would be moved aboard the army transport *Flora* and the navy steamer *Bienville*. The USS *Henry Andrew* would ferry troops from the *Bienville* to the landing site on the southwestern end of James Island, and the *Andrew* and six other ships would provide covering fires from the Stono River.[16]

The movement was conducted on June 2 and featured effective naval gunfire directed by army signal officers that served to keep the defenders at bay. DuCoin deems it an excellent example of "what could be accomplished when the services cooperated," but whatever solace Du Pont took in his contribution was dashed by the subsequent defeat at Secessionville on June 16.[17] Disgusted by the missed opportunity, Du Pont complained to Fox: "Oh those Soldiers I put them nearly on *top* of the house in Charleston, but I did not push them into the windows and they came back."[18] From his forward position on the Stono River, Commander Percival Drayton shared Du Pont's frustration, writing to Fox of "the most unfortunate and at the same time injurious evacuation of James Island by the army, as our forces were quite securely placed in an advantageous position." The result, Drayton continued, "will not only greatly inspirit the enemy, but depress our own troops who must look upon themselves as beaten off, and by a force little if at all superior to them."[19] Both Du Pont and Drayton expressed the common theme that the navy had done its duty and that it was the army that had failed.

Rather than engaging in a meaningful dialogue about joint operations, Hunter, who was "an old hand at army politics," quickly diverted attention elsewhere.[20] On June 17 he "with great regret" wrote to Secretary Stanton that he found himself "compelled to trouble you with complaints" about such pressing matters as his need for "straw or light felt hats, convinced that we could thus save the lives of many of our men, exposed as they are to an almost tropical sun." He also reminded Stanton of his need "for tents, so indispensable at this season of the year to the health and comfort of our men."[21] In another letter written sometime earlier but also received by the War Department on June 17, Hunter reiterated his "fears that this expedition would fail in consequence of my being stripped of transportation by the Quartermaster's Department, and I have not the least doubt if we had the steamers belonging here and those for which I have applied that we should to-day be in possession of Charleston. Without this transportation our different points are not in supporting distance of each other and we are entirely at the mercy of the enemy, being liable any day to be cut off in detail. I deem it a duty I owe to myself frankly to state our situation, as I have before frequently done, that reverses many not be attributable to me."[22] In this letter, rather than devoting his energies to securing a victory, Hunter was attempting to distance himself from a defeat before it even occurred.

Obviously wise to Hunter's manipulative designs, Stanton parried his transportation complaints by replying on June 19 that "it would not have been expected that a general of your experience would undertake at his own discretion, without orders and without notice to the Department, a hazardous expedition, with 'fears of failure' for want of adequate transportation, and it is therefore hoped that the statement in your letter in the last respect may be unfounded." In the wake of the Secessionville debacle "serious complaints have been made against General Benham touching his courage and good conduct, copies of which will be immediately sent to you."[23] Sensing this opportunity to assign the blame elsewhere, Hunter relieved Benham and replaced him with Brigadier General Horatio Wright.[24] Whatever the merits of this internal change in command, it did nothing to resolve the root problem of unity of effort between the army and the navy.[25] This lack of cooperation would continue to plague the Federal command at Charleston, ultimately resulting in Du Pont's relief, only to resurface with the subsequent command team of Rear Admiral John Dahlgren and Major General Quincy Gillmore.

Leadership Lessons

General of the Army George Marshall is among many great leaders who champion the philosophy to "fix the problem, not the blame."[26] A big part of the problem facing the Federals at Charleston was a lack of unity of effort between the army and the navy. In the aftermath of the defeat at Secessionville, Hunter was more interested in making his subordinate commander Benham the scapegoat for the debacle than in dealing with the problem of how to effectively wage joint warfare. While such a narrow-minded approach reveals one of Hunter's weaknesses as an operational commander, it also shows a character and leadership flaw. General of the Army Dwight Eisenhower succinctly posited that "leadership consists of nothing but taking responsibility for everything that goes wrong and giving your subordinates credit for everything that goes well."[27] Such a perspective was well beyond the capacity of the self-serving Hunter. His response to the defeat at Secessionville was a testimony to his shortcomings as both a strategist and a leader.

Du Pont may have been more astute in identifying that the problem was the failure in joint operations rather than due to any action of Benham, but Du Pont also advanced little past blaming the army for a general lack of cooperation and certainly stopped short of Marshall's admonition to "fix the problem." Indeed, Du Pont's inability to convince his superiors in Washington of the need for a joint approach to Charleston would eventually reach a catastrophic climax for the admiral.

One way leaders can avoid the recrimination and unproductive handwringing that frustrated any real improvement in Federal joint operations after Secessionville is the after action review (AAR). After action reviews are conducted as soon as possible after an event in order to capture lessons learned and foster an environment of continuous improvement. The facilitator of the AAR asks the group to answer three questions: What was supposed to happen? What actually happened and why? What can we do to improve what went wrong and sustain what went right? One of the strengths of the AAR is that the group members discover for themselves ways of making themselves and the organization better. As such, an AAR is distinct from a "critique," which usually "only gives one viewpoint and frequently provides little opportunity for discussion of events by participants."[28] After Secessionville, Du Pont and Hunter each gave their version of what happened, but there was no corporate discussion involving the commanders and other participants. The climates associated with critiques prevent candid and productive discussion and do little to promote learning, improvement, and team building.[29] Unfortunately for the Federal cause, that is largely what transpired in the wake of Secessionville.

Had the Federals conducted an AAR, they would have had to come to grips with their failure to achieve unity of effort and then been led to develop a potential solution to the problem. Because at the time of the Civil War there were "neither command arrangements nor doctrine for joint operations," Scott Stuckey observes, "successful joint operations, like much else, would have to be improvised by those on the scene."[30] By failing to engage each other in meaningful dialogue, Du Pont and Hunter abdicated this responsibility and opportunity.

While more frequent exposure to complex, multi-participant operations has helped the military and other organizations standardize procedures that foster unity of effort, the challenge remains. At the time of the Civil War, it was the operations themselves that were novel. But once such activities became routine, a host of other changes in areas such as technology, communications, values, distance, and pace have risen to further task leaders' abilities to build synergy across a broad spectrum. As organizational structures become increasingly horizontal and leadership becomes increasingly transformational, instances of the traditional hierarchical unity of command lessen. In such environments, the ability to achieve unity of effort is critical, and it is the leader's responsibility to integrate and synchronize the wide range of capabilities at his disposal. The Federal command failed this task at Charleston.

Take-aways

- Fix the problem, not the blame. The after action review process can help facilitate this.
- Even in cases where there is no hierarchical command relationship, leaders must establish unity of effort.
- Communicate and use personal relationship skills to build a team approach.

13

Gabriel Rains and Alternative Solutions

If the Federals could achieve unity of effort and take advantage of their superior navy, the Confederates at Charleston would be in trouble because they simply lacked the ships to confront the Federal fleet in the traditional way. Instead, enterprising and imaginative thinkers like Gabriel Rains developed alternative solutions to the problem.

Gabriel Rains graduated from West Point in 1827 and fought in the Second Seminole War. Commanding a company at Fort King in what is now Ocala, Florida, Rains "soon discovered he was in a hornet's nest, and so reported, but was unheeded." The Indians took advantage of their superior numbers "and they became bold accordingly." Rains reported his "men were so waylaid and killed that it became dangerous to walk even around the post, and finally two of his best men were waylaid and murdered in full view thereof." Concluding that "desperate diseases often require desperate remedies, and as the preservation of the lives of his command required it," Rains made a booby trap of an explosive shell and, most likely, a friction primer. He buried the device and successfully used it alert his men of an approaching Indian force and to frighten the attackers away. With this action, Rains claimed a pioneering role in the history of mine warfare in the U.S. military.[1]

Rains then served in the Mexican War and subsequently in various recruiting, frontier, and garrison assignments. On July 31, 1861, he resigned as a lieutenant colonel in the U.S. Army. Upon joining the Confederacy, he was appointed a brigadier general and commanded a brigade during the Peninsula Campaign; but his true passion was science, and he was less interested in, and seemingly ill-suited for, field command.[2] He did, however, demonstrate his natural calling by using "some four small shells, found abandoned by our artillery" to delay the Federal pursuit after the Confederates evacuated Yorktown and withdrew up the Virginia Peninsula in May 1862. These munitions, Rains writes, "were hastily prepared by my efforts and put in the road near a tree felled across, mainly to have a moral effect in checking the advance of the enemy (for they were too small to do more) to save our sick, wounded, and enfeebled, who straggled in our rear."[3]

Both Federal and Confederate commanders criticized this unorthodox method of warfare. Major General George McClellan complained that "the rebels have been guilty of the most murderous and barbarous conduct in placing torpedoes within the abandoned works." Accordingly, the commander of the Army of the Potomac threatened to "make the prisoners remove them at their own peril."[4] Even Major General James Longstreet, Rains's corps commander, sent subsequent instructions to Rains to "put out no shells or torpedoes behind you, as he does not recognize it as a proper or effective method of war."[5] On the other hand, Major General D.H. Hill, Rains's division commander and a notorious Yankee-hater, opined that "all means of destroying our brutal enemies are lawful and proper."[6] The conflicting assessments were resolved on June 18 when Rains was assigned to the river defenses, where the use of his torpedoes was deemed "admissible" by Secretary of War George Randolph, "because they drive off blockading or attacking fleets" rather than merely taking "life with no other object than the destruction of life."[7]

In his new role, Rains began producing "submarine mortar batteries" that had several advantages over the devices then being developed by the navy. Rains's models used readily available materials such as artillery shells and timbers. They also used contact primers to result in detonation when struck by the enemy vessel. Rains even designed a simple "emergency" torpedo that could be made out of a beer barrel and constructed in an hour. On the other hand, the more complicated navy versions required scarce insulated, waterproof wire and galvanic cells to generate electric current and an operator to initiate the explosion when the target appeared to be in the correct location.[8]

Rains was not alone in his efforts. Among his fellow laborers was Matthew Maury, founder of the Confederacy's Submarine Battery Service. As the war progressed, Maury focused on the James River, and Rains was instrumental in planning the torpedo defenses of Mobile Bay and Charleston Harbor. By his count, 123 torpedoes were planted in Charleston Harbor and the Stono River, which he boasted "prevented the capture of that city and its conflagration."[9] His indefatigable efforts were recognized in June 1864 when Rains became head of the Confederate Torpedo Bureau.

Rains's torpedoes are an excellent example of asymmetric warfare. In asymmetric warfare, the weaker of two dissimilar opponents adopts new tech-

This display of ordnance found at Charleston after the war includes torpedoes (Library of Congress, Prints & Photographs Division).

niques to exploit the dissimilarity.[10] The Federal Navy at Charleston reflected the latest technology, while the Confederate conventional naval threat there was virtually nonexistent. Symmetrically, the Confederates did not have a chance. Undeterred, Rains explained: "Iron-clads are said to master the world, but torpedoes master the iron-clads, and must so continue on account of the almost total *incompressibility* of water and the developed gasses of the fired gunpowder of the torpedo under the vessel's bottom passing through it, as the direction of least resistance." By his count, fifty-eight Federal ships were sunk by torpedoes.[11]

General P.G.T. Beauregard was unsparing in his praise for the contribution of torpedoes to the Confederate cause. Summing up his narrative "Torpedo Service in the Harbor and Water Defences of Charleston," Beauregard quoted an article entitled "Has the Day of Great Navies Past?" to testify to the asymmetric power of the torpedo:

> Think of the destruction this infernal machine effected, and bear in mind its use came to be fairly understood, and some system introduced into its arrangement, only during the last part of the war. During a period when scarcely any vessels were lost, and very few severely damaged by the most powerful guns then employed in actual war, we find this long list of disasters from the use of this new and, in the beginning, much despised comer into the arena of naval warfare. But it required just such a record as this to arouse naval officers to ask themselves the question, "Is not the days of great navies gone forever?" If such comparatively rude and improvised torpedoes made use of by the Confederates caused such damage and spread such terror among the Union fleet, what will be the consequence when skilful engineers, encouraged by governments, as they have never been before, diligently apply themselves to the perfecting of this terrible weapon?[12]

For Rains, torpedoes represented "the modern *ne plus ultra* of warlike inventions." They were the latest in a succession of developments designed to counter and defeat the existing technology.[13] Unlike evolutions such as the rifle that improved upon the musket, however, the torpedo was an asymmetric weapon that sought not to make strength stronger but to turn weakness into strength. Under the circumstances, the defenders of Charleston had few other options.

Leadership Lessons

Rains and his torpedoes represent at least two examples of effective leadership. The first is the productive use of Rains's particular skill set by the Confederacy and the second is his novel approach to offsetting the Federal advantage. Both examples represent imaginative and creative leadership.

Leaders must use the assets available to them, especially their human resources, to form the most efficient team to accomplish the mission. Rains's early stint as brigade commander was unremarkable. At Seven Pines he was ordered to conduct a flank attack which "met a most galling fire," and "a portion of his command met with a disastrous repulse." Although Major General D.H. Hill declared Rains a "gallant and meritorious officer," Hill could not help but "regret that [Rains] did not advance farther in that direction. He would have taken the Yankees in flank...."[14] Herbert Schiller interprets Hill's somewhat delicately worded report as meaning Rains's "performance was judged as somewhat lacking."[15]

When General Robert E. Lee assumed command of the Army of Northern Virginia he could have easily ignored or quietly disposed of such a lackluster subordinate. Instead, Lee saw Rains and his penchant for mines as a means of countering the Federal use of the James River as an approach toward Richmond. As Major General Dabney Maury recalled with some poetic license, Lee beseeched Rains: "The enemy have upwards of one hundred vessels in the James River, and we think that they are about making an advance that way upon Richmond, and if there is a man in the whole Southern Confederacy that can stop them, you are the man. Will you undertake it?" In Maury's version, the noble Rains responded, "I will try."[16] Rather than leaving Rains in place as an ineffective brigade commander or relieving him for his tepid showing at Seven Pines, Lee assigned Rains "to the charge of the submarine defenses of the James and Appomattox Rivers."[17]

Even after allowances are made for Maury's literary flair, the exchange still represents a valuable leadership lesson. One of John Maxwell's "seventeen indisputable laws of teamwork" is "the law of the niche." According to this law, "all players have a place where they add the most value," and it is the responsibility of the leader to put people in situations where they can maximize their effectiveness. If that does not happen, Maxwell cautions, "when people aren't where they do things well, things don't turn out well."[18] That is exactly what happened when John Pemberton was promoted and assigned to command of the Charleston defenses. Like Pemberton, Rains's talents were primarily in the technical dimension, but he was spared from the frustration of Pemberton's ill-advised command assignment because Lee put Rains in his appropriate niche. Rains was certainly not the stereotypical brigadier general. One observer described him: "a most comical looking person ... medium height, with a short, quick, jerky way of walking, and a most peculiar expression of face, the eyes and mouth of which are incessantly in motion. A great torpedo man ... is a perfect monomaniac on the subject and talks of nothing else. I saw him get one innocent and confiding young man in a corner and I am certain he torpedoed him for at least two hours."[19] That such a decidedly unique individual could make a contribution within as uncompromising an organization as the military suggests that the thoughtful leader can find most anyone their niche.

Perhaps it was Rains's lack of convention that led him to his asymmetric use of torpedoes and the second leadership lesson in this episode of the Charleston Campaign. Such a solution to the problem was certainly consistent with the teachings of Sun Tzu, a military theorist from the period of the Warring States in ancient China whose classic work is *The Art of War*. Sir Robert Fry, a retired lieutenant general in the British Royal Marines and the executive chairman of the McKinney Rogers Group of companies, notes, "Sun Tzu wrote about a world emerging from a series of strategic shocks, including the death of Confucius and the crumbling of the Chinese empire into a succession of warring kingdoms. It was the kind of time that enables revolutionary thinkers and leaders to fundamentally change the way the world works."[20] Indeed, Sun Tzu was an early advocate of asymmetry. His writings include such advice as the following: "As flowing water avoids the heights and hastens to the lowlands, so an army avoids strength and strikes weakness," "When confronted with an enemy one should offer the enemy a bait to lure him; feign disorder and strike him," and "When I have won a victory, I do not repeat my tactics but respond to circumstances in an infinite variety of ways."[21]

Today Sun Tzu's popularity extends beyond the military to such realms as business, sports, and politics. Indeed, Fry argues that *The Art of War* "offers a unique view of the world that transcends its original military focus as it discusses the notions of appropriate use of resources, of 'measuring, estimating, counting, comparing and gauging' both your own strength and that of the 'enemy'—indeed, the idea of classifying knowledge itself as a precious resource." That, Fry notes, "is all useful in business."[22]

The mismatch of naval resources left the Confederate defenders of Charleston no choice but to use asymmetric tactics, but leaders in all situations must exercise the same innovative thinking in a variety of problem-solving situations. They must carefully weigh their strengths and weaknesses, and arrive at a solution that creates an advantage that, on the surface, is not apparent. As they negotiate this process, all leaders, military and otherwise, can turn to Sun Tzu for guidance.

Fry notes that Sun Tzu "was writing about how to engage a sentient opponent and come out on top. About avoiding a draining, attritional conflict and finding another way to win. About looking at your competitor and saying, 'Where am I stronger?' And of course also saying, even though it hurts, 'Where is he stronger?,' and accepting that answer."[23] Indeed, in the cases of the "desperate diseases" Rains describes, the "desperate remedies" may well involve asymmetry.

Take-aways

- Leaders must make use of all their assets and find a niche where everyone can contribute.
- Do not discount a person in all areas because of unsuitability in one area.
- Exploit strengths and avoid weaknesses.
- Think asymmetrically, especially in unadvantageous situations.
- Be innovative in problem solving.
- Figure out what the competition expects, and then consider doing something different.

14

Samuel Du Pont and Synchronization with Superiors

An inability to solidify cooperation with the army and the constant threat posed by Rains's torpedoes vexed Du Pont and made him hesitant to attack. As there was no national level joint staff to advise the president, Du Pont was left to his own devices to explain his caution to his superiors in Washington. Sufficient tension developed that Du Pont, the head of the Blockade Board and the hero of the Port Royal Expedition, was ultimately relieved.

Naval officers on the scene were not alone in their disgust with the army's withdrawal in the wake of the defeat at Secessionville. Other observers, however, drew different conclusions from the affair. While Admiral Du Pont remained convinced that taking Charleston required a joint operation, Assistant Secretary of the Navy Gustavus Fox told Du Pont that Secessionville only proved that "you will have to do it as you have done everything else, alone."[1] "Go squarely at it by the channel," he advised Du Pont, "so as to make it *purely navy*."[2] Du Pont was left to conclude that "Fox's Navy feelings are so strong and his prejudices or dislikes of Army selfishness so great ... that he listens unwillingly to combined movements." On October 18, 1862, Du Pont again recommended to Fox that the attack on Charleston "might be a joint movement of Army and Navy," but Du Pont seemed to have lost his energy to argue. Although he had come to the conclusion that success depended on landing a large enough army force on James Island to capture Fort Johnson, which Du Pont believed to be the key to Charleston Harbor, Du Pont stopped short of insisting on such a course. After he told Fox that "certainty of success" was more important than "undivided glory," Fox agreed, saying, "Oh, yes, indeed, the success must be paramount." Yet Du Pont "failed to exploit the opening" and was "too diffident to insist on a combined operation."[3] "It is not my nature to press things," he explained to his friend Congressman Henry Winter Davis.[4]

In reality, Du Pont had serious reservations that involved considerations even deeper than his belief in joint operations. The geography of Charleston Harbor and the layers of Confederate defenses, which included an abundance of torpedoes, were serious obstacles. As early as May 1862, Du Pont had written Fox that attacking Charleston was to enter an exitless trap. There was no way to "run the gauntlet" as Admiral David Farragut had done in his bold and successful attack on New Orleans. Instead, at Charleston, Du Pont explained, "we go into a bag, no running past, for after we get up they can all play upon us."[5] Du Pont protested that "the extent and nature of the defenses of Charleston are underrated ... in comparison with which those of New Orleans were very slight."[6]

On the other hand, Secretary of the Navy Gideon Welles believed that Charleston's stout defenses could be matched by ironclads including the *New Ironsides*, the navy's most powerful monitor. Indeed there was a serious rift developing, with President Abraham Lincoln, Welles, and Fox on one side and Du Pont on the other. The civilian leadership was pushing Du Pont into an operation about which he had serious reservations and felt unprepared. In a series of meetings in Washington in October 1862, Du Pont reiterated his position that a joint operation was necessary and that no number of ships, even ironclads, could take Charleston alone. Lincoln and the Navy Department leadership, however, had already made up their minds.[7] On January 6, 1863, Welles began ordering ironclads "south to strengthen Du Pont in his attack on Charleston."[8]

Having made his case with his superiors to no avail and having accepted the realities of the civil-military relationship, Du Pont resolved "to test in every way the efficiency of the ironclads that had arrived." On January 27, he sent the ironclad *Montauk*, the gunboats *Seneca*, *Wissahickon*, and *Dawn*, and the mortar schooner *C.P. Williams* to attack Fort McAllister on the Ogeechee River, Georgia. Sunken obstacles that appeared to be torpedoes blocked the *Montauk*'s advance, so the ironclad blasted the fort at a distance for four hours with no noticeable effect. The Confederate fire was accurate, striking the *Montauk* thirteen times but doing no damage. The results seemed to support Du Pont's previous doubts of the ironclads' strengths and his belief in the necessity of joint operations. "My own previous impression of these vessels, frequently expressed to Assistant Secretary Fox," he reported, "have been confirmed, viz, that whatever degree of impenetrability they might have, there was no corresponding quality of aggression or destructiveness against forts, the slowness of fire giving full time for the gunners of the fort to take shelter in the bombproofs." Concerning the need for a cooperating land force, he added, "This experiment also convinces me of another impression, firmly held and often expressed, that in all such operations to secure success troops are necessary."⁹

The next day Du Pont learned from a runaway slave the position of the torpedoes that had blocked the previous attack. Armed with this new intelligence, the Federals tried again on February 1. The *Montauk* advanced to within 600 yards of the fort and both sides unleashed accurate fire for four hours.

The *Montauk* was hit forty-eight times but retired without serious damage. Fort McAllister was also still sound. Of the experiment Du Pont lamented, "If one ironclad cannot take eight guns, how are five to take 147 guns in Charleston Harbor?"¹⁰

Fort McAllister confirmed what Du Pont had already concluded from the Confederate repulse of the ironclads *Monitor* and *Galena* before Drewry's Bluff in the Peninsula Campaign of 1862. It "was a very ill-advised and incorrect operation to expose those gunboats before the Army could take the forts in the rear," Du Pont opined.¹¹ In his mind, the situation at Fort McAllister was no different.

Du Pont launched attacks on Fort McAllister again on February 28 and March 3 with more disappointing results. His monitors could withstand the fort's punish-

In spite of his triumphant capture of Port Royal, Admiral Du Pont fell out of favor with Secretary of the Navy Welles as the Federal offensive against Charleston languished (Library of Congress, Prints & Photographs Division).

ment, but their slow rate of fire limited their ability, in a short span of time, to inflict serious damage to shore fortifications. This inefficiency of fire would plague Federal attempts on Charleston throughout the war.[12] But while Du Pont continued to think the solution to Charleston lay in a joint operation with a robust army component, Welles was equally adamant in favoring the all-navy solution he felt was made possible by ironclads.[13]

Du Pont remained skeptical, but he agreed to try if Welles could provide the necessary quantities. "The limit of my wants in the need of ironclads," Du Pont wrote Fox on March 2, 1863, "is the capacity of the [Navy] Department to supply them."[14] Ultimately Du Pont received all but one of the navy's new ironclads, making his fleet at Charleston the first integration of the revolutionary monitor technology into the navy's larger organization. Still, Du Pont's requests for more and more resources and his continued delay in attacking caused Lincoln and Welles to liken him to the overly cautious George McClellan.[15]

In the meantime, the Confederates did not remain passive. On January 31, Flag Officer Duncan Ingraham used the cover of the morning fog to attack ten unarmored Federal vessels of the blockading squadron just off the harbor. Ingraham inflicted much damage and caused enough panic that General P.G.T. Beauregard indulged himself in the hyperbole of declaring that the blockade had been lifted.[16] Of more lasting concern however was the regular threat posed by Confederate torpedoes, which one Federal naval officer said the Confederates had "strewn about like autumn leaves."[17] A torpedo had already badly damaged the *Montauk* in the February 28 attack on Fort McAllister and the *Weehawken* and the *Patapsco* would eventually be sunk by torpedoes as well.[18]

All of this activity resulted in the Confederates being well-prepared when Du Pont made his all-out attack on Charleston at 12:10 p.m. on April 7. Du Pont's plan was to run past Morris Island without returning fire, steam into the harbor, and open fire on Fort Sumter at close range. After Fort Sumter had been reduced, Du Pont would then concentrate on the Morris Island forts. This plan ran aground when Du Pont's lead vessel encountered obstacles strung across the channel from Fort Sumter northeastward to Fort Moultrie. The ensuing delay foiled Du Pont's plan of running past the point where Confederate fire was the most concentrated. Now, at about 3:00 p.m. Du Pont's fleet was under fire from nearly a hundred Confederate guns and mortars. About fifteen minutes later, Du Pont ordered his ships to return fire. For some two hours, Confederates and Federals exchanged fire at ranges between 550 and 800 yards. The Confederate guns were especially accurate, delivering some 400 hits and heavily damaging several monitors. The volume of fire was extremely lopsided, with the Confederates firing 2,229 rounds compared to just 139 for the Federals. Du Pont broke off the action at dusk, writing Major General David Hunter, "I attempted to take the bull by the horns, but he was too much for us."[19] To his wife, Du Pont confided, "We have failed as I felt sure we would."[20]

The Confederate forts had held, and Du Pont now declared that Charleston could not be taken by a naval attack alone. He deemed the monitors "miserable failures where forts are concerned."[21] Moreover, he was afraid that the Confederates might sink and then salvage one of the ironclads, so he withdrew all except the *New Ironsides* to Port Royal. In Washington, Du Pont's prudence was perceived as defeatism. On April 12, Welles wrote in his diary:

> [Du Pont] has no idea of taking Charleston by the Navy. In this I am not disappointed. He has been coming to that conclusion for months, though he has not said so. The result of this demonstration, though not a success, is not conclusive. The monitor vessels have proved their resisting power, and, but for the submarine obstructions, would have passed the forts and gone to the wharves of Charleston. This in itself is a great achievement.[22]

For Welles, the problem was with Du Pont, and increasingly other observers shared this sentiment. In the wake of the defeat, the *Baltimore American* opined, "Oh! That we had a Farragut here to take command at once, and do what has been so weakly attempted by Admiral Du Pont."[23] Finally, on June 3, Welles informed Du Pont "… it appears that your judgment is in opposition to a renewed attack on Charleston, and in view of this fact, with your prolonged continuance of the blockade, the Department has concluded to relieve you of the command of the South Atlantic Squadron, and to order Rear-Admiral [Andrew] Foote in your place.[24]

Leadership Lessons

Du Pont's biographer Kevin Weddle tellingly titled his biography of Du Pont *Lincoln's Tragic Admiral*. Weddle convincingly describes Du Pont as a scapegoat for the overall Federal frustration with the stiff Confederate defense of Charleston and the overall inefficiencies of the Federal high command at this stage in the war.[25] Nonetheless, Du Pont's fall from grace at Charleston provides lessons about the responsibilities both parties share in the senior-subordinate relationship.

There was obviously some communications breakdown between Welles and Du Pont. After Fort McAllister, Du Pont referred to his "firmly held and often expressed" impression of the need for joint operations. Nonetheless, after the failed direct attack on Charleston, Welles thought Du Pont had been coming to the conclusion for months that the navy could not succeed alone, "though he has not said so." In the subordinate's mind, Du Pont had clearly communicated his perspective. In the senior's mind, the subordinate had kept his thoughts to himself.[26]

It is a cliché, but effective communications is really a two-way street. In this case, Welles's senior leader responsibility was to provide Du Pont with a "vision" as he had done earlier in his guidance to the Blockade Board. From this vision would then proceed the implementing strategy or plan to ensure its attainment.[27]

In expressing his vision, Welles clearly articulated his desired end state of a Charleston in Federal hands. Du Pont agreed with this end state. Where the men differed was on the strategy for achieving it. For Welles (and Fox as well), the answer involved an aggressive and unilateral naval attack that leveraged the ironclad technology. For Du Pont, it involved a joint army-navy effort that respected the strong Confederate defenses. The senior and subordinate failed to achieve consensus on this plan. Robert Schneller concludes that "the principal reason for the Union's failure to capture Charleston was the lack of coordination within the high command" and the resulting failure "to reconcile political ends and military means."[28] It is not uncommon for such a difference of opinion to occur at different levels of command. In fact, if subordinates always provide the same analysis and interpretation of a situation as the senior does, they contribute less than if they presented an alternative solution for consideration. Leaders need their subordinates to generate workable options, even if they are contrary to the boss's initial frame of reference.

To this end, General Colin Powell tells his subordinates, "When we are debating an issue, loyalty means giving me your honest opinion, whether you think I'll like it or not. Disagreement, at this state, stimulates me. But once a decision is made, the debate ends. From that point on, loyalty means executing the decision as if it were your own."[29] Good leaders know that "yes men" are of little value, so they welcome opinions and recommendations that are contrary to their own as they work through the decision-making process. Once the decision is made, however, loyalty demands teamwork and compliance in executing the decided upon course of action.

Du Pont seems to have fulfilled his obligations in Powell's equation. He expressed his concerns about an all-navy attack and the strength of the Confederate defenses and made a recommendation for a joint operation. Pursuant to Welles's vision, Du Pont conducted a test of the ironclads at Fort McAllister and again reported his concerns. Welles remained insistent, and at this point Du Pont accepted his senior's decision and attacked Charleston. He perhaps did not fully embrace Powell's admonition to execute "the decision as if it were your own," but in spite of his doubts Du Pont made an all-out attack in good faith. That he was not surprised at the repulse does not imply that he did not seek success in its execution.

Subsequent Federal commanders would also fail to defeat Charleston's defenses, suggesting that Du Pont's reluctance was justified. In fact, leaders are well-advised to take seriously the counsel of those like Du Pont who are "on the ground." Powell explains that "the people in the field are closest to the problem, closest to the situation, therefore that is where real wisdom is." For that reason, Powell advises that "the commander in the field is always right and the rear echelon is wrong, unless proven otherwise."[30] Welles's misplaced confidence in technology, his belief in the universal applicability of the tactic used at New Orleans, and his misunderstanding of the unique nature of the Charleston defenses caused him to attribute Du Pont's assessment as timidity and overcaution. According to Powell, Welles owed Du Pont the benefit of the doubt.

One way to resolve the inefficiency illustrated in the Welles-Du Pont episode is to recognize that communication is both art and science.[31] The art of communication requires such things as interpersonal skills, mutual respect, and willingness to listen. The science of communication relates more to the structure and process that allow the art to unfold. The absence of joint task forces during the Civil War stymied the process of communications between the army and the navy at Secessionville, for example. Within the navy itself, the premature disbanding of the Blockade Board eliminated an excellent forum for the discussion of the philosophic differences between Welles and Du Pont.

Take-aways

- The leader's vision must include a strategy or plan for implementation.
- The demand for teamwork exists at all levels.
- Communication is both art and science.
- Subordinates owe their seniors faithful execution of orders, but seniors owe subordinates due consideration of their situational awareness and expertise.

15

Adolphus LaCoste and Maximizing Resources

One of the casualties of Du Pont's April 7 attack was the USS *Keokuk*. Adolphus LaCoste and other enterprising Confederates conducted a remarkable salvage operation that netted two valuable 11-inch Dahlgrens from the wreck. Scarce Confederate resources necessitated such bold measures and hard work made it possible.

The USS *Keokuk* was a 677-ton ironclad, built at New York City by Charles Whitney. She was originally named the *Moodna*, but she was renamed prior to being launched in December 1862. The *Keokuk* was an experimental ironclad steamer with two stationary, cylindrical gun towers, each with three gun ports. Her armor was alternating horizontal iron bars and strips of wood. Often mistaken for a double turreted monitor, the *Keokuk's* novel and untested design made many observers skeptical. She was commissioned in early March 1863. Later that month the *Keokuk* arrived at Port Royal, South Carolina, and joined the South Atlantic Blockading Squadron in time for Admiral Samuel Du Pont's attack at Charleston on April 7.

This attack ran into trouble early when the *Weehawken*, Du Pont's lead vessel, encountered obstacles strung across the channel from Fort Sumter northeastward to Fort Moultrie. The ensuing delay left the Federal fleet exposed at the point where Confederate fire was the most concentrated. Vessels of the first division received most of the pounding, and many were disabled. The *Keokuk* was last in line in the second division. In spite of the heavy fire, she steamed ahead of the other ships and lay between 600 and 900 yards from Fort Sumter in a narrow channel. For half an hour she remained in that vulnerable position, receiving the "undivided attention" of the Confederate guns.

The *Keokuk* was hit ninety times. Her alternating armor design proved to be insufficient protection, and one-fifth of the hits she received pierced her at or below the water line. "Completely riddled," she was able to withdraw and anchor out of range. The crew then worked all night trying to plug the numerous holes in her hull, but the next morning the sea became rougher, and more and more water began to pour in. At 7:30 a.m., Commander Alexander Rhind hoisted a distress signal, and the tug *Dandelion* came to rescue the crew. All men survived, but the *Keokuk* sank in about eighteen feet of water (at high tide) 1,300 yards off of Morris Island, leaving only her stack visible above the surface. The *Keokuk* thus ended her short career after about one month of commissioned service.[1] The divers Du Pont sent to examine the wreck reported the *Keokuk* was unsalvageable. At any rate, any Federal attempt at recovery would have had to be made under the threat of the Confederate guns at Morris Island. Instead Du Pont ordered her destroyed to keep her out of enemy hands.

Captain John Rodgers of the *Weehawken* and Chief Engineers E.D. Roble and A.C. Stimers attempted a seemingly overcomplicated effort to blow up the wreck using an Ericsson torpedo raft, but this plan was thwarted by rough

This engraving published in *Harper's Weekly* depicts the *Keokuk* as she sank off Charleston on April 8, 1863 (U.S. Naval Historical Center).

seas and the uncontrollable action of the *Keokuk*. When further efforts were abandoned, the Federals showed little concern. One war correspondent reported as follows: [The *Keokuk*] "is useless to the rebels. She is filled with sand, and will be broken up or buried after the first gale. The rebels cannot raise her, and she is covered by the guns of the blockading fleet, and will ever be beyond reach."[2]

At first the Confederates seemed to concur with the Federal assessment. In the days immediately following her sinking, the *Keokuk* became somewhat of a "tourist attraction," with the Confederates contenting themselves with collecting such souvenirs as rifles, clothing, and flags. Brigadier General Roswell Ripley considered the *Keokuk* was "probably for sale," but two Confederate naval officers who visited the site pronounced the valuable 11-inch guns unrecoverable. Major D.B. Harris, chief engineer, and Lieutenant S. Cordes Boyleston were more optimistic, however, and they convinced General Beauregard to give the operation a try.[3]

The man selected to orchestrate the attempt was a civilian employee of the Ordnance Department named Adolphus La Coste. A rigger by trade, LaCoste most recently had been busying himself mounting heavy guns and otherwise moving large objects. He was by all accounts considered to be the right man for the job and given great deference in determining the particulars of the operation. LaCoste selected a handpicked crew to assist him that included his brother James, several other civilians, and some soldiers from Fort Sumter.[4]

LaCoste had a formidable task before him. Although the *Keokuk* had gone down in relatively shallow water, her two turrets, each armed with an 11-inch Dahlgren, were exposed only at low water. The result was that LaCoste and his crew would have only about two and a half hours each night to work. Furthermore, the men faced the constant possibility that the Federals might dispatch armed boats at any time to interrupt the work. LaCoste could take some comfort in the fact that one or both of the two small Confederate ironclads *Chicora* and *Palmetto State* provided some protection from a covering position near the work site, and soldiers from the First South Carolina Artillery stood guard in small boats further down the channel. Indeed, on April 20 the Federal fleet fired on the boats containing LaCoste's men and the *Chicora* fired back. Although E. Milby Burton concludes the Federals must have known work was being done on the *Keokuk*, for whatever reason they chose not to attack.[5]

The first task before LaCoste was to cut a hole in the top of the turret large enough to allow the removal of the guns. LaCoste's men were confronted with two thicknesses of inch or inch and a half iron, held up by iron girders set close together and ceiled on the underside with more iron plate. In addition to the upper and lower plating, three of the heavy girders had to be cut through, each in two places, and removed. Then the gun had to be cut free from two large cap-squares of brass that held it to the carriage. This muscle-grinding work was done in chilly water with sledge hammers, chisels, wrenches, and crowbars. It took two weeks to cut through both turrets and get the first gun ready to be hoisted out of the wreck.[6]

Each gun was over thirteen feet long and weighed 16,000 pounds. An old lightship from Rattlesnake Shoal was outfitted with two outriggers of timber fourteen inches square and twenty feet long and employed for the salvage operation. To counterbalance the weight of the gun, 1,500 sandbags were placed in the bow. The lightship was towed to the site by the steamer *Etiwan* and secured to the wreck. Then LaCoste directed his men as they labored to fasten the tackle to the gun and swing it aboard. When it was time to hoist the gun, the breech came out first, but the gun could not be sufficiently elevated for the muzzle to clear the turret. As John Johnson dramatically describes the event, LaCoste was "equal to the emergency" and "was not to be thwarted." He ordered the sandbags shifted from bow to the stern, and "the bow, heaving with the tide and becoming more buoyant every minute, gradually responded to the lightening of its load and the lifting force now exerted by the weighing down of the opposite end of the boat." Still the muzzle could not swing clear, but just as it seemed the mission would fail, a fortuitous wave lifted the lightship, derrick, and gun just enough for the gun to clear the turret. Then LaCoste and his delighted crew returned to the safety of Charleston with their prize.[7]

The expedition returned three nights later and, "as practice makes perfect," the second gun was recovered with comparative ease. In the meantime LaCoste had fallen ill, and his brother James led the second mission. With secrecy no longer necessary, the Charleston papers announced the success on May 6. Beauregard proudly reported to the secretary of war: "The two 11-inch guns from wreck of *Keokuk* have been saved by Mr. LaCoste and parties from Fort Sumter under Lieutenants Beyleston, Rhett, and Kemper. Too much praise cannot be bestowed on their zeal and energy."[8] On the Federal side, Secretary of the Navy Gideon Welles scolded Du Pont that he was personally responsible for the debacle and added that "the wreck and its important armament ought not to have been abandoned."[9]

The Confederates quickly put their new acquisitions to use. One gun was mounted on the walls of Fort Sumter at the eastern angle of the barbette battery, where it remained until the night of the September 1–2 ironclad attack. It was then brought back to Charleston and joined Battery Ramsay at White Point Garden. The second gun was mounted in Battery Bee on Sullivan's Island

and was active in Admiral John Dahlgren's attack of September 7–8. The guns recovered from the *Keokuk* were important additions to the Confederate arsenal, where, except for the British Blakelys, they were the heaviest guns in Charleston Harbor.[10]

Leadership Lessons

In his study of the siege of Charleston, Burton declares that "few episodes of the war exceeded in daring the raising of the *Keokuk's* guns."[11] With similar enthusiasm, Johnson credits the success to "the skill, daring, and perseverance of a few dauntless men."[12] Warren Ripley echoes that the recovery stands as "a monument to a group of Americans who proved that courage, ingenuity, and hard work can accomplish what many believed impossible."[13] Indeed, the work of LaCoste and his fellows is a sterling example of the problem-solving, determination, and safeguarding of resources that leaders must exhibit.

Thomas Edison believed "genius is one percent inspiration, ninety-nine percent perspiration."[14] LaCoste and his crew certainly had opportunity to exercise Edison's proscription during the recovery operation, which Johnson estimates "occupied about three weeks."[15] Much of it was labor of the most physically demanding and painfully slowest sort. LaCoste had to motivate, cajole, and inspire his men to stick to the task in spite of this hardship. That he took ill suggests he too suffered from the strain of the labor. Yet a leader must persevere and motivate his team to do so as well, especially in times of adversity.

On a much smaller scale, LaCoste modeled Earnest Shackleton's charge that "if you're a leader, a fellow that other fellows look to, you've got to keep going."[16] Shackleton was the Antarctic explorer whose 1914 expedition met disaster when his ship *Endurance* became trapped and crushed in an ice pack. Shackleton took five men with him in a small boat and spent sixteen days crossing over 800 miles of ocean to reach South Georgia. The group then trudged across the island, where they found help at a whaling station. As a result of Shackleton's heroic perseverance and leadership, his entire crew was saved.

In addition to such perseverance, LaCoste also demonstrated the leadership responsibility of optimizing available resources.[17] Air Force Materiel Command commander General Donald Hoffman likes to remind his subordinates of a New England saying that declares, "Use it up, wear it out, make it do, or do without." "Our budgets are not a growth industry," Hoffman told a gathering of his key leaders in 2010. "We have to live within our means."[18] Suffering from a weak domestic industrial base and the isolation of the blockade, the Confederacy could ill afford to ignore the opportunity to salvage the *Keokuk*'s guns. The Federal command and even two Confederate naval officers deemed the task impossible, but LaCoste proved once again what can be done by a resolute leader who puts his mind to the mission.

Take-aways

- Hard work, problem-solving, and determination allow leaders to do what others say can't be done.
- Leaders must not only accomplish the mission, they must also do it in a way that conserves resources.

16

John Dahlgren and Command Presence

After Secretary of the Navy Gideon Welles named him to replace Samuel Du Pont, Admiral Andrew Foote died before he could report to his new post. Reluctantly, Welles turned to Admiral John Dahlgren, an acknowledged ordnance expert but a man with little experience at sea. On July 6, Dahlgren assumed command of the South Atlantic Blockading Squadron. Concerns that Dahlgren's technical skills did not necessarily qualify him for command seemed warranted in his early difficulties in exerting a positive command presence.

As a captain, Andrew Foote had demonstrated a penchant for joint operations when he combined with Brigadier General Ulysses S. Grant in the Forts Henry and Donelson Campaign of February 1862. Even without any direct or formal command link (Foote had been instructed by Secretary of the Navy Gideon Welles to cooperate with the army without subordinating himself to it), Grant and Foote were able to work together closely in arranging all aspects of the attack. Their cooperation began when the pair jointly cabled Department of the Missouri commander Major General Henry Halleck with their plan. Indeed, it was Foote's endorsement that won Halleck's approval.

On February 6, Foote shelled Fort Henry into submission. Grant's land force arrived thirty minutes after the surrender and took possession of the fort. Such cooperation among the services was unusual. Scott Stuckey notes that "Foote and Grant were very different individuals ... yet they worked well together. Whatever their differences, they shared a common inclination to attack the enemy, both hating inactivity. They maintained excellent communications without undue worry as to who would get the credit—a quality rare in Civil War commanders."[1]

Foote had received a leg wound at Fort Henry from wood splinters knocked loose by a Confederate shell that struck his ship. As a result, he was recuperating at a desk job in Washington at the Bureau of Equipment and Recruiting at the time Welles was looking for a replacement for Du Pont. In addition to Foote, Rear Admirals David Farragut, Francis Gregory, and John Dahlgren, as well as (acting) Rear Admiral David Porter, were all considered as possibilities. Welles thought Farragut was the best qualified, but he could not be spared from his position in the Gulf of Mexico. Gregory was too old for active sea duty, and Porter was too junior for such an important command. Dahlgren, the chief of the Bureau of Ordnance, had been actively lobbying for the job and had President Abraham Lincoln's support, but Welles was concerned about his lack of sea service.

On the other hand, Foote had many attributes to recommend him in addition to his proven record of joint operations, his experience in command, and his ready availability. He was a friend of Welles's and was highly regarded in the navy. Such stature would be important in replacing a man like Du Pont, who still commanded a loyal following in the South Atlantic Blockading Squadron. Foote was one of very few officers who could succeed Du Pont without creating too much animosity or controversy. By late May, Welles had decided Foote was the right man for the job.[2]

With this decision resolved, Foote then suggested that Dahlgren accompany him to Charleston as commander of the ironclad fleet. Welles had only just succeeded in fending off Dahlgren's lobbying for the overall squadron command and must have been somewhat surprised by Foote's suggestion, but he acquiesced. Welles, Foote, Dahlgren, and Major General Quincy Gillmore then began a series of sessions to plan future operations. Gillmore was a veteran of the Department of the South, where he had used his technical expertise to engineer the capture of Fort Pulaski. On the strength of that feat, he had been promoted and given a division command in the Department of the Ohio. Now the War Department's frustration with Major General David Hunter gave Gillmore an opportunity to return to his old department as commander on June 12, 1863.[3]

Foote seemed content to let Dahlgren provide most of the navy's input in the discussions with Gillmore. The services agreed that the best course was to attack Morris Island and use it as a base to then neutralize Fort Sumter and capture Charleston. Beyond that general strategy, however, the consensus began to unravel. Dahlgren continued with the argument earlier advanced by Welles that the navy should attack unilaterally. Unlike Du Pont, Dahlgren was a strong proponent of ironclads and believed that with just six more of the vessels, he could successfully force his way into the harbor. The problem was that production lagged behind Dahlgren's demands, and it would be several months before sufficient ironclads would be available for Dahlgren's purposes.

Having decided to relieve Du Pont because of his reluctance to attack, the Federal high command was unwilling to remain inactive while more ironclads were built. As an alternative, Gillmore, drawing on his success at Fort Pulaski, outlined a plan to use land-based artillery at Morris Island to reduce Fort Sumter. Although Gillmore's proposal was adopted, no details were written down before Gillmore departed Washington for the Department of the South. Foote and Washington remained behind working on their plans, but Foote's old wound became infected, and he died on June 26. Even as Foote languished on his deathbed, Welles reluctantly appointed Dahlgren to command of the South Atlantic Blockading Squadron on June 21.

Gillmore had been at Hilton Head since June 11 and was already planning the attack. The momentum lost by the death of Foote further slowed the navy's planning and increased the separation between the two services' preparations. On June 13, Gillmore was already conducting a reconnaissance of Folly Island, the springboard for the attack on Morris Island.[4] As he did so, he was left to coordinate with Du Pont, who was now a lame duck commander awaiting the arrival of his replacement. Du Pont had little interest in Gillmore's preparations and resented that he now found himself having "to cooperate with him in a plan I condemned and for which I was relieved."[5]

Dahlgren finally arrived at Port Royal on the morning of July 4. He found little in the way of a transition plan between himself and Du Pont, whom Dahlgren felt had "preferred to await my arrival" rather than make any firm commitments to Gillmore.[6] Later that day and the next, Dahlgren met with Gillmore to discuss operations and found "a very loose state of things; no shape or connection."[7] The lack of written plans from the earlier meetings in Washington came back to haunt the pair. Dahlgren seemed to have gotten the impression that the navy's attack into the harbor would occur at some time distant from the army's attack on Morris Island. In Gillmore's mind, the events would be closely sequenced in one big joint operation. Thus the new Dahlgren-Gillmore command team began its dealings with a miscommunication. Four days later, the Federals attacked with the disjointed results that could only be expected from such poor coordination.[8]

All this was an inauspicious beginning to any hope of a cooperative army-navy effort, and as the campaign unfolded, things indeed went from bad to worse. At great cost, Gillmore would finally succeed in taking Morris Island, and it then came time to turn the Federal attention to Fort Sumter. By then, however, relations between Dahlgren and Gillmore had become seriously strained, and cooperation had been replaced by competition to see which service would claim the prize of capturing Fort Sumter.[9]

To that end, both men had independently developed plans to attack the night of September 8–9. When at the last moment Gillmore learned of Dahlgren's plan, he suggested that the entire effort be placed under army command. Dahlgren refused, explaining he had assembled a force of 500 sailors and marines, and he could "not consent the commander shall be other than a naval officer." After an awkward and almost comical exchange of messages designed to agree on some signal to avoid fratricide, Gillmore delayed the army's attack, ostensibly because of low tides.[10] Rather than genuine coordination, W. Chris Phelps describes the debacle as an "interservice race … narrowly won by the navy."[11]

Undeterred, Dahlgren launched an amphibious assault on the southeastern and southern face of Fort Sumter, where some 320 men of the Charleston Battalion under command of Major Stephen Elliott awaited them. After suffering 127 casualties and inflicting none on the Confederates, Dahlgren withdrew his force in failure. After the naval defeat, Gillmore opted not to launch his own attack. Even before that decision, Gillmore acknowledged that "the only arrangements for concert of action between the two parties, that were finally made, were intended simply to prevent accident or collision between them. Each party was deemed in itself sufficiently strong for the object in view."[12] Instead of developing a joint plan, Gillmore wrote Dahlgren, "We must trust to chance and hope for the best."[13] With the repulse, another chapter was recorded in the sad Federal saga of disunity of effort.

Leadership Lessons

In Dahlgren and Gillmore, the navy and army had assigned two of their best technicians and two of their biggest egos to Charleston.[14] It was an unhappy combination, and Stephen Wise notes that, "while the campaign dragged on, these two war mechanics lost track of the jointness of their venture."[15] Ultimately, Dahlgren and Gillmore would become life-long enemies.[16]

There is plenty of blame to go around, but Wise zeroes in on Dahlgren's lack of "command presence" to explain many of the admiral's relationship difficulties. Dahlgren's promotions had come from his ordnance expertise rather than sea duty, and such assignments gave him little of the confidence, assertiveness, and ability to deal with confrontation that would be required of him as a commander.[17] Du Pont probably spoke for many when he said that Dahlgren "chose one line in the walks of the profession [scientific ordnance work] while Foote and I chose another [sea duty]; he was licking cream while we were eating dirt and living on the pay of our rank."[18] Perhaps as a result, Dahlgren lacked what Belle Linda Halpern and Kathy Lubar call the "leadership pres-

Admiral Dahlgren poses beside a Dahlgren gun on the deck of the USS *Pawnee* in Charleston Harbor (Library of Congress, Prints & Photographs Division).

ence" that represents "the ability to connect authentically with the thoughts and feelings of others, in order to motivate and inspire them toward a desired outcome."[19] This weakness would plague Dahlgren throughout his tenure with the South Atlantic Blockading Squadron as an inability to inspire his officers and improve their morale.[20] At this early juncture in his command, his failure to exert a strong leadership presence manifested itself in the operation's planning stages and in the amphibious attack on Fort Sumter.

Leaders cannot be everywhere at once, and the "presence" they impart is the result of choices they make and actions they take or fail to take.[21] They must make a conscious decision to be where their presence can have the most impact. That Dahlgren contented himself to remain in Washington while Gillmore was already reconnoitering the ground on Folly Island offers some indication of Dahlgren's approach to command. His previous experience and his comfort zone were in technical, administrative, and bureaucratic fields. As such, he had little need to exert the physical presence command would require, and he no doubt thought he was doing his duty working out details in Washington. In reality, by not being physically present around Charleston in the plan's important formative stages, he was not gaining a first-hand appreciation of the situation, or building a relationship with Gillmore, or inspiring the members of his squadron. While a certain amount of behind-the-scenes analytical work is necessary, leadership also requires a physical presence at the scene of the action. At this stage of the campaign, Dahlgren had not figured out the right mix of leadership's demands for studious detachment and purposeful presence. Instead, he defaulted to his comfort zone.[22]

Dahlgren was also not present when his sailors and marines attacked on the night of September 8–9. He may have intended to observe the attack in person, but the reality was that he was still a quarter of a mile from the action when his men made contact.[23] His account of his absence has a certain hollowness when measured against the expectations of a leader in such a situation:

> Delays of various kinds prevented me from moving till about 1 o'clock, when the *Philadelphia* was put in motion and in half an hour I was well up the channel and had hardly approached Sumter when the sound of musketry announced the attack; this did not last long and was followed by shell, etc., from Moultrie. Before I could reach Sumter the conflict had ceased. It was next morning before I learned positively that our party had been repulsed with considerable loss.[24]

Dahlgren's biographer Robert Schneller offers several explanations for Dahlgren's performance. Clearly Dahlgren was sick with gastritis, and physical and mental stress had compounded the illness's effects. He constantly had to deal with his unpopularity among officers who felt he had not earned his promotion or position. He was nostalgic for the simple pleasures of his home and family. However, Schneller is quick to note that, whatever the reason, it was not a lack of courage. Dahlgren, he argues, "was a firm believer in leading from the front." Probably the best explanation is Schneller's conclusion that Dahlgren had only belatedly realized "that the tests of war were more severe than he had anticipated. The war was far less glamorous at the front than it had seemed in Washington."[25] Such conditions required a leadership presence that Dahlgren did not yet possess.

Take-aways

- A leader's physical presence is an important relational, inspirational, and motivational tool.
- Being on the scene gives the leader a unique perspective that, when combined with other information, helps him make decisions.
- Developing a leadership presence may force individuals to expand outside their familiar comfort zones.

17

Quincy Gillmore and Frame of Reference

Dahlgren's army counterpart was Major General Quincy Gillmore, one of the military's artillery and engineering technical experts. Gillmore was eager to replicate at Charleston his earlier success at Fort Pulaski, but he found that the situations were different. While he eventually succeeded in capturing Morris Island, the decisive results Gillmore hoped for eluded him, and the campaign settled into a stalemate.

Savannah, Georgia, was one of the South's largest and most important cities. It had a population of about 14,000, and before the war had exported nearly $20 million worth of cotton and lumber.[1] To protect this vibrant commercial center, Fort Pulaski sat on Cockspur Island at the mouth of the Savannah River and was in a natural defensive position for guarding the seaward approaches to Savannah, some eighteen miles inland.

In 1829, Lieutenant Robert E. Lee surveyed the fort site and designed the dike system to ensure the necessary drainage. Then in 1831, Lieutenant Joseph K.F. Mansfield began supervising the actual construction of the fort. By 1847, the basic structure of Fort Pulaski was finished. It encompassed approximately five acres and could mount up to 146 guns. The fort was surrounded by a moat seven feet deep and thirty-five feet wide. But what would prove to be the greatest obstacle to would-be attackers were the fort's brick walls, which were seven and a half feet thick and thirty-five feet high.[2] It was this barrier that caused the defenders to be so confident. In fact, in November 1861, Lee inspected Fort Pulaski and assured Colonel Charles Olmstead, the Confederate commander there, that the Federal guns on Tybee Island could "make it pretty warm for you here with shells, but they cannot breach your walls at that distance." Lee's remarks were not the result of overconfidence, wishful thinking, or personal attachment. Brigadier General Joseph Totten, the Federal Army's chief engineer, agreed that "the work could not be reduced in a month's firing with any number of guns of manageable calibers."[3]

By December, the stress and strain of sustained operations had created tension between Major General Thomas Sherman and Admiral Samuel Du Pont. Their inability to cooperate foiled their plans for a powerful coup de main against Savannah. Instead, they agreed to make a "strong feint" against Savannah, hoping it would draw Confederate troops away from Fernandina, the next Federal objective. This effort also failed when flag officer Josiah Tattnall ran past the Federal squadron and delivered six months' worth of supplies to Fort Pulaski.

In the meantime, Major General George McClellan sent word that the War Department did not consider Savannah to be worth putting under siege and instructed Sherman to concentrate his forces on Fort Pulaski, Fernandina, and maybe St. Augustine. On February 14, McClellan sent another message promising to send Sherman a siege train of heavy guns to be used in reducing Fort Pulaski.[4] The reason Sherman would need such powerful guns was that, to that point in the history of warfare, there had not been a single instance in which cannon and mortar had breached heavy masonry walls at ranges beyond 1,000 yards. Even after occupying Tybee Island, the Federals would be over a mile away from Fort Pulaski.[5]

Such a condition did not deter Captain Quincy Gillmore, the engineering officer Sherman ordered to take charge of the investment and bombardment of the Confederate stronghold. An 1849 graduate of West Point, Gillmore had both supervised harbor fortifications and taught engineering before the Civil War, so he knew what he was up against at Fort Pulaski. Nonetheless, he was a staunch believer in the power and accuracy of rifled cannon. Fort Pulaski would give him an opportunity to test his theories.

Gillmore decided to locate his batteries on the northwestern tip of Tybee Island. Throughout February and March, Gillmore's men wrestled with thirty-six siege guns and mortars, some weighing eight and a half tons. Moving them into position was no easy task. Gillmore's work parties constructed a sturdy two and a half mile road over which to transport the guns. To avoid detection by the Confederates, work along the last mile was conducted only at night and in virtual silence. The effort was superintended by Lieutenant Horace Porter, who stated he could "pay no greater tribute to the patriotism" of his work party. Porter reported "they toiled night after night, often in a drenching rain, under the guns of the fort, speaking only in whispers, and directed entirely by the sound of a whistle, without uttering a murmur."[6]

For their efforts, the Federals were able to position eleven siege batteries within two miles of Fort Pulaski. The critical element of this array were nine rifled cannon, a mix of 30-pounder Parrot guns and James guns converted from smoothbores, located at Batteries Sigel and McClellan about a mile southeast of the Confederate position.[7] The superior accuracy, range and penetrating capability of these rifled pieces was Gillmore's ace in the hole.

Just after sunrise on April 10, the Federals sent an officer to Fort Pulaski demanding its surrender.[8] Olmstead refused the offer, stating that he was there "to defend the fort, not to surrender it."[9] At 8:15, Gillmore obliged and initiated his bombardment with a single 13-inch mortar firing from Battery Halleck, located in about the middle of his line. By 9:30, Gillmore's mortars were firing at fifteen-minute intervals and his artillery at two or three times that rate. The Federal Columbiads from Batteries Lyon and Lincoln and the rifled cannons concentrated on the southeast angle of the fort. The rifled pieces first pounded the Confederate guns on the parapet and then shifted to the walls to loosen the brickwork for the Columbiads.[10] Gillmore liked what he saw. By 1:00, he reported, "it became evident that, unless our guns should suffer seriously from the enemy's fire, a breach would be effected." He could already see "that the rifled projectiles were surely eating their way into the scarp of the *pan-coupe* and adjacent south-east face."[11]

At first the defenders responded with respectable fires, but the accurate Federal shelling quickly dismounted or rendered unserviceable gun after Confederate gun. This suppression contributed to the fact that not a single Federal gun was hit by return fire. By nightfall, the southeast angle of the fort was dangerously damaged. Two embrasures had been enlarged, and the wall had been reduced to half its original seven and a half foot thickness. Olmstead recalled that "shots were shrieking through the air in every direction, while the ear was deafened by the tremendous explosions."

Confederate efforts to remount their guns and repair their positions proved fruitless. The Federals began concentrating their fires on enlarging the breach, and by noon shells were passing through the opening and exploding against the northwest powder magazine. With 40,000 pounds of powder inside the walls just waiting to ignite, Olmstead had little choice. At 2:30 he raised a white sheet over Fort Pulaski.[12]

During the thirty-hour bombardment, each side suffered one fatality. The Federals had fired 5,275 rounds, in the process silencing sixteen of the Confederate's twenty guns. By the end of the bombardment, the once-imposing moat was so filled with debris it could be crossed without getting wet. Gillmore reported that his mortars "were from some cause practically inefficient," leaving the impressive results to be from the breaching power of his artillery alone. Less than half of the Federal expenditure of ordnance had come from rifled guns, but these more accurate and powerful pieces had done a disproportionate amount of the work.[13]

Gillmore noted that his success represented "the first example, in actual warfare, of the breaching power of rifled ordnance at long range."[14] Specifically, the implications were disastrous for the Confederacy, whose coastal defense system was built around forts such as Fort Pulaski. As Daniel Brown concludes, "an entire defense system, which had taken nearly fifty years to perfect, was made obsolete in less than two days."[15]

On June 12, 1863, Gillmore, now a brigadier general, assumed command of the Department of the South, and he set out to replicate his success at Fort Pulaski against Forts Wagner and Sumter at Charleston. Incorrectly believing he was outnumbered when he in fact had twice the size of the Confederate force, Gillmore developed a plan to seize Morris Island in an assault supported by two diversions. One would be made by Colonel Thomas Higginson's 1st South Carolina Regiment. This force would move up the South Edisto River on armed transports and attempt to cut the Charleston and Savannah Railroad at Jacksonborough. The second would be a feint conducted by Brigadier General Alfred Terry's division after being transported into the Stono River and landed on the southwestern shore of James Island.

These diversions supported the main assault on Morris Island under the command of Major General Truman Seymour. Brigadier General George Strong's brigade would lead the way. Gillmore's background was as an engineer and his plan for Morris Island reflected his unfamiliarity with maneuver warfare. His diversions consumed more than 50 percent of his force and robbed him of mass at the decisive point.[16] Nonetheless, he was confident of success. On the other hand, the newly arrived Admiral Dahlgren obviously had serious reservations, declaring "the thing is rather complicated."[17]

The main attack began on July 10 when Gillmore crossed nearly 3,000 troops from Folly Island to the south end of Morris Island in an effort to overrun the Confederate positions and take the entire island. According to Stephen Wise, the battle's outcome "would depend largely on cannon power and ability of the opposing artillerists. In this realm, Gillmore and Dahlgren had complete confidence."[18]

The Federals considered it imperative to open fire first and gain surprise in support of the landing. At 5:00 a.m., Seymour gave orders to begin firing and about two hours later, he received Gillmore's signal "to land and assault the enemy's works."[19] Awaiting Seymour, the Confederates had eleven detached batteries supported by a line of rifle pits at Oyster Point. The defenders hoped to halt a Federal landing with this force, but if that failed, they would hold at Fort Wagner, further down the island about three miles north of Light-House

Inlet. Three quarters of a mile north of Fort Wagner on Cummings Point was Battery Gregg. This lightly manned position was designed to fire on enemy vessels approaching from the south in the main ship channel, but it was not expected to defend against infantry attacks.[20] Thus it was Fort Wagner, an irregular fortification built of earth and sand riveted by palmetto logs that posed the greatest challenge to Seymour. At the Battle of Sullivan's Island in 1776, South Carolinian patriots defending what became Fort Moultrie found that their fort's spongy palmetto logs and yielding sand readily absorbed shot and shell from British ships.[21] Fort Wagner's construction would allow it to withstand a similar pounding.

Fort Wagner was a massive position with parapets fifteen feet high and twelve to fourteen feet thick on top. It had a sea face measuring 210 feet along the interior crest and a land face of 600 feet. It mounted a 10-inch Columbiad and two 32-pounders on the sea face, with field guns and other 32-pounders elsewhere. In addition to this armament, it contained two bombproofs. The first was 20 × 20 feet and was positioned as a traverse protecting the three guns on the sea face from fire by land-based artillery. The second was a huge 30 × 130 foot structure parallel to the sea face. It could hold 900 men if they stood "elbow to elbow and face to back." One-third of this bombproof was designated for use by medical personnel as a hospital.

The land face was designed with reentering angles and emplacements for five guns, each protected by heavy traverses. An extension of the left flank stretched out to the high tide mark and could mount two field guns that could sweep the front of the sea face. A 300-foot long retrenchment protected the right flank, and a deep ditch that could be filled with water from Vincent's Creek created an obstacle in the front of the fort. The result of this careful design was that Fort Wagner was well-prepared to deliver deadly enfilading fires against any would-be attackers.[22]

The Federal attack enjoyed initial success, sending the Confederates in their forward rifle-pits fleeing for the shelter of Fort Wagner. There the defense rallied and the attackers soon came under fire both from grape and canister from Fort Wagner and solid shot from Fort Sumter. The attack lost its momentum and "the head of the column was halted within musket-range of Fort Wagner." There the soldiers formed a picket line across the island while their commanders pondered their next move. Strong decided to halt the day's attack "on account of the excessive heat of the weather, and consequent fatigue of our troops."[23] The Confederates took advantage of the lull to rush reinforcements to the scene.[24] The Federal diversions had failed to prevent this occurrence and merely served to deprive Gillmore of the strength he needed at Morris Island.[25] When Strong renewed his attack the next day, the Confederates were ready. This poorly planned attack was repulsed, and a duly chastened Gillmore began building a line of breastworks across the island and bringing forward the artillery he thought would shell Fort Wagner into submission.[26] With Gillmore acting as chief engineer, Batteries Reynolds, Weed, Hays, and O'Rorke were built at distances ranging from 1,330 to 1,920 yards from Fort Wagner.[27] By July 17, Gillmore had positioned forty guns of various types and calibers in his Morris Island batteries. To these were added the weight of Dahlgren's ironclads.

After rain cancelled the attack planned for July 17, Dahlgren moved his vessels into position at 11:30 a.m. the next day. The *Montauk, Catskill, Nantucket, Weehawken, Patapsco,* and *New Ironsides* anchored 1,200 yards off Fort Wagner and opened fire. As the tide rose, the vessels crept still closer to their target. By noon, all the Federal artillery on land and sea was firing, hitting Wagner at a rate of nearly a projectile every two seconds. Inside, Brigadier General William Taliaferro, whose brigade was among the reinforcements to arrive after the July 10 attack, estimated more than 9,000 shells had poured into the battery.[28] One Federal soldier preparing for the assault noted "no one would ever suppose that a human being, or a bird even, could live for a moment upon that fort."[29]

Gillmore reached the same conclusion, and he ordered the navy to hold its fire and his 6,000 infantry to move forward. Brigadier General Seymour was overall in charge of the force, which was divided into three brigades. Strong's brigade was in the lead with the 54th Massachusetts Regiment, commanded by Colonel Robert Shaw at the head of the column.

Shaw's men started forward at 7:45 p.m. and it soon became apparent that Gillmore had greatly overestimated the effects of the bombardment. Instead, as soon as the Federal barrage was lifted, a "most destructive musketry fire was instantly delivered from the parapet by the garrison, which, up to that moment, had remained safely ensconced in the bomb-proof shelter."[30] The 54th Massachusetts struck Fort Wagner in the center and was decimated. The 6th Connecticut and the 48th New York fared little better attacking the seaward salient. After the first three regiments were repulsed, the 3rd New Hampshire, the 9th Maine, and the 76th Pennsylvania also attacked. Throughout the battle, small groups of Federals reached the battery's walls but could not hold their ground. Realizing further attack was fruitless, Strong ordered a retreat.

Seymour then ordered his other two brigades forward. First came the four regiments of Colonel Haldiman Putnam. Hoping to avoid the inability to quickly reinforce that had plagued the first attack, Seymour ordered Brigadier General Thomas Stevenson's four regiments to follow closely behind. The Federal attack quickly became confused when Seymour was wounded.

As he was carried from the field, he ordered Stevenson forward, but, unbeknownst to Seymour, Gillmore had ordered Stevenson not to move.

Attacking alone, Putman's men captured a portion of the Confederate battery. Hoping to exploit this success, Gillmore ordered Stevenson forward but countermanded the order when he learned Putman had been killed in the assault. Instead, Stevenson's men began building a defensive line to protect the Federal batteries from a Confederate counterattack. By 1:00 a.m. on July 19 the fighting was over. Of the 5,000 men who made the attack, 246 were killed, 890 wounded, and 391 captured. By comparison, the Confederates suffered just 222 total casualties. Over the next two months, the Federals launched at least twenty-five separate attacks to try to capture the rest of Morris Island but without success.[31]

Leadership Lessons

Effective leaders build a personal frame of reference from schooling, experiences, self-study, and assessment. They reflect on past experience in order to learn from them and to help place the current organization and situation in strategic context.[32] However, the frame of reference is designed to expand, not limit, the leader's horizons. The leader cannot unimaginatively apply a course

Major General Gillmore in front of his headquarters tent on Morris Island (Library of Congress, Prints & Photographs Division).

of action that worked once to a new situation for which it is inappropriate. They must be mentally agile enough to understand the circumstances around them and adjust. This was Gillmore's failure. In February 1862, he had used rifled artillery to destroy the masonry walls of Fort Pulaski. Gillmore thought he could repeat this tactic at Fort Wagner, but he found that there his artillery could only plow up the fort's sand and earth walls. Behind them, the Confederate defenders remained safe and ready to receive the attack.

Because of his overconfidence in his artillery, Gillmore paid little attention to the other details of the attack. His men had no scaling ladders or trenching tools. His subordinate commanders had little knowledge of the topography or the fort's layout. There was little sophistication in the attack other than to throw one brigade after another. E. Milby Burton concludes, "General Gilmore, having reduced Fort Pulaski so easily, seems to have assumed that he would simply overwhelm the garrison in Wagner by sheer force of numbers."[33]

Gillmore drew on his past experience, but he applied it to an inappropriate situation. His frame of reference inhibited, rather than facilitated, his response to the environment. At Fort Pulaski, Gillmore had ended the era of masonry fortifications. At Fort Wagner, Stephen Wise notes, "he opened the era of trench warfare."[34]

Take-aways

- Leaders build a personal frame of reference that allows them to understand a situation in a strategic context.
- Every situation is different, and the leader uses his frame of reference to tailor his present actions, not robotically repeat his past ones.
- Leaders must be agile, imaginative, and flexible.

18

Robert Shaw and Moral Leadership

At the forefront of the failed Federal attack on Fort Wagner was the 54th Massachusetts Infantry. Although the regiment was manned by black soldiers, it was commanded by Colonel Robert Shaw, a white officer. While the 54th was a well-drilled unit, it represented much more than an effective fighting force. It was an important part in the progress of black Americans to equality.

Robert Gould Shaw was born in Boston, Massachusetts, on October 10, 1837, to parents who valued society, education, and the abolition of slavery. They were close friends of William Lloyd Garrison, editor of the *Liberator*, and young Shaw was a playmate of Garrison's two boys. Although Shaw enjoyed the comfort and luxury made available by the family's history of successful business dealings, he was raised to be a "Boston Brahmin" humanitarian who wanted to improve the lives of those less fortunate. After extensive travels throughout Europe, Shaw entered Harvard but withdrew in order to go to work at his uncles' mercantile office in New York. He was there on the eve of the Civil War and joined "the unit of high society, the ultra-exclusive Seventh New York National Guard."[1]

The Seventh New York enlisted for thirty days and then disbanded. Many of its members returned to civilian life, but Shaw gained a commission as a second lieutenant in the newly approved Second Massachusetts Infantry, one of the first three-year regiments organized during the Civil War.[2] Shaw and the regiment saw their first combat battling Major General Stonewall Jackson in the Shenandoah Valley at Front Royal and Winchester. They saw fiercer fighting at Cedar Mountain and then at Antietam. It was the strategic victory at Antietam that allowed President Abraham Lincoln to issue his preliminary Emancipation Proclamation.[3]

Although Shaw was enlightened, he was not the fervent abolitionist his parents were. He thought the Emancipation Proclamation would elicit a Confederate response so that "the evil will overbalance the good for the present." Only after the war was won did Shaw believe the proclamation would "be a great thing."[4] Nonetheless he had been an early advocate of integrating the army, having written his mother "about having negroes in our present white regiments, I think the men would object to it very strongly at first, but they would get accustomed to it in time."[5] Shaw would have a chance to act on this optimism when, in late January 1863, President Lincoln authorized Secretary of War Edwin Stanton to enlist black men into volunteer regiments.

Among those who welcomed Lincoln's decision was Massachusetts Governor John Andrew. He received with great excitement the authorization from Stanton on January 26 to raise regiments which "may include persons of African descent, to be organized into special corps." Eager to make this experiment, with all its implications for the advancement of the black population, successful, Andrew took great care in selecting the white officers that would lead the regiment. He was drawn to Shaw, both on the strength of his military record and his family's devotion to abolition.[6] On January 30, Andrew sent a letter to Shaw through his father, Francis: "I am about to organize in Massachusetts a Colored Regiment as part of the volunteer quota of this State—the commissioned officers to be white men. I have today written your Father expressing to him my sense of the importance of this undertaking, and requesting him to forward you this letter, in which I offer you the Commission of Colonel over it."[7]

Shaw's parents were thrilled by Governor Andrew's offer, and Francis Shaw immediately hand-carried the letter to Robert at the Army of the Potomac's winter camp at Stafford Court House, Virginia. To Shaw's parents' disappointment, he initially refused the offer, in large part because of his loyalty to the Second Massachusetts. Still, Shaw understood what was at stake. He explained to his father: "I would take it, if I thought myself equal to the responsibility of such a position." Francis Shaw left Virginia with a heavy heart, but Robert continued to ponder his decision. He was troubled by what appeared to be his lack of practical commitment to a noble cause. Even more, he worried what disappointment his decision would cause his fervently abolitionist mother. He wrote his fiancé, Annie Haggerty, that he feared "Mother will think I am shirking my duty." In the end, Shaw reversed his earlier decision and telegraphed his father to telegraph Governor Andrew that he would accept his offer. Shaw's biographer Russell Duncan notes that there were numerous factors that had an impact on Shaw's decision and "perhaps they all pushed and helped him to be courageous."[8]

Philosopher William James would later speak of Shaw's "lonely courage" in making this decision to leave "his warm commission in the glorious Second" and cast his lot with "this new negro-soldier venture, [where] loneliness was certain, ridicule inevitable, failure possible; and Shaw was only twenty-five; and although he had stood among the bullets at Cedar Mountain and Antietam, he had till then been walking socially on the sunny side of life."[9] Indeed, Shaw had never previously been around blacks, and he harbored many of the racial stereotypes of the day. He referred to the black recruits as "niggers" and "darkeys" and ridiculed their poor language or their attempts to pattern themselves after whites. "It is very laughable to hear the sergeants explain drill to the men," Shaw told his friend Charley Morse, "as they use words long enough for a Doctor of Divinity or anything else."[10]

But the more Shaw was around his new comrades, the more his attitude changed. By the end of March he told his mother "the intelligence of the men is a great surprise to me." To Amos Lawrence, a businessman and member of the committee charged with recruiting men for the regiment, Shaw confessed, "I am perfectly astonished at the general intelligence these darkeys display."[11] Shaw's observations may smack of condescension and the epithet in his remark to Lawrence is painfully untoward, but Shaw was no doubt coming to appreciate the potential of the black soldier—and therefore the black man. At the same time, the men of the 54th were coming to know and respect Shaw. Corporal James Gooding, for example, praised Shaw's "quick eye [that] detects anything in a moment out of keeping with order or military discipline." With such leadership and such men, the 54th quickly became a proud and efficient unit. In an impressive ceremony on May 18, Governor Andrew presented the regiment its colors, symbolizing its readiness for battle.[12]

The 54th then departed for service with the Department of the South, where commander Major General David Hunter was a strong abolitionist. Hunter had prematurely emancipated slaves in the area under his control only to have President Lincoln countermand the order. Now Hunter was eager to provide a proving ground for these "intelligent colored men from the North" who would serve alongside other black regiments in his department comprising of newly freed slaves.[13] The regiment docked at Hilton Head on June 3.

Shaw soon met Colonels James Montgomery and Thomas Higginson, who commanded the other black regiments now in the Department of the South. The 54th's first mission took it to Saint Simons Island, Georgia, for a rendezvous with Montgomery's Second Regiment of South Carolina Volunteers. Montgomery had cut his teeth in the no-holds-barred prewar Bleeding Kansas. He used the same bushwacking tactics in the present environment, and Shaw and the 54th soon found themselves involved in a raid against the small town of Darien, Georgia. Montgomery suspected the town of being a haven for blockade runners, and, although the residents had evacuated before his arrival, Montgomery proceeded to plunder it. "I shall burn this town," he told Shaw. Shaw considered the action a "dirty piece of business" that amounted to "wanton destruction." He reported to Governor Andrew that Montgomery's approach to warfare "disgusted" him, and he claimed the 54th was "superior" to Montgomery's contraband regiment and worthy of better service. To Hunter's adjutant, Shaw decried the raid as "barbarous." Instead, Shaw insisted on strict discipline among his men, partly because of his sense of morality, but also because he knew that black soldiers participating in scorched-earth tactics would only ignite racial stereotypes of blacks as savages. At the forefront of Shaw's mind was always the reality that the 54th was more than an infantry regiment. It was a social experiment of the highest order, and its conduct must be beyond reproach.[14]

Shaw got his opportunity "for better service than mere guerrilla warfare" upon his return to Hilton Head. He was ordered to prepare to support the upcoming assault on Charleston, and on July 8 the 54th prepared to embark for James Island. As if the pending battle was not enough, Shaw also had to contend with the issue of unequal pay for his soldiers. White soldiers received thirteen dollars per month, but the government had decided to pay black soldiers just ten dollars—the wage paid to laborers. Moreover, the blacks' pay was docked three dollars per month for clothing expenses instead of being supplemented by three dollars, as was the procedure for whites. Shaw considered this discrepancy to be an outrage, especially since the men had been recruited with the promise of being paid thirteen dollars per month. Shaw wrote Andrew of this "great piece of injustice," and the governor protested to President Lincoln and Secretary Stanton. It was not until September 29, 1864, that Congress finally equalized pay, and by then, the 54th had more than proven its worth at Fort Wagner.[15]

Shaw's men first saw action on July 16 when some 1,400 Confederates launched a surprise attack. Forced to fight a delaying action, the 54th retreated but prevented a route. The danger subsided when the 54th reached the protection of the navy's gunboats and the Confederates halted their attack. The 54th performed well and earned the praise of several of their white comrades. One member of the Tenth Connecticut admitted, "But for the bravery of ... the Massachusetts Fifty-fourth (colored), our whole regiment would have been captured." "They fought like heroes," he added. Even Major General Alfred Terry advised Shaw he was "exceedingly pleased" with the conduct of his regiment. Nonetheless, the 54th lost fourteen killed, eighteen wounded, and thirteen missing. There would be more casualties to come.[16]

During the night, the 54th withdrew to a transportation rendezvous point. At 11:00 p.m. on July 17, the 54th boarded the *General Hunter* and were transported to Folly Island. From there the men boarded another transport that carried them across the 500-yard inlet to Morris Island. There they waited for the order to attack Fort Wagner. As the men made their final preparations, Shaw moved forward to coordinate with his brigade commander, Brigadier General George Strong.[17] Strong had become friends with Shaw at Hilton Head and admired him. He also remembered Shaw's request "for better service than mere guerrilla warfare," and now Strong offered the 54th the honor to lead the attack. "You may lead the column if you say yes," Strong told Shaw. Recalling the fierce fight on July 16 and the subsequent match, Strong added, "Your men, I know, are worn out, but do as you choose."[18]

It was both an opportunity and a responsibility. William James later described the decision as "the grand chance ... the one chance which above all others seemed essential!" Yet, Shaw no doubt understood the danger. He confided to his friend Lieutenant Colonel Edward Hallowell: "If I could only live a few weeks longer with my wife, and be at home a little while, I might die happy, but it cannot be. I do not believe I will live through our next fight." Nonetheless, adjutant Garth Wilkinson James remembered that Shaw's face

This Currier & Ives print gloriously depicts the charge of the 54th Massachusetts against Fort Wagner (Library of Congress, Prints & Photographs Division).

brightened at Strong's offer, and even before he answered, Shaw ordered James to issue instructions to bring the regiment forward.[19]

As Shaw's men steeled themselves before launching the attack, Shaw challenged them to "take the fort or die there."[20] His biographer Peter Burchard surmises what Shaw must have felt when the attack began. "With his strong presentiments of death," Burchard believed the advance for Shaw "must have been a waking nightmare. The way grew narrower and the men on the flanks fell back. Shaw held his position in front of the center of the shrinking phalanx." When the 54th was 200 yards away, the guns of Fort Wagner erupted in a "sheet of flame, followed by running fire, like electric sparks, swept along the parapet." Soldiers remembered Shaw advancing wet to the waist with his body bent forward and his jaw firmly set. He reached the fort's ramparts, urging his men forward with his sword raised. Then in the flash of a cannon he crumpled headlong and lifeless.[21] The 54th continued forward only to be repulsed after fierce hand-to-hand fighting. The Federals that followed them suffered the same fate. The black and the white dead lay strewn together along a three-quarters of a mile stretch of sand. Of the 600 men of the 54th who charged the fort, 272 were killed, wounded or missing. Shaw was among the dead. He was buried in a common trench with the black men he led and with whom he died.[22]

There were those who considered such a final resting place to be an insult. Several among the Confederates thought it was just what a man like Shaw deserved. Others, however, held it as an unparalleled honor. Shaw's father believed there was "no holier place" for his son's body. To those who sought to remove it for a more dignified reburial, he admonished, "We mourn over our own loss & that of the Regt, but find nothing else to regret in Rob's life, death, or burial. We would not have his body removed from where it lies surrounded by his brave & devoted soldiers, if we could accomplish it by a word. Please to bear this in mind & also, let it be known, so that, even in case there should be an opportunity, his remains may not be disturbed."[23]

Leadership Lessons

Biographer Russell Duncan notes that Shaw "never had the clear-eyed crusader's vision, commitment to abolition, faith in moral uplift, or deep-thinking ability of some in the anti-slavery movement." Instead, he says, "What Shaw had was courage and loyalty. He was responsible enough to give black troops a fair trial. He did his duty to his men, his mother, and himself."[24] In the process, Shaw showed much physical courage in the attack of Fort Wagner. What is more remarkable is the moral courage he showed before that fateful day.

Rushworth Kidder defines moral courage as "the quality of mind and spirit that enables one to face up to ethical challenges firmly and confidently, without flinching or retreating."[25] Shaw had lived a life that had produced the "quality of mind and spirit" that Kidder argues moral courage requires. He had been raised by enlightened parents who had taught him and modeled for him a sense of humanity, equality, and service. He had proved his mettle in combat with the Second Massachusetts and demonstrated his ability to lead soldiers. Yet he faced one of those "right versus right" choices that Kidder correctly identifies as requiring the "toughest decisions."[26] Shaw had loyalties to the practical reality of the Second Massachusetts as well as to the potential ideal of a regiment of black soldiers and all it meant to the future. He had to choose between the two, and his initial decision and subsequent reversal testifies the difficulty of the task. Only Shaw knows exactly what made him change his mind, but if moral courage is about "taking action when your values are put to the test," Shaw choose the course that represented "the most revolutionary feature of a war that wrought a revolutionary transformation in America."[27]

While this initial decision may have been the most difficult of the ethical challenges Shaw would have to face "firmly and confidently, without flinching or retreating," others certainly followed. He had to remove himself and his men from what he considered to be the barbarous guerrilla tactics of Colonel Montgomery. He had to champion the equal pay his men had been promised as soldiers. He had to accept Brigadier General Strong's offer to lead the attack, even though Shaw knew its dangers and had an honorable excuse to avoid them. Shaw passed each of these tests with the unwavering certainty that true moral courage provides. He also demonstrated William Ian Miller's assertion that "moral courage grows by the doing of deeds that require" one to put it into practice. "Standing up for what we think is right is not easy," Miller explains, "but it may well get easier if we cultivate the habit of doing so."[28]

Kidder adds that this multiplicative effect has an impact on organizations as well. Moral courage is most often required in organizations that are in disrepair. On the other hand, Kidder argues, successful organizations "require moral courage in their leaders and then work assiduously to make sure it's rarely needed."[29] Historian James Ford Rhodes explains how Shaw's moral courage helped reshape American culture so that future such acts became decreasingly necessary:

> That a gentleman should leave a congenial place in the Second Massachusetts and part from brothers in friendship as well as brothers in arms because his antislavery sentiment impelled him to take a stand against the prejudice in the army and in the country against negro soldiers; that he brought his regiment to a fine degree of discipline; that when the supreme moment came his blacks fought as

other soldiers have always fought in desperate assaults—all this moved the hearts and swayed the minds of the Northern people to an appreciation of the colored soldier, to a vital recognition of the end to which Lincoln strove for and to the purpose of fighting out the war until the negro should be free.[30]

Similarly, Dudley Cornish explains that "Colonel Shaw and the 54th became symbols of the best that any troops, white or Negro, could do." To that end, Cornish notes the assault on Fort Wagner was "from a narrow military point of view ... without value. In a broader view, it was a valuable service."[31] This value was in settling the question of whether or not the black man would fight. "The answer," wrote a member of the Philadelphia Female Anti-Slavery Society, "is spoken from the cannon's mouth.... It comes to us from ... those graves beneath Fort Wagner's walls, which the American people will surely never forget."[32] Many more such acts of physical courage would be required to end the Civil War, but Shaw's resolute response to his individual ethical challenge helped America reduce its need for such acts of moral courage in the future.

Finally, Kidder notes that "moral and physical courage often coexist."[33] Indeed, it was perhaps Shaw's moral courage that made his physical courage possible. James Russell Lowell comes as close as any of Shaw's many eulogizers in connecting these two qualities when he writes,

> Right in the van,
> On the rampart's slippery swell,
> With heart that beats a charge, he fell
> Forward, as fits a man;
> But the high soul burns on to light men's feet
> Where death for noble ends makes dying sweet.[34]

Take-aways

- Moral and physical courage often coexist, but they are two distinct characteristics.
- Moral courage is "the quality of mind and spirit that enables one to face up to ethical challenges firmly and confidently, without flinching or retreating."
- Stronger moral courage can be developed by doing acts that require moral courage.
- Good organizations strive to achieve a culture of such ethical clarity that moral courage is seldom required.

19

William Carney and Personal Bravery

While Colonel Shaw excelled in moral courage, Sergeant William Carney is rightly singled out among the many brave men of the 54th Massachusetts for his physical courage. Taking the national colors when their original bearer was wounded, Carney carried them to the parapet of Fort Wagner before he was forced to withdraw. For his actions, Carney became the nation's first black soldier to receive the Medal of Honor.

William Carney was born into slavery in Norfolk, Virginia, in 1840. Along with his father, William, and his mother, Ann Dean, Carney was granted freedom in his owner's will in 1854. The family remained in Virginia for two more years and then moved to New Bedford, Massachusetts, after considering and rejecting Pennsylvania as a new home. Carney explained the decision by lamenting "the black man was not secure on the soil where the Declaration of Independence was written."[1] In Massachusetts, Carney proceeded to make his living doing odd jobs while hoping to save enough money to enter the Christian ministry.[2] That aspiration changed with the coming of the Civil War. Carney explained in an 1863 edition of the *Liberator*: "Previous to the formation of colored troops, I had a strong inclination to prepare myself for the ministry; but when the country called for all persons, I could best serve my God serving my country and my oppressed brothers. The sequel in short—I enlisted for the war."[3] Such decisions were crucial to the success of the 54th.

Governor John Andrew knew that if blacks failed to come forward and volunteer, whites would further characterize them as cowardly, and he applied the same thoughtful deliberation to filling the ranks of the 54th Regiment as he did in selecting its officers. He formed a special "Black Committee" of wealthy and influential men to advise, recruit, and raise money. Eventually the committee reached 100 members. George Stearns, a manufacturer of lead pipe from Medford, Massachusetts, who had purchased rifles for Free-Soilers in Kansas in the 1850s and helped finance John Brown's raid on Harpers Ferry in 1859, was selected to head the committee on recruiting. Other prominent members included John Forbes, Richard Hallowell, James Congdon, Amos Lawrence, William Bowditch, LeBaron Russell, Willard Phillips, and Francis Shaw.[4]

While other committee members focused on raising money, Stearns "took to the road to do most of the legwork in raising the regiment." He established a central recruiting office in Buffalo, New York, and successfully convinced many black leaders that the time to act was now or risk forever losing the chance. Among those who helped recruit for the 54th were William Wells Brown, John Rock, Charles Lenox Remond, Martin Delany, John Jones, Robert Purvis, O.S.B. Wall, Henry Highland Garnett, and John Mercer Langston. Carney, variously described as "strong" and "chunky," was recruited by Lieutenant James Grace along with twenty-seven other New Bedford men in February 1863.[5]

As the 54th waited for the order to assault Fort Wagner, Brigadier General George Strong rode among them and spoke words of motivation and encouragement. He pointed to Sergeant John Wall, who was holding the national colors, and asked, "If this man should fall, who will lift the flag and carry it on?" To the cheers of his men, Colonel Shaw took his cigar from between his teeth and said, "I will."[6]

Moments later, Shaw ordered the regiment "forward." At a range of 200 yards, the Confederate batteries opened fire. Shaw gave his men the command "double-quick," and they closed to within eighty yards of Fort Wagner. Then the defenders, who had been barely hurt by the nine-thousand shell artillery bombardment, opened fire. Lieutenant Grace, the man who had recruited Private Carney, recalled "our men fell like grass before a sickle."[7]

In the withering fire, Sergeant Wall fell into a shell crater and could not continue. He called for someone to take the colors, and Carney was soon there to gather them up. In the era of the Civil War, national and unit colors served a very practical purpose beyond their highly important representation of pride and loyalty. They were visual signals that served as guides for unit movements. Soldiers looked to the colors to see where to go and how to direct their actions. Indeed, in the fire and confusion, some of the 54th veered off to the right toward Fort Wagner's seaward salient. Most, however, followed Shaw and Carney toward the center. There the fighting became more intense. Even after Shaw was killed, the attack continued. Carney was able to climb the fort's wall only to be forced back to the embankment. There he planted the flag, and, though wounded, continued to fight. In the melee, the Confederates were able to seize the 54th's state colors, but Carney and his fellows kept the national colors safe.[8]

Carney recalled "the shot—grape, canister and hand grenades—came in showers, and the columns were leveled." With Shaw dead and Lieutenant Colonel Hallowell and others wounded, command fell to Captain Luis Emilio. Realizing he could not hold his position, Emilio ordered a retreat. The survivors ran a gauntlet of Confederate fire to safety. Once out of the range of the Confederate guns, Emilio gathered his men and formed a line in some rifle pits.[9]

Before Carney made his escape, he wound the colors around the flagpole. He worked

In 1900, William Carney was awarded the Medal of Honor for his heroics at Fort Wagner (courtesy Library of Congress, Prints & Photographs Division).

his way to a low protective wall and moved along it to a ditch that was waist-deep in water. Pinned down by enemy fire, he rose up to look for some way to safety when he was struck by a Confederate bullet. He later explained: "The bullet I now carry in my body came whizzing like a mosquito, and I was shot. Not being prostrated by the shot, I continued my course, yet had not gone far before I was struck by a second shot."[10]

In spite of his wounds, Carney kept moving. Shortly after being hit the second time, he saw a soldier from the 100th New York heading his way. As the two men studied their options, Carney was hit a third time as a bullet grazed his arm. The 100th soldier rendered what aid he could and helped Carney move farther to the rear. He offered to carry the colors, but Carney refused to surrender them to anyone who was not a member of the 54th Massachusetts.[11]

As the pair struggled on, another bullet hit Carney; this time grazing him in the head. The two men finally managed to reach the safety of friendly lines, and Carney was taken to the rear and turned over to medical personnel, still carrying the national colors. He had been wounded four times, twice seriously, in the ordeal, but he proudly reported to his comrades, "Boys, the flag never touched the ground."[12]

For his heroism, on May 23, 1900, Carney became the first black soldier to be awarded the Medal of Honor. His citation reads, "When the color sergeant was shot down, this soldier grasped the flag, led the way to the parapet, and planted the colors thereon. When the troops fell back he brought off the flag, under a fierce fire in which he was twice severely wounded."[13]

Leadership Lessons

Although he was just a private, Carney's citation attests to his leadership. Summarizing a leader's duties, Chris Lowney writes, "the leader figures out where we need to go, points us in the right direction, gets us to agree that we need to get there, and rallies us through the inevitable obstacles that separate us from the promised land."[14] Carney's flag pointed his regiment to the objective and gave his fellow soldiers a visual point of reference and inspiration. He "led the way."

Lowney also points out that heroic leadership of the sort Carney demonstrated under fire comes "not just as a response to crisis but a consciously chosen *approach to life.*"[15] Lowney calls this type of leadership *magis*, after the Latin word for "more." Leaders devote themselves to a routine of service, but when the opportunity arises, they must be able to surge to the magis level to meet the challenge.

Lowney argues that "magis-driven leadership inevitably leads to heroism," which begins with each person considering, internalizing, and shaping his mission until it becomes personal.[16] Carney reached this magis level. Beyond the tactical considerations of the immediate battle, Carney and his fellow black soldiers understood the national consequences of their military service. When he enlisted, Carney seized a broad opportunity to serve God, his country, and his race. When the loss of the original color sergeant gave him a more urgent opportunity, Carney rose to the occasion. Under extraordinary circumstances, Carney's actions earned him the Medal of Honor. Sometimes leadership takes such dramatic form. More often it is found in the countless small decisions that a leader makes every day to put aside self-interest and do what needs to be done to lead his organization to the objective. Carney did not begin the day of July 18, 1863, in a leadership position. He was one of many privates in the 54th just following orders. Then in the wink of an eye, a magis level leadership opportunity presented itself.

Carney's experience is not unique. On January 13, 1983, Arland Williams found himself in a similar situation that completely changed his circumstances. Shortly after take-off from Washington National Airport, the Air Florida Flight 90 on which Williams was a passenger struck the 14th Street Bridge and plunged into the icy waters of the Potomac River. One of just six people to initially survive the crash, Williams repeatedly handed rescue ropes being dropped by a hovering helicopter to other survivors rather than saving himself. When the plane's tail section shifted and sank further into the water, Williams was dragged under the water with it. He was posthumously awarded the United States Coast Guard's Gold Lifesaving Medal. On May 19, 1993, President Ronald Reagan came to Williams' alma mater, the Citadel, to deliver the commencement address. By chance, the Citadel is located in Charleston, the scene of the epic struggle in which Carney fought over 100 years before. President Reagan described how Williams rose from ordinary passenger to hero. "When the challenge came," Reagan noted, Williams "was ready." Then Reagan went on to explain how men such as Carney and Williams are able to reach such magis levels of leadership:

> For you see, the character that takes command in moments of crucial choices has already been determined. It has been determined by a thousand other choices made earlier in seemingly unimportant moments. It has been determined by all the little choices of years past—by all those times when the voice of conscience was at war with the voice of temptation—whispering the lie that it really doesn't matter. It has been determined by all the day-to-day decisions made when life seemed easy and crises seemed far away—the decisions that, piece by piece, bit by bit, developed habits of discipline or of laziness, habits of self-sacrifice or of self-indulgence, habits of duty and honor and integrity—or dishonor and shame.[17]

The capacity for magis leadership rests silently within men like Carney and Williams, waiting only for the opportunity when it is needed, as it must, because as President Reagan explained, "there is no time, at such moments, for anything but fortitude and integrity. Debate and reflection and a leisurely weighing of the alternatives are luxuries we do not have."[18] Instead Williams and Carney did what came naturally to them based on the life they had led to that point. While their actions appear herculean to others, to the individuals themselves it is merely who they are. Indeed, when Carney was asked about his heroic actions, he simply said, "I only did my duty."[19]

Take-aways

- Leaders provide direction by their personal actions and example.
- Leaders must sustain an attitude of routine and regular service but also

need to be ready to rise to the occasion in times of extraordinary circumstances.
- Individual acts of heroic leadership are the by-products of a broader character and a life well lived.
- Leadership entails personal costs that the leader must be ready to bear.

20

Clara Barton and Servant Leadership

For many a wounded soldier, Clara Barton was the "Angel of the Battlefield" (Library of Congress, Prints & Photographs Division).

Clara Barton had been at Hilton Head since April 1863. She came to Morris Island on July 14 and established a camp that provided lifesaving and tender care and comfort for the many wounded of the failed attack on Fort Wagner. Her selfless actions were in the finest traditions of servant leadership.

As the mobilization of the Civil War armies began, Clara Barton was working as a recording clerk in the U.S. Patent Office in Washington, D.C. She immediately perceived a need to provide personal assistance to the throngs of soldiers pouring into the city, and she put her feelings into action by taking supplies to the young men of the Sixth Massachusetts Infantry, who, after being attacked by Southern sympathizers in Baltimore, Maryland, were temporarily housed in the unfinished Capitol building.

Besides supplies, Barton offered personal support to the men, keeping their spirits up by reading to them, writing letters for them, keeping them company, and praying with them. As valuable as such services were, Barton felt she could better serve on the actual battlefields rather than behind the lines.

After overcoming bureaucratic resistance, Barton eventually obtained the necessary passes that allowed her to bring her supplies and work forward. She provided much-needed service following the Battle of Cedar Mountain in August 1862, and as a result of such compassion, she soon became known as the "Angel of the Battlefield." While Barton worked in conjunction with formal organizations such as the Army Medical Department and the United States Sanitary Commission, the only such civilian-run organization recognized by the federal government, she always maintained her independent and voluntary status.[1]

Barton's unofficial status caused friction between her and Dorothea Dix, who as superintendent of army nurses closely guarded her authority and was unashamedly hostile toward unaffiliated female nurses. Likewise, as an "independent Sanitary Commission of one," Barton found it difficult to compete with the economies of scale enjoyed by such large organizations.[2] Thus when her brother David was appointed as a captain in the Quartermaster Department and ordered to report to the Tenth Army Corps at Hilton Head, South Carolina, in March 1863, the opportunity to go with him gave Barton an attractive option. Not only would her brother's position give her a connection to drawing supplies from the Quartermaster Department and the medical purveyor, a posting with the Department of the South would also get her away from Dix's firm control in the area around Washington and Virginia. On March 27, Barton received orders "to report at Port Royal as a nurse," and on April 4 she departed for this new assignment aboard the *Arago*. She arrived in Port Royal three days later.[3]

At Hilton Head, Barton "found herself in the unfamiliar role of an idle and pampered woman" and assumed a rare "softened feminine guise."[4] She lived at army headquarters, dined in the officers' mess, and frequently received bouquets of roses, orange blossoms, and magnolias. Groups of soldiers would serenade her. She found Colonel John Elwell, the quartermaster, and Captain Samuel Lamb, his assistant, to be particularly pleasant company and often went on carriage or horseback rides with each. On such outings, Barton picked blackberries and brought them back to headquarters where she made blackberry shortcake for the mess. She visited Paris Island where she found blackberries as "dense as a black velvet carpet, the orange trees drooped with fruit and the magnolias were in bud." In another trip to the plantation where John Smith landed in 1607, she viewed the "most beautiful grove of live oaks." Her biographer notes "such leisure, such freedom, such feminine gratification were rare in [Barton's] life."⁵

If this new ease was novel to Barton, it was also somewhat troubling to her. "I fear I may be spending time to little purpose," she confided to her diary. "No one really needs me here...." Instead, she began to muse, "I am fearful that I should be in some other spot...." "I cannot feel settled to remain here without some object and I can see nothing," she lamented. "I feel out of place." In a June 24 letter to editor friend T.W. Meighan, Barton explained: "My business is staunching blood and feeding fainting men; my post the open field between the bullet and the hospital."⁶ Instead, in her present surroundings, she found but three occupations—"eating, sleeping, and riding."⁷

The launch of the Federal attack on Morris Island gave Barton the opportunity she wanted to restore herself to the service she considered most fulfilling, productive, and needed. As thousands of troops stationed around Hilton Head departed for Folly Island to prepare for the attack, Barton recorded in her diary, "I begin to feel we are to have work in our department." She resolved to be a part of it, and when it came time for her friend Colonel Elwell to go, she persuaded him to let her accompany him. She left aboard the *Canonicus* on July 9, and Elwell arranged for transportation of an ambulance and supplies as well. She observed the opening shots of the battle the next day from the monitor's deck. She went ashore on July 12, bearing a pass from Major General Quincy Gillmore that read, "Miss Barton, Hospital nurse authorized by the Pres. of the U.S. will receive all facilities within our lines."⁸

Dr. John Craven, medical purveyor of the Tenth Corps, had established an impressive field medical system to support the Morris Island operation. There was a beach hospital on Folly Island as well as a "front hospital" on Morris Island. On July 13, Barton travelled across a pontoon bridge from Folly to Morris Island, bringing her ambulance and saddle horse with her. She was the only female nurse on Morris Island, and she quickly established good relations with Dr. Martin Kittinger, the codirector of the field hospital. By the time Fort Wagner was attacked on July 18, Barton had been joined by Mary Gage, one of the missionary teachers she had met at Hilton Head.⁹

Barton and Gage moved to Lookout Hill, where they could witness the attack. Barton's view was such that she could see with horror when her friend Colonel Elwell was shot from his horse about 150 yards from the southeast bastion. Barton rushed to his aid and helped him make his way back to the Union lines. An amazed Elwell declared Barton "insensible to fear."¹⁰ With Elwell safe, Barton returned up the beach to help other wounded men. With Gage, she moved from body to body, calling stretcher-bearers forward when someone was found alive. One soldier recalled it was "through [Barton's] untiring efforts many a soldier was returned to his wife and family and many a soldier boy to his poor mother."[11]

Under fire, Barton and Gage made their way back to Kittinger's hospital, where they tended to the wounded and comforted the dying. As she labored through "that fearful night," Barton recalled, "it seemed as if day light would never come." When it finally did, she pitched a kitchen tent behind her sleeping tent, and she and Gage prepared what meager food they could find for their patients. Over the next few days, they helped the wounded be evacuated by hospital boat.[12]

As Gillmore continued his attempt to take Morris Island by siege tactics, Barton continued to serve the soldiers. The conditions became so difficult that she sent Gage back to Hilton Head. Now as the only female nurse, Barton worked on with

> the shelterless sands of Morris Island for my bed, my drink the tide water that leaked through the loose sands of the little island fast becoming a crowded cemetery, my shade from a scorching August sun, the friendly clouds that scud between us, my light at night the moon, a dying camp fire, and the long glowing trail of fire that followed the deadly track of the enemies shell that hissed and shrieked and burst above us. My employment—Ah: that is the only bright spot. God be praised that he selected my hands to perform that labor.[13]

Unfortunately Barton had to contend with more than just these formidable challenges. Around mid–August, Dr. Samuel Green, then in temporary command of Morris Island's hospital service, confiscated Barton's government-issued cooking and sleeping tents. Barton was devastated. She explained a year later that Green's action left her "at the mercy of the elements, which, together with my incessant toil in short time brought me [down] with acute disease."[14] As Barton lay in the hospital with diarrhea and fever, word of her condition reached Elwell, who had been evacuated to Hilton Head because of his wound. He ordered quartermaster officials on Morris Island to put Barton on a ship for Hilton Head. As sick as she was, Barton protested so vigorously that Elwell said she had to be taken "almost by force."[15]

Barton left for Hilton Head on August 18 and, upon arriving there, spent five days bedridden. By August 27, however, she felt like "her old self" and declared she would return to Morris Island as soon as possible. Although Barton had powerful friends such as Elwell and Kittinger to argue her case, she also used her store of supplies as leverage. When she did return to Morris Island on September 7, however, she was greeted by the fact that the Confederates had abandoned their positions and left the island in Federal hands.[16] It is a bittersweet victory. As Barton described it, "We have captured one fort—Gregg—one charnel house—Wagner—and we have built one cemetery, Morris

Island. The thousand little sand hills that glitter in the pale moon light are a thousand headstones, and the restless ocean waves that roll and break upon the whitened beach sing an eternal requiem to the toil-worn, gallant dead who sleep beside."[17]

The worst for Barton, however, was yet to come. On September 15 she received an order from Gillmore's assistant adjutant general:

> The Brig. Gen. Commanding is informed by the Medical Officer in Charge of the hospital on this island that your services will be no longer required in connection with the hospital in the field, as the sick and wounded are not to be retained here but will be sent immediately to Beaufort. I am instructed to say that the General appreciates the value of your kind offices to the sick and wounded soldiers, and the benevolence which has led you to sacrifice so many comforts by residing here at the actual scene of conflict, but in view of the crowded condition of the island and the many inconveniences which such a residence must entail, he deems it best that you should remove to Beaufort, where he will provide you a comfortable dwelling.[18]

Sadly complying with the order, Barton found no solace in Beaufort. There she encountered the usual hostility to unaffiliated nurses, and the hospitals were closed to her. Her protests to Gillmore drew only more frustration. Instead, she endured another season of forced leisure, broken sporadically by service to the scores of former slaves who had descended on the Hilton Head area. Finally, on December 27 she, with mixed memories, left the Department of the South.[19]

Leadership Lessons

All leaders can benefit from Barton's example of servant leadership. This is a leadership approach in which the leader meets the subordinate's legitimate needs—which might include such concerns as training, encouragement, resources, or help with personal issues—in order to allow the subordinate to better focus on and accomplish the organizational mission.[20] While the traditional authoritarian leader asks, "What can the organization do for me?" the servant leader asks, "What can I do for the organization?" The idea is that if the leader meets his subordinates' needs, they can then concentrate on, and are empowered to pursue, the organization's needs.

The idea of servant leadership was popularized by Robert Greenleaf in the 1970s, but perhaps the most familiar example of the technique is the account of Jesus washing the disciples' feet in John 13:14–15. The disciples accepted Jesus as their Lord and Master, and he certainly was in a position to have others serve him. Instead, he humbled himself to set aside his own needs to meet the needs of others. In a society where most travel was done by walking long distances in open-toed sandals over dusty roads, foot care was critical. Jesus recognized the need of his followers to have their feet washed. In the process, he not only provided a kindness, he also equipped his disciples to continue their mission by taking care of their feet.

Servant leadership requires attention to the subordinates' situations, to humility, and to hard work. The servant leader must figure out what his subordinates need, put his own needs aside, and devote time and energy to creating the environment where the subordinates are both cared for and empowered. Some leaders shy away from servant leadership because of its demands, but Major General William Cohen argues, "Many times the dilemma between accomplishing the mission and taking care of the troops is a false one. Many times both objectives can be achieved if the leader is willing to work a little harder himself."[21] Barton exhibited this type of selfless service and sacrifice on behalf of others. In going to Morris Island, she said she "went with all I had, to work where I thought I saw greatest need."[22] Her mission was "to see if perchance I can render some little comfort as the wife or mother would if she could be there" and to "give all I have of time, strength, and means."[23] To serve the soldiers, she endured their hardships and dangers, ate moldy rations, was exposed to the elements, and received no personal remuneration. What little she had she willingly shared. If she had "a mouthful of soft or palatable food to give [a wounded soldier], it looked brighter to me than gold, and no mouthful of it passed my lips—or even could until there was enough for all."[24] Barton certainly fulfilled Cohen's requirement that leaders create the opportunity to meet the needs of others by their own personal sacrifices.

Captain Samuel Lamb noted Barton's unique quality of being able to persevere through such challenges, writing, "it requires a heart and nerve that Clara alone of a thousand possesses to calmly meet the stern realities that heap themselves like thorns in the pathway of the angel of the battlefield."[25] Servant leadership is certainly not for the faint of heart, but as General Frederick Franks somewhat counterintuitively observes, "to lead is also to serve."[26] By bringing what small comfort she could to the horrors of Morris Island, Barton personified the heart of the servant leader.

Take-aways

- Leadership is service.
- Servant leaders meet their subordinates' needs so the subordinates can concentrate on the organization's mission.
- Leadership requires hard work, selflessness, and personal sacrifice.

21

Johnson Hagood and the Go-to Guy

Brigadier General Johnson Hagood assumed command of the Confederate forces at Fort Wagner on August 21, 1863. It was the latest in a series of assignments that led Stephen Wise to label the indefatigable Hagood "the department's designated troubleshooter."[1]

Johnson Hagood graduated from the South Carolina Military Academy (the Citadel) in 1847 and then studied law. He was active in the state militia before the war and held the rank of brigadier general in that organization. He was elected colonel of the 1st South Carolina Volunteers in 1861, participated in the reduction of Fort Sumter, and fought at the Battle of First Manassas. He then returned with his regiment to South Carolina in August, but in September he petitioned the secretary of war, Leroy Walker, to allow the regiment to return to Virginia, which he considered "the seat of war." Instead, it was decided that Hagood and his regiment were "indispensable" in South Carolina. Whatever remorse Hagood may have felt soon faded. Instead, he wrote, "the tide of war soon began to roll southward. Hatteras fell; South Carolina was invaded, and the defeat of our Virginia project was no longer the subject of serious regret."[2]

To meet this new threat, Hagood was placed in command of the forces on Cole's Island. When the Federals attacked Port Royal, he asked "for his regiment to be ordered to the scene of action, but without success."[3] Instead, he remained headquartered at Cole's Island until April 13, 1862, when his regiment was withdrawn as part of the effort to consolidate the Confederate defenses in response to Port Royal.[4] In these early experiences, Hagood had clearly established for himself a reputation as a man who sought active service and who would be the sort of leader to "move to the sound of the guns."

With the withdrawal from Cole's Island, Hagood was assigned to duties as provost marshal of Charleston when martial law was declared there on May 13. It was an arduous, thankless task, which Hagood entered into "with a full sense of the difficulties surrounding it."[5] His handling of thorny issues such as passports won the praise of the *Courier*, and he continued to deal effectively and deliberately with the emergencies of the situation until he was returned to his regiment on June 9.[6] This brief stint as provost marshal showed Hagood's versatility and adaptability.

In the ensuing Battle of Secessionville on July 16, Hagood again displayed his characteristic tenacity and utility to the Confederate cause. Brigadier General Nathan Evans praised Hagood's "untiring vigilance" in ordering three regiments to readiness and dispatching reinforcements to Colonel Thomas Lamar in preparation for the Federal attack. Hagood then notified Evans of the Federal advance against the Confederate right. This timely intelligence allowed Evans to order an attack and send reinforcements to the threatened area.[7] On the strength of this performance, Hagood was promoted to brigadier general on July 21. He was assigned to command the "Second Military District of the Department of South Carolina, Georgia, and Florida," which encompassed the area south of Charleston from Rantowles to the Ashepoo River. His headquarters were at Adams Run. One of Hagood's key duties in this post was to guard the Charleston and Savannah Railroad.[8]

Patrolling the extensive territory of the Second District was made more difficult by the myriad watercourses that penetrated it. A further problem was that various units continually rotated through the district, "coming and going as the emergencies of the service required." Hagood declared his duties "unobtrusive but important," but he confessed "it was not a pleasant command." "No event of military interest beyond an occasional collision of pickets marked the time," he lamented, and "service in the Second District had all the monotony of garrison life."[9]

Hagood "chafed at his life of inactivity—while the great game of war was being played so grandly in Virginia and the west." He thought he had exacted a promise from General Beauregard "to send him into one or the other of these fields with the first brigade that left the department." Instead that honor went to Brigadier General States Rights Gist, who Hagood lamented "claimed his seniority" in leading the brigade sent to Vicksburg in June 1863.[10]

Hagood's disappointment did not last long. After the Federal attack on Morris Island on July 10, he was ordered to Charleston to take command of James Island.[11] On July 12, he attended a meeting called by Beauregard to assess the situation at Charleston and develop a plan to defend Morris Island. Among the military members also at the meeting were Brigadier General Roswell Ripley, Beauregard's artillery expert, and Brigadier General William Booth Taliaferro, newly arrived commander of the forces on Morris Island. Reflecting the importance of the situation to South Carolina, Governor Milledge Bonham and Congressman William Porcher Miles were also present. Recognizing their inability to throw the Federals off Morris Island, the council resolved to strengthen Fort Wagner.[12]

Unlike the Confederates on Morris Island, Hagood's 4,700 men on James Island were in a position to launch a counterattack. From reconnaissance,

Fort Wagner as it appeared in 1865 (Library of Congress, Prints & Photographs Division).

Hagood knew that the Tenth Connecticut was in an exposed position near Grimball's Landing on the Stono River. He launched a surprise attack of about 1,400 men against this force on July 16 and only the quick reaction of the 54th Massachusetts saved the Tenth from destruction. While the attack failed to cut off the Federal force at Grimball's, it created such consternation that Major General Quincy Gillmore decided to withdraw Brigadier General Alfred Terry's division from James Island.[13] It also showed Hagood as a man of action who aggressively sought to influence the situation rather than accept an undesirable status quo.

With the Federal attack pending, Hagood was then ordered to move with the 32nd Georgia from James Island to Morris Island. When the grand assault on Fort Wagner came on July 16, Hagood and his men "aided considerably in eliminating the Union troops inside the battery."[14] Once again, Hagood displayed his characteristic knack to move to the sound of the guns.

With the repulse of this attack, Gillmore resolved to take Morris Island by siege tactics. He began erecting new batteries that kept Fort Wagner under a continual fire. The Confederates were equally determined, and Beauregard instructed his forces to hold "Morris Island at all costs for the present." It was under these circumstances that, at 2:00 a.m. on August 21, Hagood assumed command of Fort Wagner.[15]

In this difficult situation, Hagood used sharpshooters, cannons, and mortars to slow the progress of the Federal siege operation and interfere with the bombardment. His tactics were well-executed, but the Federals continued to move their zig-zag trenches forward. By the evening of August 21, the 100th New York had advanced its pickets within twenty yards of the Confederate rifle pits. In response, Hagood organized a sortie of men from the 25th South Carolina that struck the New Yorkers before they could dig in and drove them back. The respite was a brief one, however, and by the next morning, the Federals had constructed a fourth parallel.[16]

This latest Federal advance left them just 350 yards from Fort Wagner. In spite of fire from the Confederate rifle pits to their front and artillery fire from James Island, the Federal sappers continued to inch forward. By August 25, they were ready to attack. It so happened that, at the same time, the 54th Georgia was being relieved by a detachment from the 61st North Carolina. Sensing the attack, the Confederates kept both units in place and were ready. However, the men of the 3rd New Hampshire never received the final order to attack, so all that resulted was a harmless exchange of small-arms fire between the two enemies. The Federals called off the attack.[17]

The Federals had more success when they attacked again the evening of August 26. This time they captured seventy-six of the eighty-nine men of the

61st North Carolina who formed the Confederate picket line. The Federals continued to advance their lines, all the while mercilessly shelling Fort Wagner. By September 2, Hagood reported the enemy was within 80 to 100 yards of the salient. On September 4—"the rapid advance of the enemy's trenches to Battery Wagner having made it evident that before many days that work must become untenable"—Beauregard held a council of war which Hagood attended. The situation was rapidly deteriorating, but the importance of Charleston convinced Beauregard "to hold Morris Island as long as communications with it could be maintained at night by means of rowboats." He requested 200 sailors to act as oarsmen for this purpose. Confederates at Battery Gregg thwarted a Federal attack on September 5, but Federal fire still caused 100 casualties among Fort Wagner's 900 defenders. Colonel Lawrence Keitt, the fort's commander, reported that "a repetition of [such] fire ... will make the fort almost a ruin." After continued Federal pressure, Beauregard "concluded the period had arrived when it would be judicious to evacuate Morris Island." That evacuation became at 9:00 p.m. on September 6 and was concluded at about 1:30 a.m. the next day.[18]

Beauregard was extremely proud of the Confederate defense of Morris Island: "I cannot express in too strong terms my admiration for the bravery, endurance, and patriotism displayed by the officers and men engaged in these operations, who during so many days and nights withstood unflinchingly the extraordinary fire from the enemy's land and naval batteries, and repulsed with heroic gallantry every effort to surprise or carry the works by storm." Hagood was among the handful Beauregard particularly commended for "gallantry, coolness, and zeal."[19]

With the stalemate at Charleston, both sides began dispatching forces to other areas of operation. Beauregard was assigned to command the Department of North Carolina and Southern Virginia, which stretched from Wilmington, North Carolina, to the James River in Virginia. He took two brigades with him, leaving Hagood's and Brigadier General Alfred Colquitt's brigades as the only infantry around Charleston for the winter of 1863–1864.[20]

Hagood's brigade had been formed on September 30 from the Eleventh, Twenty-first, and Twenty-fifth South Carolina regiments, and the First (Charleston) Battalion and Seventh Battalion South Carolina Volunteers.[21] To ease his disappointment at not going to Vicksburg, Beauregard had once promised Hagood that when the opportunity arose he would give Hagood "a good brigade with which to take the field." Beauregard later declared the units that made up Hagood's brigade to be "the best I had."[22]

In early April, Gillmore, with the bulk of his army, was transferred to Virginia. With the Federal threat thus reduced, on April 28 Hagood began moving his brigade to Wilmington.[23] He spent the remainder of the war fighting in Virginia and North Carolina. After the war, he was active in the effort to restore home rule to South Carolina and was elected governor in 1880.[24]

Leadership Lessons

In his conduct at Charleston and elsewhere, Hagood proved himself to be the quintessential "go-to guy." He seemed up for any challenge, always eager for action, and willing to serve however and wherever he was needed. Such versatility is particularly necessary in the military, where it has been argued that the emergencies of war require a man to "become a jack of many trades and a master of several."[25] Hagood was such a man. He could operate semiautonomously in locations like Cole's Island and in a supporting role such as that at Secessionville. He could command a fixed location such as Fort Wagner or a broader expanse such as the Second District. Although most desirous of serving in combat, Hagood even showed the ability to function administratively as a provost marshal. He moved back and forth among these various roles seamlessly and with ease.

In an era of increased specialization, individuals with Hagood's broad range of capabilities have become a very valuable commodity. For example, Dick Patton, head of Egon Zehnder's Global Chief Marketing Officer Practice, notes that "more and more we are seeing major companies entrusting top marketing roles to leaders with diversified industry expertise—not necessarily in the corporation's direct business proposition." Patton argues such companies are seeking individuals with deep experience in the area of the "primary ... problem to solve," rather than specialized expertise in any one area.[26] In Hagood's case, that problem was "how to defend Charleston," and his broad skill set allowed the Confederacy to use him in a variety of roles.

Hagood's willingness, energy, versatility, and reliability made him the natural choice for the tough jobs that kept cropping up for the Confederates at Charleston. Such tasks as imposing martial law as provost marshal or superintending the evacuation of Fort Wagner were not for the faint of heart, and Hagood became the man that the Confederates counted on to handle such difficult situations.

In his classic *Message to Garcia*, Elbert Hubbard tells the story of Lieutenant Andrew Rowan, whom President William McKinley called upon to deliver a message to General Calixto Garcia, commander of the revolutionary forces during the Spanish-American War. Rowan performed this arduous and unprecedented task without fanfare or complaint, leading Hubbard to laud him as the epitome of the go-to guy. "It is not book-learning young men need, nor instruction about this or that," Hubbard claimed, "but a stiffening of the vertebrae which will cause them to be loyal to a trust, to act promptly, concentrate their energies: do the thing—'Carry the message to Garcia.'"[27] Hagood was such a man, and he carried his share of "messages to Garcia" at Charleston.

Take-aways

- Leaders must be versatile problem-solvers rather than "one trick ponies."
- Leaders establish a record of willingness and capability that makes them the organization's "go-to guy."
- Leaders have the ability to carry the message to Garcia.

22

Edward Serrell and Charles Sellmer and Problem-Solving

While his efforts to carry Fort Wagner or reduce Fort Sumter languished, Major General Gillmore turned his attention to Charleston itself. One of the weapons he brought to bear against the city was an 8-inch Parrott gun nicknamed the "Swamp Angel." While Colonel Edward Serrell overcame difficult odds to construct this Marsh Battery, Lieutenant Charles Sellmer wrestled with the tricky task of keeping the temperamental piece safely firing.

While the Federal sappers and Confederate defenders were engaged in their duel at Fort Wagner, the Federals also kept Fort Sumter under fire. On August 17, Major General Quincy Gillmore and Admiral John Dahlgren began a week-long bombardment that was executed with the precision of clockwork. Working in three shifts, the batteries kept Fort Sumter under fire from daylight until dark, while the mortars and siege guns fired day and night. Each artillery piece had a specific rate of fire and great care was taken to properly maintain each piece to prevent malfunction or damage. Additionally, the monitors *Patapsco* and *Passaic* blasted the fort with their 8-inch Parrott guns. On August 23 and again on September 1, Dahlgren attacked Fort Sumter with his ironclads. In spite of the intense pressure, the fort held.[1]

In the midst of this onslaught, on August 21 Gillmore received word that the Marsh Battery was completed and ready to fire. Shortly after the July 18 attack, Gillmore had instructed Colonel Edward Serrell, the commander of the 1st New York Volunteers, to investigate the possibility of constructing a battery in the marsh between James and Morris islands. Serrell assigned the mission to a young engineer lieutenant who quickly determined the project to be impossible. Serrell counseled the man that nothing was impossible and instructed him to requisition any necessary materials. When requests came in first for "twenty men eighteen feet long to do duty in fifteen feet of mud" and then for support from the department's surgeon to splice three six-foot men together to make the required eighteen-footers, Serrell was not amused. He removed the unwilling subordinate, who had proven himself to be "more of a wit than an officer," from the project and took it on himself with the assistance of Captain Charles McKenna, Lieutenant Nathaniel Edwards, and Lieutenant Charles Parsons.[2]

In the local parlance, the marshes of the South Carolina low country are filled with "pluff mud." Antebellum rice and cotton planters used slave labor to prepare their fields with heavy fertilizer drawn from this rich, sticky mud. Mules or oxen pulling plows had to wear special shoes that looked like miniature snowshoes to keep them from sinking into the muck.[3] Indeed, a modern-day resident notes pluff mud is "unpredictable in its sucking power; when you step in it, you could sink up to your ankles, or up to your knees, or even to your hips."[4] Such properties created obvious problems for engineers trying to support the "Swamp Angel," an 8-inch Parrott gun and carriage weighing roughly 24,000 pounds. Serrell spent seventeen days of personally slogging through the marsh and conducting tests before developing a design that Gillmore approved. Work began on August 10 with Serrell's engineers supported by fatigue parties from the 7th New Hampshire.[5]

Serrell built the battery in two parts, beginning with the parapet. Sheet pilings some twenty feet long were driven into the marsh by a hand-lever–operated driver. Then a three-sided grillage of logs two layers thick was bolted on top of the pilings. The grillage enclosed three sides of the rectangular area that would house the gun platform.[6]

Then the work crews of the 7th New Hampshire carried a total of 13,000 sandbags across a plank causeway two to four feet wide and 1,700 yards long and placed them on the grillage. It took over an hour for the men to complete this journey on the slippery boards, occasionally while under fire from the Confederate batteries on James Island. When the men finished their mission, they had moved more than eight tons of sandbags.[7]

With the parapet complete, the more complicated construction of the gun platform began. In order not to have the incredible weight of the gun disrupt the parapet, Serrell did not connect the platform and the parapet. Instead, he designed the battery so that its two parts "floated" in equilibrium on top of the marsh mud. In the rectangular area inside the grillage, the men packed down marsh grass, canvas tarpaulins, and fifteen inches of well-tamped sand. On top of this base, they then placed a close-fitting platform made from three tiers of three-inch thick planks.[8] Serrell's theory was that the weight of the sandbagged parapet would compress the mud and force it upward against the

22. Edward Serrell and Charles Sellmer

The Marsh Battery and Swamp Angel (Library of Congress, Prints & Photographs Division).

gun platform. As he described it, "It was simply a force meeting another force of a like amount in an opposite direction." This action was designed to hold the platform at a constant level. If the log foundation of the parapet sank, more sandbags could be added to raise the height of the parapet. Displaced mud would exert pressure on the grillage and also rise around the battery, forming a gooey glacis.[9]

There was little the Confederates could do to interrupt progress on the Marsh Battery except lob an occasional shell at the work parties. Still, Serrell took no chances and built a mock battery to the south of the real one in order to confuse the enemy. He also placed log-beams in the surrounding creeks and patrolled the waters with picket boats. At night, a squad of soldiers armed with seven-shot Spencer rifles guarded the battery.[10]

Although some of the soldiers derided the project as Marsh Croaker, Mud Lark, and Serrell's Folly, work progressed rapidly. By August 17, the battery was ready for its armament. First the 8,000 pound iron carriage was ferried to the site. Then the 16,300 pound, 8-in Parrott was shipped on a specially prepared boat launched from the southern end of Morris Island. The journey was slow and painstaking. The Parrott weighed the boat down so that it floated with only five inches of freeboard, and water had to be constantly pumped from the boat. Nonetheless, the gun safely arrived and was mounted four days later. When it was, Serrell's theory of downward pressure proved to work.[11]

With the battery complete, Gillmore turned his attention to Charleston itself. On August 21, he sent Beauregard a demand for the evacuation of Fort Sumter and Morris Island within four hours. If Beauregard failed to comply, Gillmore promised to open fire on Charleston. Beauregard was not present when the note reached Confederate headquarters, and, since it was unsigned, the Confederates returned it for verification. Gillmore responded by opening fire at 1:30 a.m. on August 22 with a shot aimed at the steeple on St. Michael's Church.[12]

Manning the Marsh Battery was a detachment of the 11th Maine Infantry under the command of Lieutenant Charles Sellmer. Sellmer had served nine years in the regular artillery and had attended the artillery school at Fort Monroe before the war. His detachment had been called up from Fernandina, Florida, on July 22 and had operated mortar batteries before being assigned to the Swamp Angel.[13]

Before dawn, Sellmer had fired sixteen shells into Charleston. Ten of these were incendiary rounds known as "Greek fire." Although the shells from the Swamp Angel caused fires and panic in the waterfront district, Williams Middleton reported "little or no damage has been done and not a soul hurt."[14] The next morning at 9:00, Gillmore's now-signed note again arrived at Confederate headquarters. This time Beauregard was there to receive it, and he responded with a protest against Gillmore's firing on noncombatants. He demanded that he be given time to evacuate Charleston's citizens, and Gillmore agreed to give him one day to do so. Throughout the next night, the Swamp Angel remained silent. The gun had slid out of position, and during the respite, Sellmer and his men labored to put it back in place.[15]

Sellmer's problems with the gun continued when the shelling was resumed on the evening of August 23. Many of the shells exploded in the gun, and on the sixth round, Sellmer found the cannon barrel to be moving in the breech-band. Undeterred, Sellmer tied two lanyards together and positioned his men outside the battery. If the gun burst, Sellmer figured he had created enough distance that he and his men would be out of harm's way.[16] Sellmer safely fired thirteen rounds using this technique, and then deviated from his precaution. On the next round, he remained by the gun to use the light from the flash of the discharge to check the time on his watch. Sellmer and three others suffered minor injuries when the breech exploded as the Swamp Angel's thirty-sixth and final shot was fired.[17]

The failure of the Swamp Angel seemed a harbinger for ensuing Federal efforts. A major ironclad assault on Fort Sumter on September 7 floundered

The Swamp Angel after her breech exploded (Library of Congress, Prints & Photographs Division).

in a lack of joint service cooperation. With all the ironclads now in need of extensive repairs at Port Royal, active operations ceased for several weeks. When the Federals resumed harassing the forts, the Confederates responded by shifting heavy guns from Fort Sumter to the more powerful Forts Moultrie and Johnson. They also continued to plague the Federals with torpedoes and submersibles.

Leadership Lessons

Although the Swamp Angel failed to accomplish its military objective, the leadership lessons that can be gleaned from Colonel Serrell's and Lieutenant Sellmer's problem-solving techniques should not be lost. Both men encountered obstacles that would have given less resolute individuals an excuse to quit. Instead, Serrell and Sellmer devised novel solutions to their problems.

To build the Marsh Battery, Serrell had to overcome his environment. Peter Northouse notes that "the overriding function of management is to provide order and consistency to organizations, whereas the primary function of leadership is to produce change and movement. Management is about seeking order and stability, leadership is about seeking adaptive and constructive change."[18] The young lieutenant who first declared the construction of the Marsh Battery impossible was at best a manager. He could not see past the status quo and had no capacity to positively change it. Serrell, on the other hand, followed Northouse's proscription of "seeking adaptive and constructive change." Northouse argues that leaders "act to expand the available options to long-standing problems" and "change the way people think about what is possible."[19] James Kouzes and Barry Posner agree, adding that "change is the work of leaders. It's what they do.... They experiment. They tinker."[20] "Innovation and leadership," they argue, "are nearly synonymous."[21] They certainly were for Serrell.

In the process, Serrell had to summon a host of technical and interpersonal competencies. First, he had to apply his engineering skill to design a battery that could operate in the marsh mud. Then, he had to motivate a work force to perform the herculean labor that his theory required. Through it all, he had to persevere amidst the ridicule of those who could not appreciate his vision. Serrell succeeded on all accounts. In so doing, Serrell proved Stephen Covey's argument that "all things are created twice. There's a mental or first creation, and a physical or second creation to all things."[22] Serrell had to first use his analytical skill to develop the idea for the Marsh Battery. He then had to use his action skills to make that idea a reality. A leadership failure in either of these two "creations" can doom a project. Both "creations" are required for success.

Although it required its own mental agility, Sellmer's problem-solving was largely a continuation of this second creation. Leaders inevitably encounter obstacles, challenges, and setbacks as part of any action. Sellmer could have easily used the Swamp Angel's weakened barrel as an excuse to cease firing. Instead, he developed a work-around that allowed the mission to continue while keeping his men safe. There are certainly other lessons to be learned from Sellmer's later carelessness, but he handled the initial problem with creativity and initiative. Kouzes and Posner assert that

> the study of leadership is the study of how men and women guide others through adversity, uncertainty, hardship, disruption, transformation, transition, recovery, new beginnings, and other significant challenges. It's the study of people who triumph against overwhelming odds, who take initiative when there is inertia, who confront the established order, who mobilize people and institutions in the face of strong resistance. It's also the study of how men and women, in times of constancy and complacency, actively seek to disturb the status quo and awaken others to new possibilities. Leadership, challenge, and seizing the initiative are inextricably linked. Humdrum situations simply aren't associated with award-winning performances.[23]

Serrell and Sellmer measured up to this challenge by being unwilling to accept a status quo that was inconsistent with their vision for the future. To do so, they had to both develop a solution and put it into practice. While some people may tend to be "thinkers" and other people may tend to be "doers," leaders must be both.

Takeaways

- Leaders seek adaptive and constructive change. They are not content with preserving an unsatisfactory status quo.
- "All things are created twice," and leaders must be both thinkers and doers.
- Leaders solve problems.

23

Thomas Lockwood and the Entrepreneurial Spirit

The fall of Fort Wagner and the capture of Morris Island drastically curtailed blockade running into Charleston. From their batteries at Cummings Point, Federal artillerymen now could deliver effective fire into the channel and the navy also increased its surveillance. The result was that much blockade-running activity shifted to Wilmington, North Carolina.[1] Before that, however, Charleston had played host to many bold blockade runners such as Thomas Lockwood.

In spite of the ever-tightening Federal blockade, blockade runners possessed several advantages. Blockade duty was monotonous and dreary, and it was hard for the Federals to be constantly vigilant. Blockade runners could exploit this weakness using the element of surprise to take advantage of a momentary Federal lapse in attention. Blockade runners also often had local knowledge of the intricacies of the Confederate coast and knew how to use the geography to their advantage. The Federal ships could obviously not be everywhere, and the blockade runner needed to find just one loose seam to avoid detection. Consequently, hundreds of enterprising individuals took their chances running the blockade in order to bring cargo in and out of the Confederacy. Their efforts helped satiate the South's dependence on overseas goods and also produced handsome profits for the blockade runners.

The mix of patriotism and profit attracted a wide variety of blockade runners. A few were Confederate Navy officers such as John Maffit, who commanded ships owned or leased by the government and devoted a significant portion of their cargoes to items of military necessity. One European item most needed by the Confederate Army was rifles. In fact, President Jefferson Davis dispatched Caleb Huse to Britain to secure rifles, and Huse ended up purchasing more than 100,000 Enfields for the Confederacy. Although Huse's efforts were in part hamstrung by a limited amount of specie and the Federal blockade, Confederate blockade runners still delivered some 600,000 stand of arms to the South, most of which were British Enfields.

In addition to bringing European goods to the Confederacy, blockade runners also exported Confederate products, particularly cotton. Throughout the course of the war, some million and a quarter bales of cotton safely reached Great Britain. Sales of this commodity gave the Confederate government some access to much needed specie, but early reliance on the power of "King Cotton" was clearly misplaced.

More common, however, than government organized runners were civilian captains who sailed their own vessels and specialized in luxury goods such as wine, perfume, and cigars that would fetch huge profits. A single round-trip between Wilmington, North Carolina, and Nassau could net as much as $425,000 for such entrepreneurs. Rhett Butler represents this type of blockade runner in the movie *Gone With the Wind*, and Thomas Lockwood is among those credited with being Margaret Mitchell's inspiration for the Butler character.[2]

The flamboyant Lockwood began to attract attention even while the Fort Sumter crisis was brewing. On March 12, 1861, the *New York Times* reported the following: "It is as well to note that the first vessel that carried [the new flag of the Confederate States of America] out of the port of Charleston was the steamer *Carolina*, commanded by Capt. LOCKWOOD. He delayed the hour of sailing for the purpose of being the first to carry the new flag down to Florida." The article continued: "Capt. TOM LOCKWOOD ought to be known in New York. He is one of the few live pilots that Charleston possesses." The correspondent then recounted how Lockwood, "by his untiring exertions," used the *Gordon* to pull the *Columbia* off Moultrie Beach, "after she had been given up by everyone in Charleston."[3] Before the Civil War, Lockwood had worked for the Florida Steam Packet Company, an ancillary of John Fraser and Company. He eventually became a captain of the *Carolina*, a sidewheel coastal packet built in 1852 that made regular runs carrying passengers, mail, and cargo between Charleston and Jacksonville, Florida.[4]

At the time of the Civil War, John Fraser and Company were the leading cotton shippers in Charleston. The president of the firm was George Trenholm, one of the wealthiest and most influential men in the South, whom Clifford Dowdey describes as "a man of charm and presence, and passionately devoted."[5] Like Lockwood, Trenholm is sometimes credited as being "the real Rhett Butler."[6] With offices in Charleston, New York, and Liverpool, Trenholm had access to almost unlimited credit abroad; a capacity critical to the cash-strapped Confederacy. It was a simple and tidy arrangement. Caleb Huse reported, "Fraser, Trenholm & Co. of Liverpool, John Fraser & Co. of Charleston, S. C., and Trenholm Brothers of New York, were practically one concern."[7]

Even before fighting broke out, John Fraser and Company began negotiations to provide the Confederacy with steamship service to England. Trenholm took advantage of the early uncertainty of the secession and Fort Sumter crises to ship arms from New York and Liverpool to Charleston. Most were sold for huge profits which provided Trenholm with a glimpse of the opportunity that lay ahead.[8] While Trenholm was readying vessels for blockade running, he also offered the services of his Liverpool branch as financial agents for the Confederacy. The Confederates accepted, and the letters of credit sent to England by Trenholm would provide the Confederacy the cash and credit it sorely needed.[9]

On April 17, 1861, President Jefferson Davis published an invitation to ship owners to apply for letters of marque and reprisal that would authorize them to act as privateers. Prospective privateers had to post a bond ranging from $5,000 to $10,000, depending on the size of the crew, as a guarantee they would not engage in piracy or otherwise embarrass the Confederacy. Armed with these licenses, the bearers were authorized to capture Federal commercial ships and sell them for their own profit as contraband of war. The Confederate government also promised to pay the privateers 20 percent of the value of any Federal warship they destroyed. Entrepreneurs were quick to seize this opportunity, forming syndicates to underwrite the costs of arming and manning the vessels. By May 6, the day the Confederate congress ratified Davis's announcement, more than 3,000 applications had been submitted to state and Confederate authorities.[10]

John Fraser and Company bought some of the first merchant ships seized by privateers and converted them to blockade runners. One of these was the *Gordon*, which Lockwood commanded.[11] The ship became so notorious in Northern circles she was called the *Black Witch*.[12] Federal Captain John Conley wrote to the *Gordon* "mounts two 62 and two 32 pounders, manned by 50 men; draws too much water to go over the swash, so that she can be shelled easily from the outside." In spite of Conley's rather dismissive report of the *Gordon*, Lockwood ran her through the blockade at Charleston and used her to capture the *William McGilvey*, which was then taken to Cape Hatteras and used as a storehouse.[13]

The Confederate privateers instilled panic in the northeastern coastal towns and drove up maritime insurance rates. Many American shipments were shifted to foreign vessels. In spite of pleas to devote more resources against the privateers, Secretary of the Navy Gideon Welles instead focused on strengthening the blockade. His theory was that privateering would stop once the Confederate ports were closed proved correct. By the end of 1861, most privateers, unable to penetrate the blockade with their deep-draft prizes, began shifting to the more promising venture of blockade running.[14]

The *Gordon*, subsequently renamed *Theodora*, was one of the ships that made this transition. Her powerful engine and small size made her a suitable vessel to carry James Mason and John Slidell, Confederate envoys to England and France, through the blockade. Seeing both "an opportunity to assist the Confederate government and make a quick profit," Trenholm agreed to pay one-half of the vessel's $10,000 charter fee in exchange for the privilege of using any available cargo space. Under this arrangement, Lockwood ran the *Theodora* through the blockade at Charleston on October 12, 1861. Benefiting from the cover of a rainstorm, Lockwood made Nassau but found no transatlantic transportation there for Mason and Slidell, so he sailed for Havana, Cuba. Running low on fuel, he stopped at Cardenas, Cuba, for coal. There Mason and Slidell disembarked and proceeded to Havana by train.[15]

While all this had been going on, Captain John Wilkes had been unsuccessfully searching for the Confederate cruiser *Sumter* and had taken his *San Jacinto* to Cienfuegos, Cuba, for coal. While there, Wilkes learned that Mason and Slidell were at Havana, intending to sail for St. Thomas a week later aboard the English mail packet *Trent* for the next leg of their journey. Wilkes moved to a choke point from which he could intercept the *Trent* and waited. The *Trent* set sail on November 7 and the next day Wilkes fired two shots across her bow and dispatched a boarding party to seize Mason and Slidell. He then allowed the *Trent* to continue on her way and took his two captives to Boston. Wilkes's actions touched off an international incident that threatened to bring England into the war.[16]

While Lockwood was in Cuba, he boasted that he had already run the blockade from Charleston twenty-seven times. This time, after recoaling he went to Havana and took on a cargo that included swords, pistols, lead, coffee, and 200,000 cigars. He left Havana in late October and followed the Florida coastline until he reached the intercostal waters off Georgia. He maneuvered through these protected waterways until he reached Charleston on November 4.[17]

This voyage of the *Theodora* proved to be the shape of blockade running for the rest of the war. In spite of their smaller cargo capacities, fast, shallow-draft vessels like the *Theodora* could avoid the blockade in ways larger ships could not. Furthermore, such smaller vessels were ideal for negotiating the sheltered rivers and channels that dotted the Atlantic seaboard. Finally, the practice of transshipping from intermediary ports such as Havana, Nassau, Halifax, and St. George became standard practice, and a robust network of brokers sprouted up to handle shipment arrangements on these islands. Stephen Wise opines that "the *Theodora's* voyage forecast the future of blockade running."[18]

In December 1861, John Fraser and Company bought the 165' × 29' 10' × 10' 4" steamer *Carolina*, which Lockwood had captained before the war, and renamed her the *Kate*.[19] Under Lockwood's command, the *Kate* would become "the workhorse for John Fraser and Company." Lockwood's favorite port was Charleston, although he also used Wilmington and once even entered the "sealed" port of Savannah.[20]

On January 18, 1862, Lockwood reached Nassau with the *Kate* after running the blockade at Charleston with a load of 250 bales of cotton. While he was there, the fully loaded *Gibraltar* arrived from England, but the British captain did not want to take his chances with the Federal ships anchored outside the harbor. The Trenholm firms then received permission to "break bulk" and transport the cargo piecemeal in smaller, faster ships. The *Gibraltar's* cargo was transloaded on to the *Kate* and the *Ella Warley*. Lockwood then sailed the *Kate* to the unguarded port at Mosquito Inlet, Florida. He brought with him 6,000 Enfield rifles, thirty-two bales of blankets, four cases of surgical equipment, ninety-four boxes of mess tins, fifteen cases of medicine, one barrel of medicine, 500 barrels of gunpowder, 514 boxes of cartridges, and ninety boxes of percussion caps.[21] It was all an exceedingly lucrative business. In 1862, Lockwood was receiving $2,000 in gold for every successful trip he made with the *Kate*.[22] Some of the cargos he delivered were very special, such as a powerful steam engine he brought to Charleston in July to be used on an ironclad ram being constructed.[23]

Although the number was likely exaggerated considerably, on November 14 the *Kate* was credited with making her "forty-fourth successful trip to Dixie." By then Lockwood was no longer her captain, but according to one source he had already brought her into Charleston twenty times. The *Kate* was often sighted and frequently chased, but the Federal Navy was never able to bring her to bay. Instead, the *Kate's* impressive career came to an end on November 18 when she hit a snag inside the Cape Fear River Bar. Although the vessel was a total loss, her cargo was saved. By then, Lockwood had "already reaped a large fortune during the past year" and was reportedly "gone to Canada ... to purchase a fast steamer for the blockade business."[24] Such bold exploits netted Lockwood praise, if not appreciation, even from his enemies. The *New York Times* lamented, "Let us console ourselves like Mr. Disraeli, by allowing [Lockwood's activities] to increase our respect for the energy of human nature."[25]

23. Thomas Lockwood and the Entrepreneurial Spirit 183

Leadership Lessons

While the lure of great payoffs was enticing, blockade running was certainly not for the faint of heart. Seaworthiness of vessels was often sacrificed for speed and maneuverability. Ships' profiles were kept low to avoid detection and crews' quarters were spartan in order to maximize cargo space. Furthermore, as Federal victories closed one Confederate port after another, the blockade tightened, and it became more difficult for runners to advance undetected. Men like Lockwood and Trenholm braved great uncertainty and took huge

With the Federal blockade tightening around Charleston, many blockade runners suffered the fate of this wreck off Sullivan's Island. Many others shifted their operations to Wilmington, North Carolina (Library of Congress, Prints & Photographs Division).

personal and financial risks in plying their trade. In the process, Lockwood and Trenholm no doubt displayed many strong leadership attributes including risk-taking, audacity, and planning, but among their most impressive traits was their strong entrepreneurial spirit. Rita Gunther McGrath and Ian MacMillan identify five characteristics of a habitual entrepreneur. Lockwood and Trenholm excelled in all these areas.

First, McGrath and MacMillan note that habitual entrepreneurs "passionately seek new opportunities." "They stay alert, always looking for the chance to profit from change and disruption in the way business is done." Trenholm saw the coming Civil War as an opportunity to reengineer his existing import-export business. Entrepreneurs "greatest impact occurs when they create entirely new business models," and Trenholm's acting as the Confederacy's financial agent in Europe is an excellent example.[26] Lockwood demonstrated McGrath and MacMillan's requirement for entrepreneurs to "pursue operations with enormous discipline."[27] His seamanship, timing, and patience are all hallmarks of disciplined execution of a project. Negotiating the blockade was a meticulous undertaking, and Lockwood left nothing to chance.

Entrepreneurs "pursue only the very best opportunities and avoid exhausting themselves and their organizations by chasing after every option."[28] Whether it was luxury items like cigars, key personnel like Mason and Slidell, or essential military hardware like a steam engine, Lockwood carried cargoes that maximized demand, profit, and value. The overseas needs of the Confederacy were expansive, but Lockwood focused on where "there was the most bang for the buck."

McGrath and MacMillan argue entrepreneurs must model "adaptive execution" of the sort Lockwood used to bring the *Theodora* into Charleston on November 4, 1861. The innovative techniques involved in this particular run became the pattern for future efforts. Entrepreneurs model this characteristic when they act on new ideas rather than becoming paralyzed by over-analysis and they change direction as opportunity evolves.[29] Lockwood displayed this capability when he received the *Gibraltar*'s transloaded cargo on to the *Kate*, as did Trenholm when he arranged for this procedure to occur.

Finally, habitual entrepreneurs "engage the energies of everyone in their domain." They "create and sustain networks of relationships rather than going it alone."[30] Trenholm excelled in this regard in leveraging his Charleston, New York, and Liverpool offices, as well as in developing a mutually beneficial relationship with the host of importing and exporting firms located at Nassau.

Yet, traditional measures of business success that focus on maximizing profits and shareholder value creation are no longer considered sufficient by Danna Greenberg, Kate McKone-Sweet, and H. James Wilson. Instead they call for a new generation of entrepreneurial leaders who will also maximize the common good and minimize social injustice and environmental impacts.[31] Lockwood and Trenholm might get mixed reviews when assessed against this standard.

Indeed, one criticism of the Confederate blockade running effort is that so many of the cargoes contained civilian consumer goods rather than wartime essentials. The Confederate congress responded to this situation in February 1864 by passing a law "to prohibit the importation of luxuries, or of articles not necessaries or of common use." Still, the government was slow to exert complete authority over blockade running, requiring ships to reserve only half their cargo space for government shipments.

Yet, Trenholm's defenders claim he was "above all else a Southern patriot" whose ships concentrated on carrying necessities such as weapons, munitions, salt, iron, and coal. That his firms may have netted total profits from blockade running as high as $20 million does not necessarily mean Trenholm did not "put patriotism first."[32] Indeed, he ended the war as the secretary of the treasury, where he could put his financial acumen to the good of the cause. "Unfortunately, for the Confederacy," laments Clifford Dowdey, "Trenholm came along when the country was bankrupt." Under such circumstances there was little even a man of Trenholm's manifest talents could do."[33]

Entrepreneurs possess many of the characteristics necessary to a good leader. They can use those characteristics to serve themselves, others, or a combination of both. A fair appraisal of Trenholm and Lockwood probably places them in the "combination" category, and there is certainly no criticism implied in that.

Take-aways

- Entrepreneurs pursue new opportunities with passion, discipline, selectivity, adaptive execution, and synergy.
- Entrepreneurship involves risk-taking.
- There are increasing demands for entrepreneurial leadership to include concern for the common good instead of mere profit.
- How entrepreneurs use their skills with regard to leadership is a choice they must make.

24

George Dixon and the Power of Persuasion

Although the status quo was unacceptable to them, there was little the Confederates could do to challenge the Federal siege warfare. Instead, they sought to change the situation by innovative and asymmetric thinking similar to what had brought Gabriel Rains's torpedoes to the battlefield earlier. This time, the Confederates turned to submarines, and on the night of February 17, 1864, the *Hunley* succeeded in sinking the Federal *Housatonic*.

The *Hunley* was a submarine privately built in the spring of 1863 in the machine shop of Thomas Park and Thomas Lyons at Mobile, Alabama, under the direction of Lieutenants William Alexander and George Dixon, two Confederate Army engineers. She was based on plans furnished by Horace Hunley, James McClintock, and Baxter Watson, who had earlier worked on the *Pioneer*. After successful trials in Mobile Bay, General P.G.T. Beauregard called for her to be transported to Charleston in hopes of destroying some of the Federal ships blockading the harbor. By August 15, she arrived in Charleston on board two railroad flatcars.

The *Hunley* was 40 feet long, 3.5 feet wide, and 4 feet deep. Her main hull was made out of a boiler, cut lengthwise with a twelve-inch wide longitudinal strip added to it to increase her height. A pointed bow and stern attached to the boiler gave the *Hunley* a cigar shape. Others, like Beauregard, considered her shaped like a fish and to some she was known as the "fish torpedo-boat."[1] She was designed for a crew of nine: one man to steer and the other eight to power the vessel by hand-turning a crankshaft that moved the propeller.[2]

On August 30, the *Hunley* was tied up to the wharf at Fort Johnson with her hatches open when the steamer *Etiwan* moved off without notice. The

24. George Dixon and the Power of Persuasion 187

The *Hunley* as she appeared in a 1902 drawing by R.G. Skerrett (U.S. Naval Historical Center).

ropes of the two vessels became entangled, and the *Hunley* was capsized. As the *Hunley* started going down, Lieutenant John Payne and two crewmen were able to escape. When the boat reached the bottom in twenty-four feet of water, the water pressure equalized, and Lieutenant Charles Hasker, with his leg broken, was also able to escape through a hatch. Five other men were trapped inside and were drowned. Although the local newspaper reported the accident, the type of vessel was not identified to preserve its secrecy. Nonetheless, some word of the *Hunley*'s presence leaked out from loose-lipped blockade runners, and on September 1, Admiral John Dahlgren received word from the Navy Department that the Confederates had a "submarine machine."[3]

The boat was raised, and Horace Hunley, her principal benefactor, soon came from Mobile to Charleston to plead her case. On September 19, he wrote General Beauregard, proposing to bring a crew from Mobile who were "well acquainted with the management and make the attempt to destroy a vessel of the enemy as early as practicable." Eager to do something to challenge the Federal blockade, Beauregard accepted Hunley's offer. Among the crew Hunley assembled was Lieutenant George Dixon.[4]

Little is known of Dixon's early life. He was a native of Kentucky, and his wardrobe suggests he was quite wealthy. He had been an engineer serving aboard a Mississippi riverboat when the Civil War erupted, and he enlisted in the Confederate Army. He served with the Twenty-First Alabama at Shiloh, where he was severely wounded in his upper left thigh. The injury could have been much worse had not a twenty-dollar U.S. gold coin in Dixon's pocket deflected the musket ball's trajectory. In May 1862, Dixon was promoted to lieutenant based on his service at Shiloh.[5] After Shiloh, Dixon returned to Mobile, where he became aware of the work on a submarine being done at the Park and Lyons shop. He soon attached himself to the project. It was most likely either Dixon or James McClintock who commanded the boat during its trials in Mobile. As a result of Hunley's request to Beauregard, Dixon obtained a twenty-day leave from his duties at Mobile to report to Charleston.[6]

Dixon quickly took charge of the *Hunley*'s new crew and began training. According to Beauregard, "as originally designed, the torpedo was to be dragged astern upon the surface of the water; the boat, approaching the broadside of the vessel to be attacked, was to dive beneath it, and, rising to the surface beyond, continue its course, thus bringing the floating torpedo against the vessel's side, when it would be discharged by a trigger contrived to go off by the contact."[7] A common drill for practicing this technique was to dive underneath the CSS *Indian Chief*, a three-masted schooner anchored in the harbor, in a mock attack. The *Hunley* would tow a dummy torpedo attached to some hundred feet of rope and resurface on the opposite side of the *Indian Chief*.[8]

On October 15 Dixon was for some reason unavailable to command the *Hunley*. He may have returned briefly to Mobile or simply been about other business in Charleston. Regardless of the reason, Horace Hunley took command of the vessel that day and attempted the mock attack on the *Indian Chief*. The *Hunley* dived underneath the ship's starboard side but never resurfaced. Hunley and seven other men lost their lives. Three weeks later, the *Hunley* and the dead bodies were recovered.[9]

In the wake of this second disaster, Beauregard was ill-disposed to press his luck again. When the *Hunley* was recovered, he was noticeably affected. He reported "the spectacle was indescribably ghastly; the unfortunate men were contorted into all kinds of horrible attitudes; some clutching candles, evidently endeavoring to force open the man-holes; others lying in the bottom tightly grappled together, and the blackened faces of all presented the expression of their despair and agony." "After this tragedy," Beauregard "refused to permit the boat to be used again."[10] "I can have nothing more to do with that Submarine boat," he declared. "'Tis more dangerous to those who use it than to the enemy."[11]

By numerous accounts, Dixon was a man of impressive persuasive abilities, and he plied Beauregard with the best of his skills.[12] Declaring Dixon "a brave and determined man," Beauregard eventually assented to returning the *Hunley* to action, "not as a submarine machine, but in the same manner as the *David*," which operated low in the water as a surface vessel.[13]

24. George Dixon and the Power of Persuasion

Having obtained Beauregard's permission to operate the *Hunley*, Dixon still faced the daunting task of finding crew members for a vessel that had become known as "the peripatetic coffin" and "the murdering machine."[14] Dixon sought Beauregard's permission to look for new recruits aboard the *Indian Chief*, but Beauregard was reluctant. However, after several refusals, he finally acquiesced, but he also insisted potential crew members be made fully aware of the *Hunley*'s history. Lieutenant William Alexander, Dixon's second-in-command, recalled that Beauregard "strictly enjoined upon us to give a full and clear explanation of the desperately hazardous nature of the service required."[15]

Even in complying with Beauregard's full-disclosure requirement, Dixon and Alexander were able to recruit James Wicks, Arnold Becker, Joseph Ridgaway, and Frank Collins from the *Indian Chief*. Another crewmember known only as Lumpkin also likely came from the *Indian Chief*. On February 5, Alexander "received an order which at the time was a blow to all my hopes" to return to Mobile to work on a breech loading, repeating cannon. Dixon was promised two men to replace Alexander, and within a few days Corporal C.F. Carlson was recruited from Company A, South Carolina Artillery, along with another man known only as Miller.[16]

Dixon methodically trained his crew, enhancing their confidence and skills. Beauregard seemed pleased with the progress Dixon had made and on December 14, 1863, he ordered Dixon to "take command and direction of the submarine torpedo-boat *H.L. Hunley* and proceed to-night to the mouth of the harbour, or as far as capacity of the vessel will allow, and ... sink or destroy any vessel of the enemy with which he can be in contact." If the *Hunley* actually ventured out that night, it is not noted in any of the war's official records.[17]

What is known is that on the night of February 17, 1864, Dixon led the *Hunley* in an attack against the 1,934-ton screw Federal sloop *Housatonic*. By this time Admiral Dahlgren had received several firsthand accounts from deserters of the *Hunley*'s activities. On January 7, he warned his command of an enemy vessel "which is nearly submerged and can be entirely so. It is intended to go under the bottoms of vessels and there operate." He ordered all his ironclads to have their own boats in motion, their fenders rigged with netting dropped overboard from the ends, the howitzers loaded at all times, and a calcium light ready. He also cautioned against anchoring in the deepest part of the channel in order to limit the amount of space for the "Diver" to operate.[18]

These warnings, supplemented by the fact that "the night was bright and moonlit," allowed the *Housatonic* to spot the *Hunley* at a distance of about 100 yards. The alarm was sounded and the *Housatonic* engaged her attacker with small arms and tried to escape, but it was too late. The *Hunley* exploded her 130-pound spar torpedo, and the *Housatonic* became the first ship in the history of naval warfare to be sunk by a submarine. The blast, however, likely damaged the *Hunley* as well, and she sunk while returning to shore. Her entire crew was lost.

Leadership Lessons

In the attack, Beauregard credited Dixon with acting with his "characteristic coolness and resolution."[19] The same could be said of Dixon's conduct as a persuader. Not only did he convince a reluctant Beauregard to authorize operation of the *Hunley*, Dixon also was somehow able to recruit a third crew after two incidents of drownings.

Persuasion often smacks of unsavory salesmanship, manipulation, and chicanery, but many leadership definitions also invoke the word. John Gardner, for example, defines leadership as "the process of persuasion or example by which an individual (or leadership team) induces a group to pursue objectives held by the leader or shared by the leader and his or her followers."[20] Gardner notes that sometimes leadership involves giving orders and coercion, but that in most cases persuasion is the preferred technique.[21] Certainly in dealing with a superior officer like Beauregard, persuasion was Dixon's only option.

Kurt Mortensen defines persuasion as "the process of changing or reforming attitudes, beliefs, opinions, or behaviors toward a predetermined outcome through voluntary compliance." It is distinct from negotiating, which "suggests some degree of backing down or meeting in the middle." Instead, persuasion is "actually convincing the opposing party to abandon their previous position and embrace yours."[22] Persuasion is what Dixon needed to get Beauregard to change his mind about employing the *Hunley*.

Persuasion requires clear and consistent communication. In spite of numerous refusals, Dixon repeatedly stated his case to Beauregard with conviction and persistence. Yet Dixon was well aware he had no power to coerce Beauregard. "Singularly among Confederate officers in Charleston," declares Tom Chaffin, "Beauregard could afford the potential risks to his stature posed by the submarine boat's continued operations."[23] Dixon would have to use the reasoned logic of persuasion to convince rather than compel. Somehow, he would have to persuade Beauregard to accept the risk.

Allan Cohen and David Bradford note the successful persuasion of a superior often requires establishing an interdependent or partnership relationship in which the subordinate's proposal also offers a supportive way for the senior to be more effective.[24] Beauregard describes Dixon's request to put the *Hunley* back in action as coinciding with the appearance of the *Housatonic*, "which lay at the time in the north channel opposite Beach Inlet, materially obstructing the passage of our blockade-runners in and out." Desiring to rid himself of this Federal threat, Beauregard "consented to [the *Hunley*'s] use for this purpose."[25] Dixon's objective benefited from being supportive of Beauregard's objective, and this relationship facilitated the persuasion.

Dixon would need more persuasive skill in recruiting a third crew. Beauregard had made it very clear that the men would not only have to be volunteers, they would also have to be fully informed of the risks involved. To convince men to leave the relatively comfortable life aboard the *Indian Chief* for such hazardous and uncertain duty as the *Hunley* offered would require all Dixon's persuasive skills.

Cohen and Bradford note that such a difficult task can be accomplished if the leader "can give people what they need." By knowing "the concerns, objectives, and styles of the people you want to influence," persuaders can increase their ability to build "win-win relationships."[26] Lieutenant Alexander offers some insight into the tactic Dixon may have used in this regard. "In spite of the many fatalities which [the *Hunley*] had caused," Alexander writes, "I don't believe a man considered the danger which awaited him." Instead, Dixon appears to have tapped into a mix of patriotism, glory, and adventure in persuading his recruits. As Alexander explains, "The honor of being the first to engage the enemy in a novel way overshadowed all else."[27] Dixon persuaded the recruits to do want he wanted by simultaneously offering them something they wanted.

Take-aways

- Especially in the team-centered construct of most modern organizations, persuasion rather than coercion is an important leadership skill.
- Persuasion requires consistent and clear communication.
- Bosses can be persuaded by presenting proposals that also make them more effective.
- It is easier to persuade people if you understand their own concerns, objectives, and styles.

Part Three

Summary

25

The Fall of Charleston

On December 21, 1864, Lieutenant General William Hardee evacuated Savannah, Georgia. The next day, Major General William Sherman moved in to occupy the city, wiring President Abraham Lincoln, "I beg to present you, as a Christmas gift, the City of Savannah, with 150 heavy guns and plenty of ammunition, and also about 25,000 bales of cotton."[1] Where Sherman would go next was anyone's guess, but Charleston was certainly an option. The city had already felt the impact of Sherman's march through Georgia as generals and troops had been relocated elsewhere to provide what little resistance they could.[2] Now Charleston's citizens braced for the worst.

Sherman, however, had other ideas. On December 31, he confided to Admiral David Porter, commander of the North Atlantic Blockading Squadron, that he planned to march through South Carolina, "tearing up railroads and smashing things generally, feign on Charleston, and rapidly come down upon Wilmington from the rear, taking all their works in reverse."[3] Still Major General Henry Halleck mused to Sherman, "Should you capture Charleston, I hope by some accident the place may be destroyed, and if a little salt should be sown upon its site it may prevent the growth of future crops of nullification and secession."[4] Sherman replied, "I will bear in mind your hint as to Charleston and don't think salt will be necessary. When I move the Fifteenth Corps will be on the right of the Right Wing, and their position will bring them naturally, into Charleston first; and if you have watched the history of that corps you will have remarked that they generally do their work up pretty well. The truth is the whole army is burning up with insatiable desire to wreak vengeance upon South Carolina. I almost tremble at their fate."[5]

On January 2, 1865, the first of Sherman's troops crossed the Savannah River and made a lodgment on the South Carolina side. Heavy rains had turned the low country roads into bogs and made movements slow and laborious. By

January 20, the bulk of Sherman's army was in South Carolina, but the saturated ground dissuaded Sherman from any campaign angled toward Charleston.[6] Instead, it was Columbia that felt the promised wrath of the Federal Army.

When Major General Quincy Gillmore left Charleston for Virginia, Major General John Foster had succeeded him as commander of the Department of the South. Now, in a move that did not please Foster, Admiral John Dahlgren, and others, Gillmore was ordered to relieve Foster on January 30. Gillmore then proceeded to keep Charleston under heavy bombardment, and the Federals made a few unremarkable amphibious demonstrations. On February 14, General Beauregard realized the end was at hand and sent instructions for the evacuation of Charleston. That evacuation was accomplished on the night of February 17–18.

Federal troops raced for the honor of being the first to enter the city. Among them was Lieutenant Colonel Augustus Bennett of the 21st U.S. Colored Troops. As Bennett cautiously moved into the city with a small force of about twenty-five men, he was approached by city alderman George Williams. Williams handed Bennett a note from Mayor Charles Macbeth announcing, "The military authorities of the Confederate States have evacuated the city. I have remained to enforce law and preserve order until you take such steps as you may think best."[7] It was over. As one veteran blockader recorded, "And thus, after a siege which will rank among the most famous in history, Charleston became ours."[8]

Fires and explosions rocked the city. The one that destroyed the gunboat *Palmetto State* soon ensconced itself in the subsequent lore of the Lost Cause. This ironclad ram had been built in January 1862 in Charleston using money raised from women who had sold their jewelry. Along with her sister ship the *Chicora* she had launched the surprise attack on the Federal blockade on January 31, 1863, that emboldened Beauregard to crow that the blockade was lifted. Now Captain John Randolph Tucker ordered her destroyed to prevent her capture. As E. Milby Burton describes the scene, "Those who saw it said that the smoke from the explosion formed a perfect palmetto tree. In a few moments it wavered, gradually fell apart, and drifted away, almost as a symbol of what was happening to the state."[9]

Conclusions About Leadership During the Charleston Campaign

Much of the Charleston Campaign involved some sort of stalemate. It began with a standoff between Robert Anderson's beleaguered force at Fort

Sumter and the surrounding South Carolinians and Confederates. The Federal blockade that shortly followed created another tense equilibrium. The siege operations that defined much of the campaign were yet another form of stalemate. In the end, Charleston proved "too strong from the sea," and the stalemate was broken only by the impending approach of Major General William Sherman in the dying days of the Confederacy.[10]

The fact that so much of the Charleston Campaign involved some sort of stalemate has interesting implications for a study of leadership. Leadership is about generating positive change to alter an unsatisfactory status quo. Because of their objective of restoring the Union, the Federals especially bore this burden.

The status quo was more acceptable to the Confederates whose aim was merely to "hold on to the de facto independence already obtained." To do so, Robert Doughty explains, "all they had to do was to continue the struggle long enough for the North to tire of the war and accept the fact of secession."[11] Rather than defeating the Federals, all the Confederates at Charleston had to do was to hang on.

In many ways, the result was a cycle of action and reaction in which the Federals tried to break the stalemate and the Confederates countered to restore it. Daring blockade runners like Thomas Lockwood sought to bring much needed materiel to the Confederacy from Europe. To limit such opportunities, Gideon Welles created the Blockade Board, and the Federals seized Port Royal. Responding to this threat to the Confederate coast, Robert E. Lee developed a plan to consolidate and prioritize the Confederate defenses. The Federals tried to approach Charleston from the rear with an attack on James Island only to be thwarted by Thomas Lamar's stubborn defense at Secessionville. Welles reinforced Samuel Du Pont's fleet with the latest ironclad technology, and the Confederates countered asymmetrically with Gabriel Rains's torpedoes. Quincy Gillmore attacked Morris Island, and the Confederates responded by strengthening Fort Wagner. The Federals expanded and tightened their blockade, and the Confederates struck back with George Dixon's *Hunley*. Every time the Federals took action to alter the status quo, the Confederates countered in an effort to restore it or at least challenge the Federal initiative.

Another theme that emerges from the campaign is that leaders are problem-solvers. James Buchanan's laissez-faire approach did little to improve the crisis unfolding at Charleston. Robert Anderson addressed his security problem by moving his force from Fort Moultrie to Fort Sumter. Adolphus LaCoste used manpower and muscle to salvage the *Keokuk*'s guns; a task others had deemed impossible. Edward Serrell solved the problem of how to build the Marsh Battery in the pluff mud with his ingenuity. Then Charles Sellmer kept the Swamp Angel firing by devising a work-around to the safety issue. The Charleston Campaign showcases the determination, creativity, and will of several leaders who refused to be stymied by a problem.

Unity of effort and cooperation was also of critical importance at Charleston. At the higher levels, teamwork was often illusive. John Pemberton and Francis Pickens shared little personal chemistry. Samuel Du Pont had difficulties vertically with Gideon Welles and laterally with David Hunter. Army-navy disunity then continued with John Dahlgren and Quincy Gillmore. At lower levels, however, it was teamwork that often made mission accomplishment possible. Robert Smalls and his close band of family and friends, LaCoste's salvage team, and the crew of the *Hunley* all worked together to prove what a small group can achieve.

As in most all situations, interpersonal skills proved to be significant factors. Men like Buchanan, Pemberton, and Dahlgren had personalities that diminished their leadership execution. On the other hand, Smalls, Lamar, Shaw, Barton, and Dixon were able to magnify what they could accomplish by their boldness, charisma, character, selflessness, and persuasion.

Leadership has been called "the most dynamic element of combat power."[12] The vignettes presented here show how various leaders approached their duties during the Charleston Campaign. The lessons drawn from their actions, however, extend far beyond the battlefield to all aspects of human interaction.

Some Reminders of the Charleston Campaign

The Civil War still defines much of what Charleston is today. Even the history buff with the mildest interest could spend weeks exploring its treasures. The purpose of this small section is not to pretend to be a tour guide of Civil War Charleston but to highlight a few of the reminders associated with the vignettes in this volume.

For those particularly interested in Robert Anderson, the National Park Service administers sites at Fort Sumter and Fort Moultrie. The Fort Sumter National Monument is obviously the more spectacular of the two, but it is accessible only after a boat ride of some two and a half hours. The boats offer excellent sightseeing of Charleston Harbor during the ride to the fort and can be boarded at the end of Calhoun Street.

For visitors looking for a more accessible alternative, the Fort Moultrie site at 1214 West Middle Street on Sullivan's Island is also very interesting.

25. The Fall of Charleston

Fort Moultrie's service spanned 171 years, from 1776 to 1947, so the exhibits include much more than just its Civil War service. Moreover, a visit to Fort Moultrie is easily combined with a trip to the beach.

Both Forts Sumter and Moultrie offer informative and detailed displays of the artillery pieces that played such an important part in the Charleston Campaign. An equally impressive display can be found in White Point Gardens at the Battery. Included among the many pieces there are one of the *Keokuk*'s guns salvaged by Adolphus LaCoste and his team. White Point Gardens also includes many impressive monuments, including one to "The Confederate Defenders of Charleston."

On James Island, Fort Lamar Heritage Preserve provides a glimpse into the Battle of Secessionville and the exploits of Thomas Lamar. The site is small but provides a good opportunity to inspect some of the earthworks as well as an appreciation of how canalized the attack must have been by the terrain. It can be reached by taking South Carolina Road 171 onto James Island and going south to Grimball Road. Turn left and continue to Secessionville Road (also called Battery Island Drive). Turn right and go south to Fort Lamar Road. Turn left, and the Heritage Preserve is on the left. (Bring bug spray!)

The *Hunley* is on display at the Warren Lasch Conservation at the old Charleston Naval Base in North Charleston. Tour times are limited, as scientists work to preserve the fragile relic, but a replica is on display outside the Charleston Museum at 360 Meeting Street downtown. A solemn burial site for George Dixon and other crew members is at the Magnolia Cemetery, somewhat off the normal Charleston beaten path, on 70 Cunnington Street. The cemetery contains some 1,700 Confederate graves.

Two historical markers were placed to honor Robert Smalls in conjunction with the 150-year anniversary of his daring escape with the *Planter*. One is at Waterfront Park off Cumberland Street and the other at 40 East Bay Street. The "Seizure of the *Planter*" marker reads:

> Early on May 13, 1862, Robert Smalls, an enslaved harbor pilot aboard the *Planter*, seized the 149-foot Confederate transport from a wharf just east of here. He and six enslaved crewmen took the vessel before dawn, when its captain, pilot, and engineer were ashore. Smalls guided the ship through the channel, past Fort Sumter, and out to sea, delivering it to the Federal fleet which was blockading the harbor.
> Northern and Southern newspapers called this feat "bold" and "daring." Smalls and his crew, a crewman on another ship, and eight other enslaved persons including Smalls' wife, Hannah, and three children, won their freedom by it. Smalls (1839–1915) was appointed captain of the *Planter* by a U.S. Army contract in 1863. A native of Beaufort, he was later a state legislator and then a five-term U.S. Congressman.

Indeed, there is much more to commemorate Smalls a convenient drive from Charleston in his hometown of Beaufort.

Morris Island is uninhabited and accessible only by boat. From the northeastern end of Folly Island, Lighthouse Inlet Heritage Preserve includes much of the area occupied by the Federal troops in preparation for their attack. In 1989, Hurricane Hugo ravaged the area and the next year, the Charleston Museum, with the help of numerous volunteers, salvaged what they could. Many of the artifacts recovered from that effort are currently on display at the museum.

Fort Wagner and the graves of Robert Shaw and his fellow members of the 54th Massachusetts are now under water as Morris Island has suffered from much erosion. There is, however, a historical marker in nearby Mount Pleasant that reads, "The Whilden House served as Union headquarters after the fall of Mount Pleasant in February 1865. Among the occupying troops was the first black volunteer 54th Mass. regiment. Under the command of Colonel Robert Gould Shaw, this unit was made famous by its assault on Battery Wagner in February 1865. The regiment mustered out in Mount Pleasant in August 1865."

Countless other small reminders of the principal characters of *Military Leadership Lessons of the Charleston Campaign* are ubiquitous. The Citadel football stadium is named in honor of Johnson Hagood. One of Charleston's busiest streets is (Thomas) Lockwood Avenue. Robert E. Lee's brief stay in Charleston as a guest at the Mills House is the subject of a Mort Kunstler painting and a room in the hotel bears Lee's name. The Civil War is an inescapable part of the Charleston landscape.

These testaments to the long and hard fought Charleston Campaign mean different things to different observers. In the context of this book, each represents some human dimension of leadership—good, bad, and mixed. The lessons they teach are timeless and transcend armed struggle and combat to inform every aspect of life. In the example of these men and women of the past, today's leaders can find inspiration, ideas, and warnings that will help them succeed in the challenges before them.

Notes

Introduction

1. E. Milby Burton, *The Siege of Charleston: 1861–1865* (Columbia: University of South Carolina Press, 1970), xvi.

Chapter 1

1. "Bugle Notes," (West Point, NY: The Staff, 1979), 274, 275.
2. John Scharf, *History of the Confederate States Navy from Its Organization to the Surrender of Its Last Vessel* (New York: Rogers & Sherwood, 1887), 67.
3. Ibid., 675.
4. Robert G. Poirier, *By The Blood of Our Alumni: Norwich University Citizen Soldiers in the Army of the Potomac, 1861–1865* (Boston: Da Capo, 1999), iii, 289, 298, 316.
5. Burton, 289–290.
6. Herman Hattaway and Archer Jones, *How the North Won: A Military History of the Civil War* (Champaign: University of Illinois Press, 2004), 17.
7. Kevin Dougherty, *Civil War Leadership and Mexican War Experience* (Jackson: University Press of Mississippi, 2007), xi.
8. W. Chris Phelps, *Charlestonians in War: The Charleston Battalion* (Gretna, LA: Pelican, 2004), 19, 60–61.
9. Russell Weigley, *The History of the United States Army* (New York: MacMillan, 1967), 99.
10. Quincy Gillmore, "The Siege and Capture of Fort Pulaski," in *Battles and Leaders of the Civil War*, vol. 2, ed. Robert Johnson and Clarence Buel (New York: Century, 1887), 10.
11. Daniel Brown, "Fort Pulaski," in *The Civil War Battlefield Guide*, ed. Frances Kennedy (Boston: Houghton Mifflin, 1990), 36–40.
12. Mallory to Conrad, May 10, 1861; *Official Records of the Union and Confederate Navies in the War of the Rebellion*, Series 2, Vol. 2 (Washington, D.C.: United States Naval War Records Office, 1922), 67–69 (hereinafter *OR, Navies*).
13. Mallory to his wife, August 31, 1862, Stephen Mallory Papers, P.K. Yonge Library, University of Florida.
14. Stephen Wise, *Gate of Hell: Campaign for Charleston Harbor, 1863* (Columbia: University of South Carolina Press, 1994), 23.
15. *OR Navies*, Series I, Vol. 13, p.712.
16. Du Pont to Benjamin Gerhard, February 19, 1863; Tucker, 92; Weddle, 183–184.
17. Christopher Gabel, *Staff Ride Handbook for the Vicksburg Campaign, December 1862-July 1863* (Fort Leavenworth, KS: Combat Studies Institute, 2001), 80.
18. Warren Ripley, *Artillery and Ammunition of the Civil War* (New York: Van Nostrand Reinhold, 1970), 109–110.
19. Wise, 156.
20. Ibid., 148, 170.
21. Ibid., 21; Andrew Billingsley, *Yearning to Breathe Free: Robert Smalls of South Carolina and His Families* (Columbia: University of South Carolina Press, 2007), 77.
22. Wise, 20.
23. Edwin Bearss. "The Vicksburg River Defenses and the Enigma of 'Whistling Dick," *Journal of Mississippi History* 29 no. 1 (January 1957), 26.
24. W.A. Swanberg, *First Blood: The Story of Fort Sumter* (New York: Dorset, 1957), 287.
25. Ibid., 309.

26. "The Charleston Blockade: An Important Capture; The British Steamer *Princess Royal* Taken; Whitworth Guns, Rifles, Powder, and Steam Engines on Board," *New York Times*, February 3, 1863, http://www.nytimes.com/1863/02/03/news/ccharlestoblockade-important-capture-british-steamer-princess-royal-taken.html (accessed December 7, 2012).
27. Quincy Gillmore, *Engineer and Artillery Operations Against the Defences of Charleston Harbor in 1863* (New York: D. Van Nostrand, 1865), 154.
28. Ibid., 330.
29. James Hazlett, Edwin Olmstead, and M. Hume Parks, *Field Artillery Weapons of the Civil War* (Champaign: University of Illinois Press, 2004), 149–150.
30. "Big Guns at Gettysburg," Gettysburg National Military Park, Department of the Interior, http://www.nps.gov/archive/gett/soldierlife/artillery.htm (accessed 19 December 2008); Gabel, 26.
31. *The War of the Rebellion: A Compilation of the Official Records of the Union and Confederate Armies*, Series 1, Vol. 28, Part 2 (Washington, D.C.: Government Printing Office, 1901), 377 (hereinafter *OR*).
32. Wise, 20.
33. *OR*, Series 1, Vol. 28, Part 2, p. 220.
34. George Brooke, ed., *Ironclads and Big Guns of the Confederacy : The Journal and Letters of John M. Brooke* (Columbia: University of South Carolina Press, 2002),139–140.
35. Philip Katcher, *American Civil War Artillery, 1861–65: Heavy Artillery* (New York: Osprey, 2001),5–6; Ripley, 71.
36. Wise, 22.
37. Mark Boatner, *The Civil War Dictionary* (New York: David McKay, 1959), 707.
38. Michael Ryan, "The Historic Guns of Forts Sumter and Moultrie," monograph, 1997, pp. 21, 31.
39. Thomas Wilhelm, *A Military Dictionary and Gazetteer* (Philadelphia: http://books.google.com/books/about/A_Military_Dictionary_and_Gazetteer.html?id=GHcrAAAAMAAJL.R. Hamersley, 1881), 385.
40. Boatner, 119.
41. Ripley, 267.
42. Boatner, 119.
43. Patrick Brennan, *Secessionville: Assault on Charleston* (Boston: Da Capo, 1996), 172–173.
44. Ripley, 45.
45. Gillmore, "Charleston," 234.
46. Ibid., 234; Wise, 120, 142.
47. Gillmore, "Charleston," 36, 59.
48. Gabel, 30–31.
49. Gillmore, "Charleston," 20.
50. Ibid., 128.
51. Ulysses Grant. *Personal Memoirs of U.S. Grant* (New York: Da Capo, 1982), 522; Ripley, 59.
52. Wise, 179.
53. Percival Drayton to Edwin Hoyt, February 28, 1863, in Drayton, *Naval Letters*, 29–30: Weddle, 182.
54. I.B. Holley, *Technology and Military Doctrine: Essays on a Challenging Relationship*, "Insights on Technology and Doctrine" (Maxwell Air Force Base, AL: Air University Press, 2004): 79–89.
55. Kevin Weddle, *Lincoln's Tragic Admiral: The Life of Samuel Francis Du Pont* (Charlottesville: University of Virginia Press, 2005), 107.
56. Scott Stuckey, "Joint Operations in the Civil War," *Joint Forces Quarterly* (Autumn-Winter, 1994–1995): 98–99.
57. Hattaway and Jones, 127.
58. *New York Tribune*, June 9, 1862.
59. Gustavus Fox, *Confidential Correspondence of Gustavus Vasa Fox*, ed. Robert Thompson and Richard Wainwright (New York: De Vinne, 1918), 128.
60. *OR*, Series 1, Vol. 14, Part 1, pp. 523–524.
61. Weddle, 156.
62. The title of Douglas Bostick's *Charleston Under Siege: The Impregnable City* (History Press, 2010) comes from John Dahlgren's declaration that Fort Sumter was "nearly impregnable."
63. Rod Andrew, *Wade Hampton: Confederate Warrior to Southern Redeemer* (Chapel Hill: University of North Carolina Press, 2008), 84.
64. Howard Westwood, "Generals David Hunter and Rufus Saxton and Black Soldiers," *South Carolina Historical Magazine* 86, no. 3 (July 1985), 165.
65. Beaufort, *Free South*, August 23, 1862.
66. Wise, 138.
67. Ibid., 233, 240.
68. Ibid., 43.
69. Phelps, 55–56.
70. Andrew, 86.
71. Phelps, 64–66.
72. Ibid., 68–69.
73. Ibid., 73–77.
74. Quoted in Phelps, 73.

Notes — Chapters 2, 3, 4

75. The World War II siege of Stalingrad would be a notable exception.

Chapter 2

1. Spencer Tucker, *A Short History of the Civil War at Sea* (Wilmington, DE: Scholarly Resources, 2002), 89–90; Weddle, 143.
2. Fox, 149.
3. Tucker, 90–91; Weddle, 177–178.
4. Tucker, 91.
5. Fox, 121–122.
6. Tucker, 91–92; Weddle, 155, 160, 164.
7. Du Pont to Benjamin Gerhard, February 19, 1863; Tucker, 92; Weddle, 183–184.
8. Tucker, 97–99; Weddle, 191–193, 195.
9. Tucker, 99–100; Weddle, 188, 203–204.
10. Tucker, 101.
11. Ibid.
12. Ibid.
13. Ibid., 102; Ivan Musicant, *Divided Waters: The Naval History of the Civil War* (Edison, NJ: Castle Books, 1995), 402–404.

Chapter 3

1. Ezra Warner, *Generals in Blue: Lives of the Union Commanders* (Baton Rouge: Louisiana State University Press, 1964), 8.
2. Boatner, 58–59; Warner, *Blue*, 30.
3. Fox, 160; Weddle, 163.
4. Tucker, 3, 100; Weddle, 162–163; Boatner, 218.
5. Boatner, 252.
6. Daniel Ammen, "Du Pont and the Port Royal Expedition," in *Battles and Leaders of the Civil War*, vol. 1 (Edison, NJ: Castle, rpt. 1887), 690.
7. Weddle, 160, 165, 167.
8. Bruce Catton, *This Hallowed Ground* (Garden City, NY: Doubleday, 1956), 85.
9. Weddle, 213.
10. Musicant, 56, 58–59.
11. Fox, 126.
12. Du Pont to John Rodgers, January 6, 1863, Rodgers Family Papers, Library of Congress.
13. Boatner, 343.
14. Ibid., 418–419.
15. Robert Browning, *Success Is All That Was Expected: The South Atlantic Blockading Squadron During the Civil War*, (Washington, D.C.: Brassey's, 2002), 91.
16. Weddle, 206–207; Clarence Macartney, *Mr. Lincoln's Admirals* (New York: Funk & Wagnalls, 1956), 10; Boatner, 900–901.
17. T. Harry Williams, *Napoleon in Gray* (Baton Rouge: Louisiana State University Press, 1955), 45–50, 65.
18. Ibid., 163–165, 206–207; Boatner, 55.
19. C. Vann Woodward, ed., *Mary Chesnut's Civil War* (New Haven, CN: Yale University Press, 1981), 153.
20. Ezra Warner, *Generals in Gray: Lives of the Confederate Commanders* (Baton Rouge: Louisiana State University Press, 1959), 121–122.
21. Peter Chaitin, *The Coastal War* (Alexandria, VA: Time-Life Books, 1984),156.
22. Warner, *Gray*, 232–233.
23. Chesnut, 327.
24. Clifford Dowdey, *The Seven Days* (New York: Fairfax Press, 1978), 96.
25. Douglas Southall Freeman, *Lee's Lieutenants*, vol. 1 (New York: Charles Scribner's Sons, 1942), 268.
26. Henry Ravenel, *Ravenel Records* (Atlanta, Georgia: Franklin Printing, 1898), 61–62.
27. Warner, *Gray*, 257.
28. *OR*, Series 1, Vol. 14, p. 616.

Chapter 4

1. Jean Baker, *James Buchanan: The 15th President, 1857–1861*. American Presidents Series (New York: Times Books, 2004), xviii. Indeed, Buchanan can be found consistently at the bottom of polls ranking the performance of U.S. presidents. See Baker, 146.
2. Allan Nevins, *The Emergence of Lincoln: Prologue to the Civil War, 1859–1861* (New York: Charles Scribner's Sons, 1950), 361.
3. Swanberg, 28.
4. Grant, 114.
5. Swanberg, 29.
6. Grant, 114.
7. Swanberg, 29.
8. Nevins, 374.
9. Grant, 115.
10. Edward Pollard, *Lee and His Lieutenants* (New York: E.B. Treat, 1867), 790.
11. Abner Doubleday, *Reminiscences of Fort Sumter and Moultrie in 1860-'61* (New York: Harper & Bros, 1876), 28.
12. Swanberg, 26–29.
13. Horatio King, *Turning on the Light: A Dispassionate Survey of President Buchanan's Administration, from 1860 to Its Close* (Philadelphia: J.B. Lippincott, 1895), 120.

14. King, 121.
15. Swanberg, 18–22, 32–33; Doubleday, 30–31; Nevins, 349.
16. Doubleday, 42; Swanberg, 35–36.
17. Swanberg, 33.
18. Pollard, 799. For the record, Buchanan denied having ever made any pledges that Anderson would remain in place. See Pollard, 800.
19. Nevins, 370.
20. Ibid., 374.
21. Ibid., 375.
22. Ibid.
23. Ibid., 378–379.
24. Edwin Bearss, "Civil War Operations in and around Pensacola," *Florida Historical Quarterly* 36, no. 2 (Oct 1957): 140.
25. Arthur Wilcox and Warren Ripley, *The Civil War at Charleston* (Charleston: Post-Courier, 1986), 10.
26. Swanberg, 127.
27. *OR*, Series 1, Vol.1, p. 132.
28. Swanberg, 128.
29. Baker, 141.
30. Swanberg, 153.
31. Ibid., 153.
32. Nevins, 361.
33. Baker offers an interesting perspective that Buchanan's chief failing "was not inactivity, but rather a partiality for the South" (141).
34. Baker, 141.
35. King, 121.
36. Peter Northouse, *Leadership: Theory and Practice* (Thousand Oaks, CA: Sage, 2004), 179.
37. Baker, 151.
38. Quoted in Baker, 151.
39. Ibid., 140.
40. Ibid.

Chapter 5

1. *OR*, Series 1, Vol. 1, p. 73.
2. Doubleday, 18.
3. Ibid., 19.
4. *OR*, Series 1, Vol. 1, p. 71.
5. Doubleday, 41–42.
6. Warner, *Blue*, 7.
7. Swanberg, 2.
8. Samuel Crawford, *The Genesis of the Civil War: The Story of Sumter, 1860–1861* (New York: Charles L. Webster, 1887), 7.
9. *OR*, Series 1, Vol. 1, p. 70.
10. Doubleday, 19.
11. Swanberg, 4.
12. Crawford, 56.
13. *OR*, Series 1, Vol. 1, pp. 74–75.
14. Ibid., 76.
15. FM 6-0, *Mission Command: Command and Control of Army Forces* (Washington, D.C.: Department of the Army, 2003), G-4.
16. Ibid., 2–7.
17. *OR*, Series 1, Vol. 1, p. 79.
18. Swanberg, 41.
19. *OR*, Series 1, Vol. 1, p. 82.
20. Ibid., 74.
21. Ibid., 82.
22. Ibid., 81–82.
23. Ibid., 82.
24. Ibid., 88.
25. Ibid., 89.
26. Ibid., 89–90.
27. Ibid., 92–93.
28. Swanberg, 51.
29. Crawford, 74.
30. Eba Anderson Lawton, *Major Robert Anderson and Fort Sumter* (New York: Knickerbocker Press, 1911), 9.
31. *OR*, Series 1, Vol. 1, p. 103.
32. Swanberg, 90.
33. *OR*, Series 1, Vol. 1, p. 105.
34. Doubleday, 62.
35. *OR*, Series 1, Vol. 1, p. 2.
36. Ibid., 109–110.
37. Narrative of William Henry Trescott, in *American Historical Review* 13: 544.
38. *OR*, Series 1, Vol. 1, p. 118.
39. Ibid.,124.
40. Ibid., 2.
41. Ibid.,232.
42. Ibid., 235.
43. Ibid., 291.
44. Ibid., 13.
45. Swanberg, 292.
46. *OR*, Series 1, Vol. 1, p. 13.
47. Crawford, 424.
48. Ibid., 425.
49. Ibid., 426. See also OR, Series 1, Vol. 1, p. 60.
50. Stephen Lee, "The First Step in the War," in *Battles and Leaders of the Civil War: From Sumter To Shiloh*, ed. Robert Underwood Johnson and Clarence Clough Buel (Whitefish, Montana: Kessinger, 2004), 76.
51. *OR*, Series 1, Vol. 1, p. 18.
52. Warner, 8.
53. Rushworth Kidder, *How Good People Make Tough Choices: Resolving the Dilemmas of Ethical Living* (New York: Harper Perennial, 2009), 6.

Chapter 6

1. Kevin Weddle, "The Blockade Board of 1861 and Union Naval Strategy," *Civil War History* 48, no. 2 (June 2002), 123.
2. Ibid.," 131.
3. Robert Selph Henry, *The Story of the Mexican War* (New York: Frederick Ungar, 1950), 210.
4. Weddle, "Blockade," 131–132. For a more specific study of Du Pont, see Kevin Weddle, *Lincoln's Tragic Admiral: The Life of Samuel Francis Du Pont* (Charlottesville: University of Virginia Press, 2005). For more on the influence of Du Pont's experience in Mexico see Kevin Dougherty, *Civil War Leadership and Mexican War Experience* (Jackson: University Press of Mississippi, 2007).
5. Hugh Slotten, *Patronage, Practice, and the Culture of American Science: Alexander Dallas Bache and the U.S. Coast Survey* (New York: Cambridge University Press, 1994), 110.
6. Weddle, "Blockade," 133.
7. Ibid., 131.
8. Welles to Du Pont, Bache, Davis and Barnard, June 25, 1861, *Confidential Letter Book of the Secretary of the Navy: Correspondence of the Secretary of the Navy*, quoted in Weddle, "Blockade,"134.
9. Ibid., 134.
10. James McPherson, *The Illustrated Battle Cry of Freedom: The Civil War Era* (New York: Oxford University Press, 2003), 303.
11. Shelby Foote, *The Civil War: A Narrative*, vol. 1 (New York: Random House, 1963), 115.
12. *OR*, Series 1, Vol. 53, p. 64.
13. Ibid., 72–73.
14. Weddle, "Blockade,"137; Rowena Reed, *Combined Operations in the Civil War* (Annapolis: Naval Institute Press, 1978), 8–9.
15. *OR Navies*, Series I, Vol. 16, pp. 618–630; Weddle, "Blockade,"138; Musicant, 63.
16. Weddle, 139.
17. Ibid., 125.
18. Ibid., 141–142.
19. McPherson, 313.
20. Weddle, 142.
21. Ibid., 142.
22. Jay Conger, *The Charismatic Leader* (San Francisco: Jossey-Bass, 1989), 41.
23. U.S. Army War College, *Strategic Leadership Primer* (Carlisle Barracks, PA: U.S. Army War College, 1998), 19.
24. Bern Anderson, *By Sea and by River: The Naval History of the Civil War* (New York: Da Capo, 1962), 40.
25. FM 6–22, *Army Leadership* (Washington, D.C.: Headquarters, Department of the Army, 2006), 12–1.
26. Weddle, "Blockade," 142.
27. John Niven, *Gideon Welles: Lincoln's Secretary of the Navy* (New York: Oxford University Press, 1973), 359.
28. Fox, 156.
29. Samuel F. Du Pont to Sophie Du Pont, January 25, 1863, Du Pont, *Letters*, 2: 379.
30. Weddle, "Blockade,"125.
31. Donald Stoker, *The Grand Design: Strategy and the U.S. Civil War* (New York: Oxford University Press, 2010), 95.

Chapter 7

1. Weddle, *Lincoln's Tragic Admiral,* 140–141; Foote, vol. 1, 119–120; Pollard 194; Anderson 57–58; Emory Thomas, *The Confederate Nation, 1861–1865* (New York: Harper and Row, 1979), 125.
2. Emory Thomas, *Robert E. Lee* (New York: W.W. Norton, 1995), 212.
3. *OR*, Series 1, Vol. 6, Part 1, p. 357.
4. Russell Weigley, *The American Way of War* (Bloomington: University of Indiana Press, 1973), 101–102.
5. Wise, 10.
6. Douglas Southall Freeman, *R.E. Lee: A Biography,* vol. 1 (New York: Charles Scribner's Sons, 1934), 610; Clifford Clifford and Louis Manarin, eds., *The Wartime Papers of R.E. Lee* (New York: Bramhall House, 1961), 82.
7. "Charleston & Savannah Railroad Annual Report, 1861," p. 4,. quoted in H. David Stone, *Vital Rails: The Charleston & Savannah Railroad and the Civil War in Coastal South Carolina* (Columbia: University of South Carolina Press, 2008), 64.
8. Stone, 70–71; Anderson, 59.
9. Stone, 74.
10. Wise, 10. See also Stone, 80.
11. *OR*, Series 1, Vol. 6, p. 344.
12. Ibid., 323.
13. Earl Hess, *Field Armies and Fortifications in the Civil War: The Eastern Campaigns, 1861–1864* (Chapel Hill: University of North Carolina Press, 2005), 242.
14. *OR*, Series 1, Vol. 6, p. 335.
15. Ibid., 336.
16. Ibid., 364.
17. Ibid., 390.

18. Ibid., 394.
19. Ibid., 398.
20. Ibid., 400.
21. Ibid., 402.
22. Stephen Covey, *The 7 Habits of Highly Effective People* (New York: Simon and Schuster, 1989), 157.

Chapter 8

1. Michael Ballard, *Pemberton: The General Who Lost Vicksburg* (Jackson: University Press of Mississippi, 1991), 86.
2. Ballard, *Pemberton*, 86.
3. Ibid., 88.
4. *OR*, Series 1, Vol. 6, p. 395.
5. Michael Ballard, *Vicksburg: The Campaign That Opened the Mississippi* (Chapel Hill: University of North Carolina Press, 2010), 24.
6. Pickens to Davis, June 12, 1862, quoted in Ballard, *Pemberton*, 104.
7. *OR*, Series 1, Vol. 14, pp. 490–491.
8. Ibid,. 514.
9. Ibid., 517.
10. Ibid., 401–402.
11. Ballard, *Pemberton*, 104.
12. Ibid., 97.
13. *OR*, Series 1, Vol. 14, pp. 424–425.
14. Ballard, *Pemberton*, 99–100.
15. Ibid., 88–89.
16. Ibid., 101. See Wise, p. 12, for a critical assessment of Ripley.
17. *OR*, Series 1, Vol. 14, p. 484.
18. Ibid., 495.
19. Ibid., 509.
20. Ibid., 524.
21. Ibid., 247.
22. Ibid., 560.
23. Woodward, 375.
24. John Marsalek, ed., *The Diary of Miss Emma Holmes, 1861–1866* (Baton Rouge: Louisiana State University Press, 1979), 177.
25. John G. Pressley, "Extracts from the Diary of Lieutenant Colonel John G. Pressley," *Papers of the Southern Historical Society*, vol. 14 (Richmond, VA: William Jones, 1886), 37.
26. Ballard, *Pemberton*, 90.
27. *OR*, Series 1, Vol. 14, p. 570.
28. Northouse, 36–38.
29. "Strategic Leadership Primer," v.
30. Ibid.,11.
31. Ballard, *Pemberton*, 104.
32. William Cohen, *The Stuff of Heroes: The Eight Universal Laws of Leadership* (Atlanta: Longstreet, 1998), 5.
33. Ibid., 141–142.
34. Oren Harari, *The Leadership Secrets of Colin Powell* (New York: McGraw-Hill, 2002), 215.
35. Ibid., 216.
36. Ballard, *Pemberton*, 129.
37. John Maxwell, *The 17 Indisputable Laws of Teamwork* (Nashville: Thomas Nelson, 2001), 33–34.
38. See also Kevin Dougherty, *The Campaigns for Vicksburg, 1862–63: Leadership Lessons* (Philadelphia: Casemate, 2011), 53–62.

Chapter 9

1. Billingsley, 22, 104–105.
2. Ibid., 27, 105.
3. Burton, 94.
4. Billingsley, 43.
5. Ibid., 52.
6. Ibid.
7. Ibid., 55.
8. This entire account of the escape of the *Planter* is paraphrased from Billingsley, 55–60, and Burton, 94–96.
9. *OR*, Series 1, Vol. 14, pp. 983–986.
10. Edward Miller, *Gullah Statesman: Robert Smalls from Slavery to Congress, 1839–1915* (Columbia: University of South Carolina Press, 1995), 9–12.
11. Ibid., 12.
12. Ibid., 15.
13. Ibid., 27.
14. FM 100–5, *Army Leadership* (Washington, D.C.: Department of the Army, 1999), 2–12.
15. Ballard, *Pemberton*, 101.
16. *Holy Bible* (NIV), Esther 4:14.

Chapter 10

1. Warner, *Gray*, 106–107; Walter Cisco, *States Rights Gist: A South Carolina General of the Civil War* (Gretna, LA: Pelican, 2008), 52–55.
2. *OR*, Series 1, Vol. 2, p. 973.
3. P.G.T. Beauregard, "The First Battle of Bull Run," in *Battles and Leaders of the Civil War: From Sumter to Shiloh*, ed. Robert Underwood Johnson and Clarence Clough Buel, vol. 1 (New York: Century, 1884–1887), 210.
4. Cisco, 68.
5. Ibid., 68–69.
6. *OR*, Series 1, Vol. 6, p. 345.
7. Eisenhower quoted in Edgar Puryear,

American Generalship: Character Is Everything; The Art of Command (Novato, CA: Presidio Press, 2001), 188.
    8. Cisco, 72.
    9. *Charleston Mercury*, March 25, 1862, quoted in Cisco, 72.
    10. Warner, *Gray*, 48–49; Cisco, 66–67; Douglas Southall Freeman, *The South to Posterity* (New York: Charles Scribner's, 1939), 124; Walter Edgar, *The South Carolina Encyclopedia* (Columbia: University of South Carolina Press, 2006), 164–165.
    11. Woodward, 265, 692.
    12. Cisco, 68.
    13. Ibid., 70.
    14. James Chesnut Jr. to William Porcher Mills, March 14, 1862, William Porcher Mills Papers, Southern Historical Collection.
    15. Brennan, 33–35.
    16. *OR*, Series 1, Vol. 14, p. 499.
    17. Ibid., 500.
    18. Cisco, 67.
    19. Field Manual 6–22, *Army Leadership* (Washington, D.C.: Department of the Army, 2006), 8–11.
    20. Ibid., 8–11.
    21. Gregg Martin et al., "The Road to Mentoring: Paved with Good Intentions," in *Strategic Leadership Selected Readings*, ed. Jeffrey Johns (Carlisle Barracks, PA: U.S. Army War College, 2003), 351.
    22. Quoted in Puryear, 188.
    23. Martin, 339–340.
    24. Puryear, 189.
    25. Chesnut, 692.
    26. Puryear, 189.

Chapter 11

    1. Brennan, 117–136.
    2. Ibid., 140.
    3. *OR*, Series 1, Vol. 14, p. 352.
    4. Ibid.,46.
    5. Brennan, 32, 158–159.
    6. *OR*, Series 1, Vol. 14, p. 500.
    7. Brennan, 158–159.
    8. *OR*, Series 1, Vol. 14, p. 91.
    9. Ibid., 46.
    10. Ibid.,51.
    11. Ibid., 91.
    12. Ibid., 94.
    13. Burton, 98.
    14. *OR*, Series 1, Vol. 14, p. 355.
    15. Ibid., 90, 92.
    16. Cisco, 79.
    17. Brennan, 121, 305.
    18. Ibid., 121.
    19. *OR*, Series 1, Vol. 14, p. 96.
    20. *Edgefield Advertiser*, October 22, 1862, quoted in Brennan, 306.
    21. Northouse, 171–172.
    22. Ibid., 171.
    23. Conger, 33.
    24. Northouse, 171–172.
    25. Conger, 33.
    26. Northouse, 172.
    27. Ibid.
    28. Conger, 34.
    29. Ibid., 109, 132–133.
    30. Northouse, 172.
    31. Conger, 31.
    32. Dowdey, 81. In this case, Dowdey is specifically referring to Brigadier General Lawrence Branch.

Chapter 12

    1. Niven, 357.
    2. Reed, xiii.
    3. Niven, 480–81.
    4. Stuckey, 94.
    5. Edward Miller, *Lincoln's Abolitionist General: The Biography of David Hunter* (Columbia: University of South Carolina Press, 1997), 103.
    6. Stuckey, 98–99.
    7. Joint Pub 3–0, *Doctrine for Joint Operations* (Washington, D.C.: Joint Chiefs of Staff, February 1995), A-2.
    8. Miller, *Hunter*, 96.
    9. Francis DuCoin, "Assailing Satan's Kingdom: Union Combined Operations at Charleston," in *Union Combined Operations in the Civil War (The North's Civil War)*, ed. Craig Symonds (New York: Fordham University Press, 2010), 77.
    10. Miller, *Hunter*, 98.
    11. Letters, Du Pont to his wife, March 31, 1862.
    12. Ibid., April 4, 1862.
    13. Fox, 119.
    14. Letters, Du Pont to his wife, May 11, June 3, 1862.
    15. Fox, 121.
    16. DuCoin, 76–77.
    17. Ibid., 77.
    18. Fox, 149.
    19. Ibid., 133–134.
    20. Burton, 143.
    21. *OR*, Series 1, Vol. 14, p. 353.
    22. Ibid.,354.

23. Ibid., 354–355.
24. Ibid., 355; see also Burton, 143.
25. The revocation of the hapless Benham's appointment as brigadier general was canceled on February 13, 1863 (see *OR*, Series 1, Vol. 14, p. 979).
26. Puryear, 285.
27. Ibid., 285.
28. TC 25–20, *A Leader's Guide to After-Action Reviews* (Washington, D.C.: Department of the Army, 1993), 1.
29. Ibid., 1.
30. Stuckey, 98–99.

Chapter 13

1. Gabriel Rains, "Torpedoes," *Southern Historical Society Papers* 3, 1877, http://www.perseus.tufts.edu/hopper/text?doc=Perseus%3Atext%3A2001.05.0118%3Achapter%3D5.39
2. Freeman, *Lee's Lieutenants*, vol. 1, p. 268.
3. *OR*, Series 1, Vol. 11, Part 3, p. 516, and Gabriel Rains and Peter Michie, *Confederate Torpedoes: Two Illustrated 19th Century Works with New Appendices and Photographs*, ed. Herbert Schiller (Jefferson, NC: McFarland, 2011), 3.
4. *OR*, Series 1, Vol. 11, Part 3, p. 135.
5. Ibid., 509.
6. Ibid., 510.
7. Ibid., 510.
8. Rains and Michie, 5, 26.
9. Rains, "Torpedoes."
10. Clinton Ancker, "Doctrine for Asymmetric Warfare," *Military Review* (July-August 2003), 18.
11. Rains, "Torpedoes."
12. Pierre Gustave Toutant Beauregard, "Torpedo Service in the Harbor and Water Defences of Charleston," *Southern Historical Society Papers* 5, 1878, http://www.perseus.tufts.edu/hopper/text?doc=Perseus%3Atext%3A2001.05.0040%3Achapter%3D2.10%3Asection%3Dc.2.10.38%3Apage%3D156.
13. Rains, "Torpedoes."
14. *OR*, Series 1, Vol. 11, Part 1, p. 944.
15. Rains and Michie, 4; see also Freeman, *Lee's Lieutenants*, 268.
16. Rains, "Torpedoes."
17. *OR*, Series 1, Vol. 11, Part 3, p. 608.
18. Maxwell, 33–34.
19. Quoted in Wise, 170.
20. Robert Fry, "Sun Tzu: The Best Leadership Teacher of All Time?" *Forbes*, July 27, 2010, http://www.forbes.com/2010/07/27/sun-tzu-art-of-war-leadership-managing-advice.html.
21. Sun Tzu, *The Art of War*, trans. Samuel Griffith (New York: Oxford University Press, 1971), 101, 66, 100.
22. Fry.
23. Ibid.

Chapter 14

1. Fox, 142.
2. Ibid., 119.
3. Ari Hoogenboom, *Gustavus Vasa Fox of the Union Navy: A Biography* (Baltimore: Johns Hopkins University Press, 2010), 168.
4. Du Pont to Davis, October 25, 1862.
5. Fox, 121, 122.
6. James McPherson, *War on the Waters: The Union and Confederate Navies, 1861–1865 (Littlefield History of the Civil War Era)* (Chapel Hill: University of North Carolina Press, 2012), 142.
7. Weddle, 166–168.
8. Gideon Welles, *Diary of Gideon Welles, Secretary of the Navy Under Lincoln and Johnson*, vol. 1 (New York: Houghton Mifflin, 1911), 217.
9. *OR Navies*, Series I, Vol. 13, p. 543.
10. Du Pont to Benjamin Gerhard, February 19, 1863; see also Tucker, 92; Weddle, 183–184.
11. Du Pont to Sophie Du Pont, May 29, 1862.
12. Tucker 94; Weddle, 184.
13. Tucker, 91–92; Weddle, 155, 160, 164.
14. *OR Navies*, Series I, Vol. 13, p. 712.
15. Welles, 265, 440.
16. OR *Navies*, Series 1, Vol. 13, p. 601.
17. Weddle, 182.
18. Tucker, 93.
19. *OR, Navies*, Series 1, Vol. 14, p. 437.
20. Du Pont to Sophie, April 8, 1863, in Du Pont, Letters 3: 3–5; Tucker 97–100; Weddle 188, 191–195, 203–204.
21. *OR, Navies*, Series 1, Vol. 14, p. 437.
22. Welles, 267.
23. *OR Navies*, Series I, Vol. 14, p. 58.
24. Ibid., 230.
25. Weddle, 198–207.
26. Weddle correctly concludes that "for months, Du Pont had gone to great pains to inform both Fox and Welles of his reservations and concerns over the efficacy of the monitors and the difficulty of the mission" (199).

27. Strategic Leadership Primer, 19.
28. Robert Schneller, *A Quest for Glory: A Biography of John A. Dahlgren* (Annapolis: Naval Institute Press, 1996), 312, 313.
29. Harari, 172–173.
30. Ibid., 181.
31. See, for example, P.S. Perkins, *The Art and Science of Communication: Tools for Effective Communication in the Workplace* (New York: Wiley, 2008).

Chapter 15

1. Burton, 138–139, 145; USS *Keokuk*, Mariner's Museum, http://www.marinersmuseum.org/uss-monitor-center/uss-keokuk-originally-named-moodna (accessed June 7, 2013); Kevin Dougherty, *Ships of the Civil War* (New York: Sterling, 2013), 54.
2. John Johnson, *The Defense of Charleston Harbor, Including Fort Sumter and the Adjacent Islands, 1863–1865* (Charleston, SC: Walker, Evans and Cogswell, 1890), 65.
3. Burton, 145–146; Wilcox and Ripley, 45.
4. Burton, 146; Johnson, 65.
5. Burton, 146; Johnson, 66.
6. Burton, 147; Johnson, 66–67.
7. Burton, 147; Johnson, 69–71; Wilcox and Ripley, 45.
8. *OR, Navies*, Series 1, Vol. 14, Part 1, p. 926; Burton, 147–148; Johnson, 70–71.
9. *OR, Navies,* Series 1, Vol.14, p. 300.
10. Johnson, 71.
11. Burton, 148.
12. Johnson, 71.
13. Wilcox and Ripley, 45.
14. M.A. Rosanoff, "Edison in His Laboratory," *Harper's Weekly* 165 (September 1932), 406.
15. Johnson, 71.
16. Margot Morrell and Stephanie Capparell, *Shackleton's Way: Leadership Lessons from the Great Antarctic Explorer* (New York: Viking, 2001), 194.
17. Field Manual 6-22, *Army Leadership* (Washington, D.C.: Department of the Army, 2006), 9–5.
18. Ron Fry, "AFMC commander tells senior leaders to conserve resources, money," http://www.afmc.af.mil/news/story.asp?id=123201701 (accessed June 10, 2013).

Chapter 16

1. Stuckey, 94.
2. Wise, 36.
3. Ibid., 36.
4. *OR*, Series 1, Vol. 28, p. 4.
5. Du Pont Letters, vol. 3, p. 183.
6. Madeleine Vinton Dahlgren, *Memoir of John A. Dahlgren, Rear-admiral United States Navy* (Boston: J. R. Osgood, 1882), 396.
7. Ibid., 396.
8. Schneller, 257–258.
9. Burton, 194.
10. Gillmore, 77; *OR Navies*, Series I, Vol. 14, pp. 608–609.
11. Phelps, 146.
12. Gillmore, 77–78.
13. *OR Navies,* Series I, Vol. 14, p. 609.
14. Wise, 34, 164; see also Schneller, 254.
15. Wise, 164.
16. Schneller, 288, 368–369.
17. Wise, 164.
18. Fox, 160.
19. Belle Linda Halpern and Kathy Lubar, *Leadership Presence* (New York: Gotham Books, 2003), 8.
20. Schneller, 314.
21. Halpern and Lubar, 3.
22. It should be noted that Halpern and Lubar (3) contend that presence can be developed but to do so requires someone with Dahlgren's background and propensities "to go places and do things that feel uncomfortable, at least initially."
23. Schneller, 265.
24. *OR Navies,* Series 1, Vol. 14, p. 611.
25. Schneller, 266–267, 310.

Chapter 17

1. Browning, 58.
2. *OR*, Vol. 6, Part 1, pp. 148–149.
3. Gillmore, "Fort Pulaski," 1; Kevin Dougherty, "Rifled Artillery's First Breach of Masonry," in *Forward Observer*, April 1992, 6.
4. Browning, 63–66.
5. *OR*, Vol. 6, Part 1, p. 155.
6. Gillmore, "Fort Pulaski," 2–3.
7. *OR*, Vol. 6, Part 1, p. 157.
8. Ibid.
9. Gillmore, "Fort Pulaski,"8.
10. *OR*, Vol. 6, Part 1, pp. 158–159.
11. Gillmore, "Fort Pulaski," 7–9; Browning, 92.
12. Gillmore, "Fort Pulaski," 9; Browning, 92.
13. Gillmore, "Fort Pulaski," 8–10.

14. Ibid., 10–11.
15. Brown, 36–40.
16. Wise, 63–64.
17. Dahlgren, 397.
18. Wise, 66.
19. *OR*, Vol. 28, Part 1, p. 354.
20. Wise, 59–61.
21. This incident of the battle inspired the palmetto on the state flag and South Carolina's nickname as the "Palmetto State."
22. Hess, 253–254;Wise, 59–61; E.K. Bryan and E.K. Meadows, "Defense of Fort Wagner, Morris Island, 8 July 1863," in *History of the Several Regiments*, vol. 5, ed, Walter Clark (Goldsborough, NC: Nash Brothers, 1901), 162.
23. *OR*, Vol. 28, Part 1, p. 355.
24. Ibid., 186–193.
25. Wise, 75.
26. *OR*, Vol. 28, Part 1, pp. 13–15.
27. Ibid., 14.
28. Ibid., 417.
29. Abraham Palmer, *The History of the Forty-Eighth Regiment of New York Volunteers* (Brooklyn, NY: Veteran Association of the Forty-Eighth Regiment, 1885), 99.
30. *OR*, Vol. 28, Part 1, pp. 15–16.
31. Tucker, 101.
32. FM 6–22, 12–10.
33. Burton, 164. See also Wise, 117–118.
34. Wise, 117.

Chapter 18

1. Russell Duncan, *Where Death and Glory Meet: Colonel Robert Gould Shaw and the 54th Massachusetts Infantry* (Athens: University of Georgia Press, 1999), 3–24.
2. Ibid., 28–29.
3. Ibid., 36–42.
4. Ibid., 47.
5. Peter Burchard, *One Gallant Rush: Robert Gould Shaw and His Brave Black Regiment* (New York: St. Martin's, 1965), 59.
6. Duncan, 51–53.
7. Ibid., 54–55.
8. Ibid., 54–58.
9. Burchard, 72.
10. Duncan, 77.
11. Ibid., 77.
12. Ibid., 78–79, 84.
13. Duncan, 87–88.
14. Ibid., 92–98; Cornish, 149–150.
15. Duncan, 105–106.
16. Ibid., 107–108; Cornish, 151–152; *OR*, Series 1, Vol. 28, Part 1, p. 586.
17. Duncan, 109–110; Cornish, 152–153.
18. Duncan, 110; Cornish, 152–153: Burchard, 133.
19. Duncan, 110–111; Burchard, 133.
20. Duncan, 114.
21. Burchard, 137–138.
22. Ibid, 142; Duncan, 115.
23. Duncan, 119–120.
24. Ibid., 125–126.
25. Rushworth Kidder, *Moral Courage* (New York: William Morrow, 2006), 72.
26. Ibid., 87.
27. "Taking Action When Your Values Are Put to the Test" is the subtitle of Kidder's *Moral Courage*. The second quote is from James McPherson, *Drawn with the Sword: Reflections on the American Civil War* (New York: Oxford University Press, 1996), 109.
28. Quoted in Kidder, 32.
29. Kidder, 181.
30. Quoted in Cornish, 155.
31. Cornish, 155.
32. Quoted in McPherson, *Drawn*, 103.
33. Kidder, 25.
34. Quoted in McPherson, *Drawn*, 103–104.

Chapter 19

1. Duncan, 67.
2. Burchard, 141: Kai Wright, *Soldiers of Freedom: An Illustrated History of African Americans in the Armed Forces* (New York: Black Dog & Leventhal, 2002), 87.
3. Thomas Hammond, "William H. Carney's Grit at Fort Wagner Earned Him the Distinction of Being the First Black Soldier to Receive the Medal of Honor," *America's Civil War* 20, no. 1 (March 2007): 69.
4. Duncan, 59–63: Burchard, 77–78.
5. Duncan, 62, 66: Wright, 87. See Duncan (p. 67) for "strong" and Chaitin (p. 126) for "chunky."
6. Burchard, 136; Wise102.
7. Duncan, 112.
8. Wise, 104.
9. Luis Emilio, *A Brave Black Regiment: The History of the Fifty-Fourth Regiment of Massachusetts Volunteer Infantry, 1863–1865* (New York: Da Capo, 1995), 84: Wise, 104–105: Burchard, 141: Wright, 87
10. Hammond, 69.
11. Ibid., 69.
12. Wright, 87
13. "Congressional Medal of Honor Society: Carney, William H," http://www.cmohs.

org/recipient-detail/224/carney-william-h.php (assessed February 8, 2013).
14. Chris Lowney, *Heroic Leadership: Best Practices from a 450-Year-Old Company That Changed the World* (Chicago: Loyola Press, 2005), 14.
15. Ibid., 242.
16. Ibid., 243.
17. "Keepers of the Peace," Ronald Reagan Commencement Address, McAlister Field House, May 15, 1993, http://www.free-enterprise-foundation.org/regeantranscript.html (accessed June 2, 2013).
18. Ibid.
19. Hammond, 69.

Chapter 20

1. American Red Cross, "Founder Clara Barton," http://www.redcross.org/about-us/history/clara-barton (accessed May 13, 2013).
2. Stephen Oates, *A Woman of Valor: Clara Barton and the Civil War* (New York: Free Press, 1994), 8–10, 23, 125–126.
3. Ibid., 126–127, 131–134.
4. Ishbel Ross, *Angel of the Battlefield: The Life of Clara Barton* (New York: Harper & Brothers, 1956), 57–58.
5. Ross, 58–60; Oates, 141–143.
6. Ross, 60; Oates, 157–158.
7. Oates, 156.
8. Ibid., 161–162.
9. Ibid., 164–165.
10. Ibid., 173.
11. Ibid., 173–174.
12. Ibid., 176–177.
13. Ibid., 180.
14. Ibid., 180–181.
15. Ibid., 181.
16. Ibid., 181–185.
17. Ibid., 186.
18. Ibid., 186–187.
19. Ibid., 188, 193, 207.
20. James Hunter, *The Servant: A Simple Story About the True Essence of Leadership* (Roseville, CA: Prima, 1998), 125.
21. Cohen, 175–176.
22. Oates, 200.
23. Wise, 186.
24. Ibid., 187.
25. Ross, 64.
26. Tom Clancy and Frederick Franks, *Into the Storm: A Study in Command* (New York: Berkley Trade, 2007), 261.

Chapter 21

1. Wise, 75.
2. Johnson Hagood, *Memoirs of the War of Secession* (Columbia, SC: The State, 1910), 50–51.
3. Hagood, 53.
4. Warner, *Gray*, 121; Wise, 12; Hagood, 52, 60.
5. Hagood, 73.
6. Ibid., 79, 89.
7. *OR*, Series 1, Vol. 14, p. 91.
8. Hagood, 98–101.
9. Ibid., 108, 111.
10. Ibid., 112, 210: Cisco, 88.
11. Wise, 74.
12. Ibid., 82.
13. *OR*, Series 1, Vol. 28, Part 1, p. 586; Wise, 86–89; Duncan, 107–108; Cornish, 151–152.
14. Wise, 97; Burton, 166; Hagood, 142.
15. Burton, 172; Wise 168; *OR*, Series 1, Vol. 28, Part 1, p. 437.
16. Wise, 168–169; *OR*, Series 1, Vol. 28, Part 1, pp. 437–444.
17. Wise, 173.
18. Hagood, 156–166.
19. Ibid., 167.
20. Ibid., 217.
21. Ibid., 195.
22. Ibid., 210.
23. Ibid., 217.
24. Warner, *Gray*, 122.
25. *The Armed Forces Officer* (Washington, D.C.: Department of Defense, 1975), 179.
26. Bruce Rogers, "Which CMO Skill Is More Valuable: Industry Expert or Versatile Leader?" *Forbes*, April 30, 2013, http://www.forbes.com/sites/brucerogers/2013/04/30/which-cmo-skill-is-more-valuable-industry-expert-or-versatile-leader/ (accessed June 5, 2013).
27. Elbert Hubbard, *A Message to Garcia* (White Plains, NY: Peter Pauper Press, 1982), 19.

Chapter 22

1. Wise, 154–161: Tucker, 101.
2. William Stryker, "The Swamp Angel," in *Battles and Leaders of the Civil War*, (New York: Thomas Yoseloff, 1956), 4:74; Wise, 148, 169; *OR*, Vol. 28, Part 1, p. 234.
3. Theodore Rosengarten, *Tombee: Portrait of a Cotton Planter* (New York:

William Morrow, 1986), 60; Edgar, 267–268: Guion Griffis Johnson, *A Social History of the Sea Islands* (Chapel Hill: University of North Carolina Press, 1930), 50–59.
 4. Cathy Miller, "Why Pluff Mud?" http://pluffmudperspectives.blogspot.com/p/why-pluff-mud.html (accessed June 5, 2013).
 5. Wise, 148; Wilcox and Ripley, 53–54; *OR*, Vol. 28, Part 1, p. 230.
 6. Stryker, 73; Wise, 148–149.
 7. Stryker, 73; Wise, 149; *OR*, Vol. 28, Part 1, pp. 234–235.
 8. Stryker, 73; Wise, 149; Wilcox and Ripley, 54; *OR*, Vol. 28, Part 1, p. 234.
 9. Stryker, 74; Wilcox and Ripley, 54.
 10. Wise, 149; *OR*, Vol. 28, Part 1, pp. 234, 236.
 11. Wise, 150.
 12. Ibid., 169–170.
 13. Ibid., 150: *OR*, Vol. 28, Part 1, p. 234.
 14. Wise, 170–171.
 15. Ibid., 171.
 16. Ibid., 171.
 17. Ibid., 172.
 18. Northouse, 8.
 19. Ibid., 10.
 20. James Kouzes and Barry Posner, *The Leadership Challenge* (San Francisco: Jossey-Bass, 2012), 209.
 21. Ibid.,182.
 22. Covey, 99.
 23. Kouzes and Posner, 160–161.

Chapter 23

 1. Stephen Wise, *Lifeline of the Confederacy Blockade Running During the Civil War* (Columbia: University Press of South Carolina, 1991), 124
 2. Dougherty, *Encyclopedia of the Confederacy* (San Diego: Thunder Bay Press, 2010), 35–37; Time-Life Books, eds., *The Blockade: Runners and Raiders* (Alexandria, VA: Time-Life Books, 1983), 86–101; Thomas Boaz and Ethel Trenholm Seabrook Nepveux, "Dashing Blockade Runner: Captain Thomas J. Lockwood," *Military Images* 25 (May-June 2004): 5–9.
 3. "From Charleston," *New York Times*, March 12, 1861, http://www.nytimes.com/1861/03/12/news/charleston-fight-tariff-restlessness-palmetto-army-sumpter-with-p-intense.html?pagewanted=1 (accessed June 16, 2013).
 4. Margaret Eastman, *Old Charleston Originals: From Celebrities to Scoundrels* (Charleston, SC: History Press, 2011), 63; Wise, *Lifeline*, 307.
 5. Clifford Dowdey, *The Land They Fought For* (Garden City, NY: Doubleday, 1955), 331.
 6. E. Lee Spence, *Treasures of the Confederate Coast: The Real Rhett Butler and Other Revelations;* (Charleston, SC: Narwhal Press, 1995) 13–14.
 7. Wise, *Lifeline*, 9; J.S. Rogers, "Maj. Huse of the Secret Service," *Confederate Veteran* 13, no. 2 (February 1905), 65.
 8. Wise, *Lifeline*, 47.
 9. Ibid., 47.
 10. Dougherty, *Encyclopedia*, 222.
 11. Eastman, *Old Charleston Originals*, 63; Wise, *Lifeline*, 307.
 12. Eastman, *Old Charleston Originals*, 63.
 13. *OR, Navies*, 67–68.
 14. Dougherty, *Encyclopedia*, 222.
 15. Wise, *Lifeline*, 57.
 16. Dougherty, *Encyclopedia*, 276–277; Eastman, *Old Charleston Originals*, 63; *OR Navies*, 124, 129–130; Wise, 57.
 17. Wise, *Lifeline*, 57–58.
 18. Ibid., 58, 64.
 19. Ibid., 307.
 20. Ibid.,, 68.
 21. *OR, Navies*, 284–285; Eastman, *Old Charleston Originals*, 63; Wise, *Lifeline*, 60.
 22. Andrea Mehrlander, *The Germans of Charleston, Richmond and New Orleans During the Civil War Period, 1850–1870* (Berlin, Germany: De Gruyter, 2011), 214.
 23. Wise, *Lifeline*, 68.
 24. Mehrlander, 214; *OR Navies*, 556, Wise, *Lifeline*, 68, 307.
 25. Eastman, *Old Charleston Originals*, 63.
 26. Rita Gunther McGrath and Ian MacMillan, *The Entrepreneurial Mindset: Strategies for Continuously Creating Opportunity in an Age of Uncertainty* (Cambridge, MA: Harvard Business Review Press, 2000), 2–3.
 27. Ibid., 3.
 28. Ibid.
 29. Ibid.
 30. Ibid.
 31. Danna Greenberg et al., *The New Entrepreneurial Leader: Developing Leaders Who Shape Social and Economic Opportunity* (San Francisco: Berrett-Koehler, 2011), 1.
 32. Time-Life, eds., *The Blockade: Runners and Raider*, 98.
 33. Dowdey, *Land*, 331–332.

Chapter 24

1. Beauregard, "Torpedo," 152.
2. Dougherty, *Ships,* 216.
3. Burton, 230–232.
4. Burton, 232; Richard Bak, *The CSS Hunley* (Dallas: Taylor, 1999), 88.
5. Tom Chaffin, *The H.L. Hunley: The Secret Hope of the Confederacy* (New York: Hill and Wang, 2008), 148–149; R. Thomas Campbell, *The CSS H.L. Hunley: Confederate Submarine* (Shippensburg, PA: Burd Street Press, 2000), 29.
6. Campbell, 31; Chaffin, 149.
7. Beauregard, "Torpedo," 153.
8. Chaffin, 150.
9. Chaffin, 150–151; Burton, 233–234.
10. Beauregard, "Torpedo," 153.
11. Chaffin, 162.
12. See Chaffin, 162–163; Bak, 103–105, for commentary on Dixon's powers of persuasion.
13. Beauregard, "Torpedo," 154.
14. Bak, 101.
15. William Alexander, "The Heroes of the *Hunley,*" *Munsey's* 29, (September 1903), 748.
16. Alexander, 749; Campbell, 82; Burton, 234–235; Chaffin, 169. It should be noted that there are many contradictory reports of the details of the Hunley's crew. Contributing to the confusion is that *OR, Navies* (Series 1, Vol. 15, p. 337) lists "C. Simkins" rather than "Lumpkin." That same source spells "Ridgaway" as "Ridgeway" and does not list Miller.
17. William Beard, "The Log of the C.D. Submarine," *U.S. Naval Institute Proceedings* 42, no. 2 (September-October 1916), 1552.
18. *OR Navies,* Series 1, Vol. 15, pp. 226–227.
19. Beauregard, "Torpedo," 154.
20. John Gardner, *On Leadership* (New York: Free Press, 1989), 1.
21. Ibid., 72.
22. Kurt Mortensen, *Maximum Influence: The 12 Universal Laws of Power Persuasion* (New York: AMACOM, 2004), 9.
23. Chaffin, 168.
24. Allan Cohen and David Bradford, *Influence Without Authority* (New York: Wiley, 2005), 169.
25. Beauregard, "Torpedo," 153–154.
26. Cohen and Bradford, 56–57.
27. Alexander, 749.

Chapter 25

1. *OR,* Series 1, Vol. 44, Part 1, p. 783.
2. Burton, 304.
3. *OR,* Series 1, Vol. 44, Part 1, p. 843.
4. Ibid., 741.
5. Ibid., 799.
6. W. Scott Poole, *South Carolina's Civil War: A Narrative History* (Macon, GA: Mercer University Press, 2005), 144.
7. *OR,* Series 1, Vol. 53, Supplements, 61; Burton, 319.
8. Charles Cowley, *Leaves from a Lawyer's Life Afloat and Ashore* (Lowell, MA: Penhallow, 1879), 167.
9. Burton, 321.
10. Kevin Dougherty, *Strangling the Confederacy* (Philadelphia: Casemate, 2010), 146.
11. Robert Doughty, *American Military History and the Evolution of Western Warfare* (Lexington, MA: D.C. Heath, 1996), 106.
12. Field Manual 3–0, *Operations* (Washington, D.C.: Department of the Army, 2001), 4–7.

Bibliography

Alexander, William. "The Heroes of the *Hunley*." *Munsey's* 29 (September 1903).
Ammen, Daniel. "Du Pont and the Port Royal Expedition." In *Battles and Leaders of the Civil War*. Vol 1. 1887. Edison, NJ: Castle, 1985.
Ancker, Clinton. "Doctrine for Asymmetric Warfare." *Military Review* (July-August 2003): 18–25.
Anderson, Bern. *By Sea and By River: A Naval History of the Civil War*. Westport, CT: Greenwood, 1962.
Andrew, Rod. *Wade Hampton: Confederate Warrior to Southern Redeemer*. Chapel Hill: University of North Carolina Press, 2008.
Bak, Richard. *The CSS* Hunley. Dallas, TX: Taylor, 1999.
Baker, Jean. *James Buchanan: The 15th President, 1857–1861*. American Presidents Series. New York: Times Books, 2004.
Ballard, Michael. *Pemberton: The General Who Lost Vicksburg*. Jackson: University Press of Mississippi, 1991.
_____. *Vicksburg: The Campaign That Opened the Mississippi*. Chapel Hill: University of North Carolina Press, 2010.
Beard, William. "The Log of the C.D. Submarine." *U.S. Naval Institute Proceedings* 42, no. 2 (September-October 1916): 1545–1557.
Bearss, Edwin. "Civil War Operations in and Around Pensacola." *Florida Historical Quarterly* 36, no. 2 (Oct 1957): 125 165.
_____. "The Vicksburg River Defenses and the Enigma of 'Whistling Dick.'" *Journal of Mississippi History* 29, no. 1 (January 1957): 21–30.
Beauregard, Pierre Gustave Toutant. "The First Battle of Bull Run." In *Battles and Leaders of the Civil War: From Sumter to Shiloh*. Edited by Robert Underwood Johnson and Clarence Clough Buel. New York: Century, 1884–1887.
_____."Torpedo Service in the Harbor and Water Defences of Charleston." *Southern Historical Society Papers*. Vol. 5 (1878).
Beringer, Richard, et al. *Why the South Lost the Civil War*. Athens: University of Georgia Press, 1986.
"Big Guns at Gettysburg." Gettysburg National Military Park, Department of the Interior. http://www.nps.gov/archive/gett/soldierlife/artillery.htm (accessed 19 December 2008).
Billingsley, Andrew. *Yearning to Breathe Free: Robert Smalls of South Carolina and His Families*. Columbia: University of South Carolina Press, 2007.
Boatner, Mark. *The Civil War Dictionary*. New York: David McKay, 1959.
Boaz, Thomas, and Ethel Trenholm Seabrook Nepveux. "Dashing Blockade Runner: Captain Thomas J. Lockwood." *Military Images* 25 (May-June 2004): 5–9.
Bostick, Douglas. *Charleston under Siege: The Impregnable City*. Charleston, SC: History Press, 2010.
Brennan, Patrick. *Secessionville: Assault on Charleston*. Boston: Da Capo, 1996.

Brooke, George, ed. *Ironclads and Big Guns of the Confederacy: The Journal and Letters of John M. Brooke*. Columbia: University of South Carolina Press, 2002.
Brown, Daniel. "Fort Pulaski." In *The Civil War Battlefield Guide*. Edited by Frances Kennedy. Boston: Houghton Mifflin, 1990.
Browning, Robert. *Success Is All That Was Expected: The South Atlantic Blockading Squadron During the Civil War*. Washington, D.C.: Brassey's, 2002.
Bryan, E.K., and E.K. Meadows. "Defense of Fort Wagner, Morris Island, 8 July 1863." Edited by Walter Clark. *History of the Several Regiments* 5. Goldsborough, NC: Nash Brothers, 1901.
"Bugle Notes." West Point, NY: The Staff, 1979.
Burchard, Peter. *One Gallant Rush: Robert Gould Shaw and His Brave Black Regiment*. New York: St. Martin's, 1965.
Burton, E. Milby. *The Siege of Charleston, 1861–1865*. Columbia: University of South Carolina Press, 1970.
Campbell, R. Thomas. *The CSS H.L. Hunley: Confederate Submarine*. Shippensburg, PA: Burd Street, 2000.
Catton, Bruce. *This Hallowed Ground*. Garden City, NJ: Doubleday, 1956.
Chaffin, Tom. *The H.L. Hunley: The Secret Hope of the Confederacy*. New York: Hill and Wang, 2008.
Chaitin, Peter. *The Coastal War*. Alexandria, VA: Time-Life Books, 1984.
Cisco, Walter. *States Rights Gist: A South Carolina General of the Civil War*. Gretna, LA: Pelican, 2008.
Clancy, Tom, and Frederick Franks. *Into the Storm: A Study in Command*. Putnam, 1997. New York: Berkley, 2007.
Cohen, Allan, and David Bradford. *Influence without Authority*. New York: Wiley, 2005.
Cohen, William. *The Stuff of Heroes*. Marietta, GA: Longstreet, 1998.
Conger, Jay. *The Charismatic Leader*. San Francisco: Jossey-Bass, 1989.
Covey, Stephen. *The 7 Habits of Highly Effective People*. New York: Simon and Schuster, 1989.
Cowley, Charles. *Leaves from a Lawyer's Life Afloat and Ashore*. Lowell, MA: Penhallow, 1879.
Crawford, Samuel. *The Genesis of the Civil War: The Story of Sumter, 1860–1861*. New York: Charles L. Webster, 1887.
Dahlgren, Madeleine Vinton. *Memoir of John A. Dahlgren, Rear-admiral, United States Navy*. Boston: J.R. Osgood, 1882.
Doubleday, Abner. *Reminiscences of Fort Sumter and Moultrie in 1860-'61*. New York: Harper & Bros, 1876.
Dougherty, Kevin. *The Campaigns for Vicksburg, 1862–63: Leadership Lessons*. Philadelphia: Casemate, 2011.
_____. *Civil War Leadership and Mexican War Experience*. Jackson: University Press of Mississippi, 2007.
_____. *Encyclopedia of the Confederacy*. San Diego: Thunder Bay, 2010.
_____. "Rifled Artillery's First Breach of Masonry." *Forward Observer*, April 1992, 6–8.
_____. *Ships of the Civil War*. New York: Sterling, 2013.
_____. *Strangling the Confederacy*. Philadelphia: Casemate, 2010.
_____. *Weapons of Mississippi*. Jackson: University Press of Mississippi, 2010.
Doughty, Robert. *American Military History and the Evolution of Western Warfare*. Lexington, MA: D.C. Heath, 1996.
Dowdey, Clifford, and Louis Manarin, eds. *The Wartime Papers of R.E. Lee*. New York: Bramhall, 1961.
Dowdey, Clifford. *The Land They Fought For*. Garden City, NY: Doubleday, 1955.
_____. *The Seven Days*. New York: Fairfax, 1978.
DuCoin, Francis. "Assailing Satan's Kingdom: Union Combined Operations at Charleston." In *Union Combined Operations in the Civil War (The North's Civil War)*. Edited by Craig Symonds. New York: Fordham University Press, 2010.
Duncan, Russell. *Where Death and Glory Meet: Colonel Robert Gould Shaw and the 54th Massachusetts Infantry*. Athens: University of Georgia Press, 1999.
Eastman, Margaret. *Old Charleston Originals: From Celebrities to Scoundrels*. Charleston, SC: History Press, 2011.

Edgar, Walter. *The South Carolina Encyclopedia*. Columbia: University of South Carolina Press, 2006.
Emilio, Luis. *A Brave Black Regiment: The History of the Fifty-Fourth Regiment of Massachusetts Volunteer Infantry, 1863–1865*. New York: Da Capo, 1995.
Flanagan, E.M. "Hands-On Leadership." In *Army* (April 1992): 54–55.
Field Manual 3-0, *Operations*. Washington, D.C.: Department of the Army, 2001.
Field Manual 6-0, *Mission Command: Command and Control of Army Forces*. Washington, D.C.: Department of the Army, 2003.
Field Manual 6-22, *Army Leadership*. Washington, D.C.: Department of the Army, 2006.
Field Manual 100-5, *Army Leadership*. Washington, D.C.: Department of the Army, 1999.
Foote, Shelby. *The Civil War: A Narrative*. 3 vols. New York: Random House, 1963.
Fox, Gustavus. *Confidential Correspondence of Gustavus Vasa Fox*. Edited by Robert Thompson and Richard Wainwright. New York: De Vinne, 1918.
Freeman, Douglas Southall. *Lee's Lieutenants: A Study in Command*. 3 vols. New York: Charles Scribner's Sons, 1942–1944.
_____. *R.E. Lee: A Biography*. 4 vols. New York: Charles Scribner's Sons, 1934.
_____. *The South to Posterity*. New York: Charles Scribner's, 1939.
Fry, Robert. "Sun Tzu: The Best Leadership Teacher of All Time?" *Forbes*, July 27, 2010.
Fry, Ron. "AFMC Commander Tells Senior Leaders to Conserve Resources, Money." Air Force Material Command, April 27, 2010.
Gabel, Christopher. *Staff Ride Handbook for the Vicksburg Campaign, December 1862- July 1863*. Fort Leavenworth, KS: Combat Studies Institute, 2001.
Gardner, John. *On Leadership*. New York: Free Press, 1989.
Gillmore, Quincy. *Engineer and Artillery Operations against the Defences of Charleston Harbor in 1863*. New York: D. Van Nostrand, 1865.
_____. "The Siege and Capture of Fort Pulaski." In *Battles and Leaders of the Civil War*. Vol. 2. Edited by Robert Johnson and Clarence Buel. New York: Century, 1887.
Grant, Ulysses. *Personal Memoirs of U.S. Grant*. New York: Da Capo, 1982.
Greenberg, Danna, et al. *The New Entrepreneurial Leader: Developing Leaders Who Shape Social and Economic Opportunity*. San Francisco: Berrett-Koehler, 2011.
Greenleaf, Robert. *Servant Leadership*. Mahwah, NJ: Paulist, 2002.
Hagood, Johnson. *Memoirs of the War of Secession*. Columbia, SC: The State, 1910.
Halpern, Belle Linda, and Kathy Lubar. *Leadership Presence*. New York: Gotham, 2003.
Hammond, Thomas. "William H. Carney's Grit at Fort Wagner Earned Him the Distinction of Being the First Black Soldier to Receive the Medal of Honor." *America's Civil War* 20, no. 1 (March 2007): 69.
Harari, Oren. *The Leadership Secrets of Colin Powell*. New York: McGraw-Hill, 2002.
Hattaway, Herman, and Archer Jones. *How the North Won: A Military History of the Civil War*. Chicago: University of Illinois Press, 1983.
Hazlett, James, Edwin Olmstead, and M. Hume Parks. *Field Artillery Weapons of the Civil War*. Champaign: University of Illinois Press, 2004.
Henry, Robert Selph. *The Story of the Mexican War*. New York: Frederick Ungar, 1950.
Hess, Earl. *Field Armies and Fortifications in the Civil War: The Eastern Campaigns, 1861–1864*. Chapel Hill: University of North Carolina Press, 2005.
Holley, I.B. "Insights on Technology and Doctrine." In *Technology and Military Doctrine: Essays on a Challenging Relationship*. Maxwell Air Force Base, AL: Air University Press, 2004.
Hoogenboom, Ari. *Gustavus Vasa Fox of the Union Navy: A Biography*. Baltimore: Johns Hopkins University Press, 2010.
Hubbard, Elbert. *A Message to Garcia*. White Plains, NY: Peter Pauper, 1982.
Hunter, James. *The Servant: A Simple Story About the True Essence of Leadership*. Roseville, CA: Prima, 1998.
Johnson, Guion Griffiss. *A Social History of the Sea Islands*. Chapel Hill: University of North Carolina Press, 1930.
Johnson, John. *The Defense of Charleston Harbor, Including Fort Sumter and the Adjacent Islands, 1863–1865*. Charleston, SC: Walker, Evans and Cogswell, 1890.
Joint Publication 3-0. *Doctrine for Joint Operations*. Washington, D.C.: Joint Chiefs of Staff, 2011.

Katcher, Philip. *American Civil War Artillery, 1861–65: Heavy Artillery.* New York: Osprey, 2001.
Kidder, Rushworth. *How Good People Make Tough Choices: Resolving the Dilemmas of Ethical Living.* New York: Harper Perennial, 2009.
———. *Moral Courage.* New York: William Morrow, 2006.
King, Horatio. *Turning on the Light: A Dispassionate Survey of President Buchanan's Administration from 1860 to Its Close.* Philadelphia: J.B. Lippincott, 1895.
Kouzes, James, and Barry Posner. *The Leadership Challenge.* San Francisco: Jossey-Bass, 2012.
Lawton, Eba Anderson. *Major Robert Anderson and Fort Sumter.* New York: Knickerbocker, 1911.
Lee, Stephen. "The First Step in the War." In *Battles and Leaders of the Civil War: From Sumter to Shiloh.* Edited by Robert Underwood Johnson and Clarence Clough Buel. Whitefish, MT: Kessinger, 2004.
Lowney, Chris. *Heroic Leadership.* Chicago: Loyola, 2003.
Macartney, Clarence. *Mr. Lincoln's Admirals.* New York: Funk & Wagnalls, 1956.
Marsalek, John, ed. *The Diary of Miss Emma Holmes, 1861–1866.* Baton Rouge: Louisiana State University Press, 1979.
Martin, Gregg, et al. "The Road to Mentoring: Paved with Good Intentions." In *Strategic Leadership Selected Readings.* Edited by Jeffrey Johns. Carlisle Barracks, PA: U.S. Army War College, 2003.
Maxwell, John. *The 17 Indisputable Laws of Teamwork.* Nashville: Thomas Nelson, 2001.
McPherson, James. *Drawn with the Sword: Reflections on the American Civil War.* New York: Oxford University Press, 1996.
———. *The Illustrated Battle Cry of Freedom: The Civil War Era.* New York: Oxford University Press, 2003.
———. *War on the Waters: The Union and Confederate Navies, 1861–1865 (Littlefield History of the Civil War Era).* Chapel Hill: University of North Carolina Press, 2012.
Mehrlander, Andrea. *The Germans of Charleston, Richmond and New Orleans During the Civil War Period, 1850–1870.* Berlin, Germany: De Gruyter, 2011.
Miller, Edward. *Gullah Statesman: Robert Smalls from Slavery to Congress, 1839–1915.* Columbia: University of South Carolina Press, 1995.
———. *Lincoln's Abolitionist General: The Biography of David Hunter.* Columbia: University of South Carolina Press, 1997.
Morrell, Margot, and Stephanie Capparell. *Shackleton's Way: Leadership Lessons from the Great Antarctic Explorer.* New York: Viking, 2001.
Mortensen, Kurt. *Maximum Influence: The 12 Universal Laws of Power Persuasion.* New York: AMACOM, 2004.
Musicant, Ivan. *Divided Waters: The Naval History of the Civil War.* Edison, NJ: Castle Books, 1995.
Nevins, Allan. *The Emergence of Lincoln: Prologue to the Civil War, 1859–1861.* New York: Charles Scribner's Sons, 1950.
Niven, John. *Gideon Welles: Lincoln's Secretary of the Navy.* New York: Oxford University Press, 1973.
Northouse, Peter. *Leadership: Theory and Practice.* Thousand Oaks, CA: Sage, 2004.
Oates, Stephen. *A Woman of Valor: Clara Barton and the Civil War.* New York: Free Press, 1994.
Official Records of the Union and Confederate Navies in the War of the Rebellion. 30 vols. Washington, D.C.: United States Naval War Records Office, 1922.
Palmer, Abraham. *The History of the Forty-Eighth Regiment of New York Volunteers.* Brooklyn, NY: Veteran Association of the Forty-Eighth Regiment, 1885.
Perkins, P.S. *The Art and Science of Communication: Tools for Effective Communication in the Workplace.* New York: Wiley, 2008.
Phelps, W. Chris. *Charlestonians in War: The Charleston Battalion.* Gretna, LA: Pelican, 2004.
Poirier, Robert. *By The Blood of Our Alumni: Norwich University Citizen Soldiers in the Army of the Potomac, 1861–1865.* Boston: Da Capo, 1999.
Pollard, Edward. *Lee and His Lieutenants.* New York: E.B. Treat, 1867.
Poole, W. Scott. *South Carolina's Civil War: A Narrative History.* Macon, GA: Mercer University Press, 2005.
Pressley, John G. "Extracts from the Diary of Lieutenant Colonel John G. Pressley." In *Papers of the Southern Historical Society.* Vol. 14. Richmond, VA: William Jones, 1886.

Puryear, Edgar. *American Generalship: Character Is Everything: The Art of Command.* Novato, CA: Presidio, 2001.
Rains, Gabriel, and Peter Michie. *Confederate Torpedoes: Two Illustrated 19th Century Works with New Appendices and Photographs.* Edited by Herbert Schiller. Jefferson, NC: McFarland, 2011.
Rains, Gabriel. "Torpedoes." *Southern Historical Society Papers.* Vol. 3 (1877).
Ravenel, Henry. *Ravenel Records.* Atlanta: Franklin, 1898.
Reagan, Ronald. "Keepers of the Peace." Commencement Address, McAlister Field House, The Citadel, May 15, 1993.
Reed, Rowena. *Combined Operations in the Civil War.* Annapolis, MD: Naval Institute Press, 1978.
Ripley, Warren. *Artillery and Ammunition of the Civil War.* New York: Van Nostrand Reinhold, 1970.
Rogers, Bruce. "Which CMO Skill Is More Valuable: Industry Expert or Versatile Leader?" *Forbes,* April 30, 2013.
Rogers, J.S. "Maj. Huse of the Secret Service." *Confederate Veteran* 13, no. 2 (February 1905): 65.
Rosanoff, M.A. "Edison in His Laboratory." *Harper's Weekly* 165 (September 1932), 402–417.
Rosengarten, Theodore. *Tombee: Portrait of a Cotton Planter.* New York: William Morrow, 1986.
Ross, Ishbel. *Angel of the Battlefield: The Life of Clara Barton.* New York: Harper & Brothers, 1956.
Ryan, Michael. "The Historic Guns of Forts Sumter and Moultrie," National Park Service, 1997.
Scharf, John. *History of the Confederate States Navy from Its Organization to the Surrender of Its Last Vessel.* New York: Rogers & Sherwood, 1887.
Schneller, Robert. *A Quest for Glory: A Biography of John A. Dahlgren.* Annapolis, MD: Naval Institute Press, 1996.
Slotten, Hugh. *Patronage, Practice, and the Culture of American Science: Alexander Dallas Bache and the U.S. Coast Survey.* New York: Cambridge University Press, 1994.
Spence, E. Lee. *Treasures of the Confederate Coast: The Real Rhett Butler and Other Revelations.* Charleston, SC: Narwhal Press, 1995.
Stoker, Donald. *The Grand Design: Strategy and the U.S. Civil War.* New York: Oxford University Press, 2010.
Stone, H. David. *Vital Rails: The Charleston & Savannah Railroad and the Civil War in Coastal South Carolina.* Columbia: University of South Carolina Press, 2008.
"Strategic Leadership Primer." Carlisle Barracks, PA: United States Army War College, 1998.
Stryker, William. "The Swamp Angel." In *Battles and Leaders of the Civil War.* New York: Thomas Yoseloff, 1956.
Stuckey, Scott. "Joint Operations in the Civil War." *Joint Forces Quarterly* (Autumn/Winter, 1994–1995): 92–105.
Sun Tzu. *The Art of War.* Translated by Samuel Griffith. New York: Oxford University Press, 1971.
Swanberg, W.A. *First Blood: The Story of Fort Sumter.* New York: Dorset, 1957.
Training Circular 25–20. *A Leader's Guide to After-Action Reviews.* Washington, D.C.: Department of the Army, 1993.
Thomas, Emory. *The Confederate Nation, 1861–1865.* New York: Harper and Row, 1979.
_____. *Robert E. Lee.* New York: W.W. Norton, 1997.
Time-Life Books, eds. *The Blockade: Runners and Raiders.* Alexandria, VA: Time-Life Books, 1983.
Tucker, Spencer. *A Short History of the Civil War at Sea.* Wilmington, DE: Scholarly Resources, 2002.
United States Department of Defense. *The Armed Forces Officer.* Washington, D.C.: Armed Forces Information Service, 1975.
Warner, Ezra. *Generals in Blue: Lives of the Union Commanders.* Baton Rouge: Louisiana State University Press, 1964.
_____. *Generals in Gray: Lives of the Confederate Commanders.* Baton Rouge: Louisiana State University Press, 1959.
The War of the Rebellion: A Compilation of the Official Records of the Union and Confederate Armies. 127 vols. Washington, D.C.: Government Printing Office, 1901.
Weddle, Kevin. "The Blockade Board of 1861 and Union Naval Strategy." *Civil War History* 48, no. 2 (June 2002): 123–142.
_____. *Lincoln's Tragic Admiral: The Life of Samuel Francis Du Pont.* Charlottesville: University of Virginia Press, 2005.
Weigley, Russell. *The American Way of War.* Bloomington: University of Indiana Press, 1973.
_____. *The History of the United States Army.* New York: MacMillan, 1967.

Welles, Gideon. *Diary of Gideon Welles: Secretary of the Navy under Lincoln and Johnson.* New York: Houghton Mifflin, 1911.
Westwood, Howard. "Generals David Hunter and Rufus Saxton and Black Soldiers." *South Carolina Historical Magazine* 86, no. 3 (July 1985):165–181.
Wilcox, Arthur, and Warren Ripley. *The Civil War at Charleston.* Charleston, SC: Post-Courier, 1986.
Wilhelm, Thomas. *A Military Dictionary and Gazetteer.* Philadelphia: http://books.google.com/books/about/A_Military_Dictionary_and_Gazetteer.html?id=GHcrAAAAMAAJL.R. Hamersley, 1881.
Williams, T. Harry. *Lincoln and His Generals.* New York: Alfred A. Knopf, 1952.
_____. *Napoleon in Gray.* Baton Rouge: Louisiana State University Press, 1955.
Wise, Stephen. *Gate of Hell: Campaign for Charleston Harbor, 1863.* Columbia: University of South Carolina Press, 1994.
_____. *Lifeline of the Confederacy: Blockade Running During the Civil War.* Columbia: University Press of South Carolina, 1991.
Woodward, C. Vann, ed. *Mary Chesnut's Civil War.* New Haven, CT: Yale University Press, 1981.
Wright, Kai. *Soldiers of Freedom: An Illustrated History of African Americans in the Armed Forces.* New York: Black Dog & Leventhal, 2002.

Index

after action review (AAR) 108–109
Alexander, William 186, 189, 191
Anaconda Plan 19–20
Anderson, Robert 1, 8, 26, 31, 32, 41, 45, 47–50, 52–64, 90, 92, 196, 197, 198
Andrew, John 23, 36, 145–147, 152
artillery 14; rifled 11–12, 14, 15, 16, 30, 35, 137–139, 143; smoothbore 15, 16, 17
asymmetry 10, 18–19, 111–115
authoritarian leadership 162

Bache, Alexander 65–66, 70
Barnard, John 66, 104
Barton, Clara 22, 158–163, 198
Battery Bee 126
Battery Gregg 28, 140, 161, 168
Battery Haskell 16
Battery Simpkins 16
Beauregard, Pierre Gustave Toutant 8, 16, 26, 30, 37–38, 40, 41, 42, 60–62, 83, 91, 92, 113, 119, 125, 126, 165–168, 174, 186–191, 196
Bee, Barnard 91
Benham, Henry 27, 32, 33, 36, 88, 96–97, 99–100, 106, 108
Benjamin, Judah 76
Black, Jeremiah 49, 51
black regiments, formation of 23, 145, 152–153
CSS *Black Witch* see CSS *Gordon*
Blakely, Alexander 15
Blakely rifles 15
Blockade Board 19, 26, 34, 37, 65–70, 104, 121–122, 197
blockade, declaration of 19, 65
blockade running and runners 178–179, 183
Bonham, Milledge 41, 166
Brooke, John 16
Brooke rifles 16

USS *Brooklyn* 49, 50
Buchanan, James 26, 40, 45–51, 57–60, 197, 198
Buell, Don Carlos 56–57
Butler, Rhett 179

Cameron, Simeon 59–60
canister 17, 100, 102
Capers, Ellison 94
Carney, William 22, 152–157
CSS *Carolina* 179, 182, 184
Castle Pinckney 28, 52, 54, 87
charismatic leadership 102–103, 104
Charleston: defenses 28, 117; significance 20–21
Charleston and Savannah Railroad 73–75, 77, 165
Charleston Battalion 10, 24, 99, 102
Chesnut, James 38, 60–61, 90–95
Chesnut, Mary 38, 41, 82, 91–92, 94
CSS *Chicora* 13, 125, 196
The Citadel 1, 8–9, 21, 50, 156, 200
Coehorn mortar 18
Cole's Island 75–76, 81, 87–88, 94, 96, 97, 164–165, 169
Columbiads 16–17
command (leader) presence 129, 132–135
commander's intent 55
Craven, John 160
Crawford, Samuel 54, 61, 63
cronyism 94
Cummings Point 140, 178

Dahlgren, John 15, 30–31, 33, 35, 108, 127, 129–135, 136, 139, 171, 187, 189, 196, 198
Dahlgren guns 15, 33
Darien, Georgia 146–147
CSS *David* 18–19, 41–42, 188
Davis, Charles 34, 66

Index

Davis, Jefferson 37, 38, 39, 45, 46, 77, 78–79, 82, 83, 90, 92–93, 178, 180
Department of the South 23
Dix, Dorothea 159
Dixon, George 186–191, 197, 199
Doubleday, Abner 47, 52–54
Du Pont, Samuel 8, 10, 13–14, 15, 19, 20, 26–30, 33–34, 35, 36, 37, 66, 68, 73, 88, 105–109, 116–122, 123, 124, 126, 129–131, 132, 137, 197, 198

Eisenhower, Dwight 91, 108
Elwell, John 159–161
Emancipation Proclamation 144–145
Emilio, Luis 154
entrepreneurial leadership 184–185
Evans, Nathan 97, 99, 100, 165

Farragut, David 28, 68, 117, 119, 130
54th Massachusetts Volunteer Regiment 23, 36, 141, 144–151, 152–155, 167, 200
Floyd, John 16, 32, 46–49, 52–59, 64
Folly Island 69, 75, 131, 134, 139, 143, 160, 200
Foote, Andrew 30, 33, 119, 129–131, 132
Fort Johnson 28, 31, 75, 97–101, 116, 175, 186
Fort Lamar *see* Tower Battery
Fort Lamar Heritage Preserve 199
Fort McAllister 13–14, 18, 28–30, 117–119, 120–121
Fort Moultrie 17, 26, 28, 31, 41, 47, 52–57, 63, 75, 119, 123, 134, 140, 175, 197, 198–199
Fort Pemberton 93
Fort Pulaski 10, 11–12, 18, 30, 32, 35, 36, 39, 73, 75, 80, 105, 106, 130, 131, 136–139, 143
Fort Ripley 28
Fort Sumter 1, 9, 13, 15, 16–17, 22, 25, 26, 28, 30–31, 32, 34, 37, 38, 39, 41, 42, 45–50, 52–63, 65, 75, 87, 88, 90, 92, 101, 119, 123, 125, 126, 130, 131, 132, 133, 134, 139, 140, 164, 171, 174–175, 179, 196–197, 198–199
Fort (Battery) Wagner 9, 18, 28, 30–31, 36, 42, 139–143, 144, 147–151, 158, 160, 161, 166–169, 171, 178, 197, 200
Foster, John 23, 196
Fox, Gustavus 21, 27, 28, 34–35, 59–60, 65, 70, 105–106, 116, 117, 119, 121
frame of reference 1, 142–143

Gage, Mary 160–161
Gaillard, Peter 24, 99–100
Gardner, John 47, 52–54
Garrison, William Lloyd 144

Gillmore, Quincy 10, 12, 16, 18, 23, 30–31, 35, 36, 108, 130–134, 136–143, 160–162, 167–168, 171–172, 174, 196, 197, 198
Gilmer, Jeremy 18
Gist, William 25, 90
Gist, States Rights 38, 90–95, 96, 98, 165
Goodlette, Spartan 99
CSS *Gordon* 179–184
Grace, James 153
Grant, Ulysses 34, 46, 129
Greek Fire 15, 174
Green, Samuel 161
Greenleaf, Robert 162
Grimball's Plantation 96–97, 167
guns, described 17

Hagood, Johnson 9, 24, 38, 97, 99, 164–170, 200
Hallowell, Richard 153, 154
USS *Harriett Lane* 61
Hatch, Lewis 97–98
Haynesworth, George 9
Higginson, Thomas 139, 146
Holmes, Emma 82
Hough, Daniel 26, 63
USS *Housatonic* 19, 31, 189–191
howitzers, described 17
Huger, Benjamin 47, 55
Humbert, J.B. 17, 100, 102
CSS *Hunley* 19, 31, 186–191, 197, 198, 199
Hunley, Horace 186–188
Hunter, David 8, 20, 22, 27, 33, 35–36, 88, 96–100, 104–109, 119, 130, 146–147, 198
Huse, Caleb 178–179, 180

CSS *Indian Chief* 189, 191
initiative 89
ironclads 12–14, 28–31, 37, 112, 117–120, 130–131

James, Charles 16
James Island 27–28, 38, 61, 75, 76, 86, 90, 93–95, 96–100, 107, 116, 147, 165–167, 171–172, 197, 199
James rifles 16
Jesus 162–163
John Fraser and Company 179–182
Johnston, Joseph 78, 90, 93
joint operations 19–20, 30–31, 34, 35, 104–109, 116–122, 129, 131–132

CSS *Kate* see CSS *Carolina*
Keitt, Lawrence 168
USS *Keokuk* 15, 123–128, 197, 199
Kittinger, Martin 160–161

LaCoste, Adolphus 123–128, 197, 198, 199

laissez-faire leadership 51, 197
Lamar, Thomas 9, 17, 22, 27, 39, 94, 96–103, 104, 165, 197, 198, 199
Lamb, Samuel 159, 163
law of the niche 114
leadership, defined and described 7, 197, 198
Lee, Robert 21, 27, 39, 40, 41, 72–77, 78, 79, 80, 82, 91, 136, 197, 200
Lee, Stephen 60, 62
Lighthouse Inlet 93, 139–140, 200
Lincoln, Abraham 13, 19–20, 21, 25, 28, 33, 34, 35, 36, 37, 41, 45, 47, 51, 60, 65, 70, 117, 119, 130, 144–145–147, 151, 195
Lockwood, Thomas 178–185, 197, 200

Macbeth, Charles 52, 79–80, 196
magis leadership 155–157
Magnolia Cemetary 199
Magrath, A.G. 80, 82
Mallory, Stephen 12
management (versus leadership) 85, 175–177
Marsh Battery 15, 171–176, 198
Mason, James 181, 184
Maury, Matthew 111
McClellan, George 39, 119, 137
McClintock, James 186, 188
McEnery, John 99–100
McGowan, John 50
McKee, John 86
Medal of Honor 154, 155
mentorship 90, 94–95
Message to Garcia 169–170
Mexican War, influence of 7, 10, 33–34
Miles, William 62, 80, 82, 93, 166
USS *Monitor* 13
USS *Montauk* 13–14, 18, 29–30, 117–119, 141
Montgomery, James 146–147, 150
moral courage 58, 64, 149–151
Morris Island, South Carolina 15, 17–18, 28, 30, 39, 41, 50, 75, 101, 119, 124, 130, 131, 136, 139–143, 158, 160–161, 163, 165–168, 171, 173–174, 178, 197, 200
mortars, described 18

USS *Nantucket* 8
USS *New Ironsides* 120, 141
Norwich University 9

Olmstead, Charles 136–138
optimism 84

CSS *Palmetto State* 13, 125, 196
Parrott, Robert 14–15
Parrott guns 14–15
USS *Pawnee* 61, 133

Pemberton, John 1, 21, 38, 39–40, 42, 77, 78–85, 89, 91, 96–97, 100, 114, 198
persuasion 190–191
physical courage 149, 151, 152
Pickens, Francis 8, 39, 40–41, 76, 77, 78–83, 91, 101, 198
CSS *Pioneer* 186
USS *Planter* 27, 36, 80, 86–89, 199
Port Royal, South Carolina 10, 12, 21, 26–27, 31, 34, 35, 39, 66, 67, 68, 70, 72–75, 88, 116, 119, 123, 131, 159, 175, 197
Porter, Fitz John 52–54
potential, as a basis for promotion 85
Powell, Colin 84, 121–122
prioritization 73, 77
privateers 180–181
Pryor, Richard 62
Putman, Haldiman 141–142

Rains, Gabriel 18, 40, 41, 110–115, 116, 186, 197
Randolph, George 111
Ravenel, St. Julien 41–42
Reagan, Ronald 156
Requa guns 18
Rhind, Alexander 124
right-versus-right dilemmas 64, 150–151
Ripley, Roswell 42, 75–76, 77, 81–82, 83, 125, 165–166
Rodman, Thomas 17
Rodman guns 17
Rowan, Andrew 169

Scott, Winfield 19, 47, 49, 104
secession 21, 25–26, 45
Secessionville, South Carolina 9, 17, 27, 32, 36, 39, 42, 82, 90, 93–94, 96–102, 104, 105, 107, 116, 122, 165, 169, 197, 199
Sellmer, Charles 171–177, 198
Serrell, Edward 171–177, 197
servant leadership 158, 162–163
Seymour, Truman 9, 139–142
Shackleton, Earnest 127
Shaw, Robert 23, 36, 141, 144–151, 152–154, 200
Sherman, Thomas 36, 105, 137
Sherman, William 25, 31, 195, 197
siege operations 14
skills approach to leadership 83–85
Slidell, John 181, 184
Smalls, Robert 22, 27, 36, 86–89, 90, 198, 199–200
Smith, Alexander 99–100
Smith, William Duncan 96
Stanton, Edwin 49, 88, 104, 107, 147
Star of the West 1, 9, 26, 41, 49–50, 59
steam power 10–11

Index

Stearns, George 153
Stevens, Isaac 96, 99
Stevenson, Thomas 141–142
Stone Fleet 27, 75
Strong, George 139–141, 148–149, 153
submarines and submersibles 10, 18–19, 22, 31, 41–42, 175, 186–191
Sullivan's Island, South Carolina 17, 28, 126, 140, 183, 198
Sun Tzu 114–115
Surf Battery 17–18
Swamp Angel 15, 30, 171–175, 197

Taliaferro, William 141, 166
Terry, Alfred 139, 147, 167
CSS *Theodora* see CSS *Gordon*
Thompson, Jacob 46, 50
torpedoes and mines, 10, 13–14, 18, 22, 30, 31, 40, 41, 110–115, 116, 117–119, 175, 186, 188, 190, 197
Totten, Joseph 75, 77
Tower Battery 93, 96–101
transactional leadership 51
transformational leadership 51, 109
Trenholm, George 179–185
Trent Affair 181
Tucker, John Randolph 13, 196

United States Military Academy 7–8, 9
United States Naval Academy 7–8

unity of effort (or lack of) 20, 27–28, 30–31, 35, 104–109, 110, 129, 137, 174–175, 198

CSS *Virginia* (USS *Merrimack*) 12–13
vision, strategic 70–71, 121, 122
VUCA (volatility, uncertainty, confusion, ambiguity) 84

USS *Wabash* 88
Wagner, Thomas 100
Walker, Leroy 60, 90, 164
Warren Lasch Conservation 199
Watson, Baxter 186
USS *Weehawken* 18, 119, 123, 124, 141
Welles, Gideon 13, 19, 28, 34–35, 37, 65–70, 104, 117–122, 126, 129–131, 197, 198
White Point Battery (Battery Ramsay) 28, 126, 199
Whitworth guns 15–16
Wigfall, Louis 61–62
Williams, Arland 156
Williams, Gilbert 97
Wright, Horatio 96–97, 100, 107

yes men 121
Young, Gourdin 61–62

www.ingramcontent.com/pod-product-compliance
Ingram Content Group UK Ltd.
Pitfield, Milton Keynes, MK11 3LW, UK
UKHW041951140426
5217IPUK00015B/744